A WARRIOR'S WAY

AVIGDOR KAHALANI

S.P.i.
BOOKS
A division of Shapolsky Publishers, Inc.

S.P.I. BOOKS
A division of Shapolsky Publishers, Inc.

ISBN 1-56171-239-6

For any additional information, contact:

S.P.I. BOOKS/Shapolsky Publishers, Inc.
136 West 22nd Street
New York, NY 10011
212/633-2022 / FAX 212/633-2123

Printed in Canada

10 9 8 7 6 5 4 3 2 1

CONTENTS

INTRODUCTION
    BY HERMAN WOUK VII

FOREWORD BY
    YITZHAK RABIN IX

1. DEPARTED COMRADES 1
Back from the Yom Kippur War 1
Post-War Days 8
Missing in Action 10
To leave or not to leave 16

2. A MATTER OF
    HOME AND ROOTS 23

3. INTO UNIFORM 30
Induction 32
To be a fighter, to be a "tankist" 35

4. OFFICER CANDIDATE SCHOOL 42
Armored officer training 48

5. BACK TO THE 82ND BATTALION . 52
On Alert in the North 60

6. THE FIRST
    PATTON BATTALION 69
A Tank Company of My Own 73

7. THE SIX DAY WAR 76

Monday, June 5, 1967 79
Up in Flames 103
Protecting the Troops 107
To the hospital 109
Combat Medicine 115

8. IN THE HOSPITAL 118

Disability 137

9. RECUPERATION 139

Young leaders 143

10. THE 77TH BATTALION —
"OZ 77" 147

En route to the battalion 147
Second-in-command 151
Battalion commander 155

11. THE YOM KIPPUR WAR 161

Rosh Hashana 5734 162
Yom Kippur, October 6, 1973 168
Sunday, October 7, 1973 173
Monday, October 8, 1973 178
Tuesday, October 9, 1973 179
Courage and fear 189
Counterattack 191
The war winds down: October 13-24, 1973 199
Friendship and comradeship-in-arms 200
Citations 205
Medals and Citations 209

12. REHABILITATING
THE ARMORED CORPS 213

Reconstructing a Reserve Training Base 220
Officer placement 225
To the Golan Heights via Israel TV 233

13. THE SEVENTH BRIGADE 237

The Four Officers Affair 244
Command and leadership 250
Routine in a wasteland of basalt 253

14. TO THE UNITED STATES
FOR STUDY 261

Innocent abroad 263

15. DIVISION COMMANDER
— A MAILED FIST 271

A division in a field of basalt.. 276
Confrontation with the Druse 281
Operation "Hotem" ("Official Seal") 290
On routine, on alert... 295
Discipline 298

16. PEACE FOR GALILEE
— THE WAR IN LEBANON 301

Sunday, June 6, 1982 311
The Arnon Highlands
and Beaufort Castle Fall 333
Perseverance 342
Monday, June 7, 1982 349
Sidon falls: June 8-9, 1982 362
Wednesday, June 9 384
Combat reaction syndrome 398
The war winds down 400

17. FROM THE BASALT STONES TO
THE
IRON TRIANGLE 408

Schedules 411

18. EPILOGUE 418

Officers at the crossroads 418

INTRODUCTION
BY
HERMAN WOUK

Brigadier General Avigdor Kahalani, the author of
A Warrior's Way, is a famous war hero, as well as a
distinguished Israeli military writer. His previous
work, *The Heights of Courage*, an account of the epic
tank battle on the Golan in the Yom Kippur War, is
an outstanding narrative of modern battlefield experiences. A bestseller in Israel, translated into other
languages, it describes a single critical struggle in
October, 1973, lasting only a few days, during which
the survival of the Jewish state actually hung in the
balance.

For his part in winning that battle against the
suprise Syrian onslaught, he received his country's
highest combat decoration, the Itur G'vura, or Medal
of Heroism, the Israeli equivalent of the Congres-
sional Medal of Honor. At the height of the Golan
battle, when the Syrian forces at the last moment
broke and retreated, the exausted Kahalani, whose
famed battalion had stood in the breach and barely
survived decimation, received this message from his
commander: "You have saved Israel." In the heat of
combat, such praise, though coming from the heart,
might have been exaggerated. But perhaps it stated a
simple fact for some military historians, writing in
cool retrospect, have repeated the assessment.

So much for the background of this author, a sabra
of Yemenite descent, with a record of valor in several

wars. Today Kahalani continues his dedicated public service as a member of the Knesset, the Israeli parliament.

In *A Warrior's Way*, Avigdor Kahalani writes a more intimate and philosophical work, exploring the nature of the fighting man and the realities of combat. For any reader curious about the extraordinary successes and the rare heartstopping failures of Zahal, the Israel Defense Forces, this frank book will be exciting and revealing.

I have known Avigdor Kahalani for years, I have much profited by studying his writings, and I am proud to have him for a friend. Prime Minister Rabin's eloquent Foreword about him says it all, but I feel privileged to add my words of admiration, and to recommend *A Warrior's Way* to American readers.

Herman Wouk
October, 1993

FOREWORD
BY YITZHAK RABIN

The Israelis are not born for war and most of them do not see their future in the army. Young Israelis want to be professionals, to work, to enjoy life — to live.

The on-going existential threat to the state of Israel compels the Israeli youth during his military service, with all its difficulties, to ask himself questions which affect his own existence. Great challenges stand before him. By virtue of his duty to the state, he must sacrifice his individualism and his personal life, and become one of many; to prevent the annihilation of the State of Israel, he must guarantee its existence. In this century, there has been virtually no other nation whose existence is constantly in jeopardy.

That is what happened to Avigdor Kahalani. The difficult security situation and the various wars always thrust him on the front line of fire, at the point of danger. His was among the first tanks which faced the barrage of enemy fire in the Six Day War. He fought on the front line in the War of Attrition. He straddled — with his comrades in the Yom Kippur War — the tin walls between man and armour, between life and death, between the possibility of facing a bitter end or fighting until victory.

The story of Avigdor Kahalani, which is captured in these pages, reveals the life of a courageous young Israeli who was forced to defend his country and to expose himself for many years in the turret of the tank; to fight for his life and see his comrades fall; to grit his teeth; to hide the scars of war on his body and the pain in his soul. It is committed to that goal.

Yitzhak Rabin

1. DEPARTED COMRADES

Back from the Yom Kippur War

At the crack of dawn we sped toward Nes Ziona, the farming town where I was born and raised. I entered the neighborhood that was so much a part of my life; my heart pounded. I grew excited as the moment of reunion with my family drew near. My brother Emmanuel was dead. They had told me a few hours earlier, and it weighed heavily on my mind. I wanted to know more about his last moments, yearned to hear how he had fought. I knew only that he had been in a tank crew in the Sinai, facing the Egyptians. The thought of seeing my parents again agitated me. Yanush, Col. Avigdor Ben-Gal, my commander, had given me to understand that they had made every effort to bring me home from the war when they learned my brother had perished.

Even though the car was comfortable and spacious, I could not fall asleep during the nighttime drive. Israel's highways looked no different than ever, apart from the unusually heavy military traffic. I asked the driver to stop at my house, not far from my parents' home. I was surprised to see the roof covered with shingles; I had left it bare when I had gone to war. The shingles I had abandoned in a heap next to the house now rested in exemplary order where they belonged. Giving the quiet yard a quick reconnaissance, I saw I had no reason to worry about the impending winter rains.

My neighbor, a pensioner named Shlomo, followed me into the yard and greeted me with agitation. He told me that Dalia had taken the kids to her parents in Jerusalem. Her younger brother, Ilan, had been killed, and she wanted to share the ritual seven days' bereavement with them. Her parents had been visiting mine, commiserating with them for their loss, when a phone call delivered them the same bitter news. I did not have to look for Dalia; I knew she was with them. I wondered how her parents would overcome their anguish: Ilan was their second son to fall in Israel's wars.

"How did the roof tiles get up there?" I asked Shlomo.

"Civil Defense people came and put them up; the mayor told them to. We were all worried about the rain," answered Shlomo, proud of the fact that it had been done.

"They saved me some work."

I was dying to stay home a little longer, to rest, to pull myself together, but I knew that there was no use in postponing the terribly hard task that lay before me: the inevitable meeting with my parents.

The car skidded into the yard and stopped behind the house. I heard the sound of morning prayers inside: the regular worshipers of the neighborhood synagogue had moved the service into my parents' home, as is customary for the newly bereaved. Hearing that I had arrived, my father stepped into the yard. There I faced him, in my dirty, sooty tank overalls. An eighteen-day growth of beard covered my face; surely it intensified his feelings. His cheeks were framed with white stubble. His eyes were red, his face fallen. "Thank you for coming, for making the effort. Finally they agreed to let you go," he said with a touch of sarcasm, restraining his agitation. "So what do you say?" he continued after embracing me, eyes flashing with joy and sadness, tears glistening. "Emmanuel's gone, and all this time I was worried about you. I knew you're always the first to jump into the fire."

Inside the house, the men glanced at us through the windows in mid-prayer. My driver, embarrassed by his presence at this conversation, backed away.

Emmanuel had followed me into the Armored Corps; I had pulled strings to get him out of Ordnance and into a tank. He fell during what should have been his honeymoon.

I said nothing, wanting to see my mother first. She ran to me in anguish and clutched me about the neck. I could do nothing to staunch her tears. Suddenly she looked older than she was.

"At least God kept you alive for me," she sobbed, refusing to let go. My brother Arnon, an ordinance man in my battalion during the war, was also home. I could not remember having given him permission to leave the battalion. My sister Ilana had come from faraway Arad to be at my parents' side. A short time later all of them began urging me to go to Jerusalem to be with Dalia and the kids, Dror and Vardit.

After talking it over at length on the phone, I did just that. I found Dalia pale as chalk. Her parents, to judge by their appearance, would never get over the loss. Their entire family gathered from all over the country, letting togetherness mitigate their agony. Everybody insisted that I describe the ordeal I had gone through on the Golan Heights. Their only source of information had been the media, and they yearned for a first-hand, personal account.

Quickly we began to discuss why this war had been thrust upon us, and everyone's accusing eyes had one target: the government. I was disinclined to look for people to blame; the content of the talk was far from me. I found it uncomfortable to be at home, with my family, while my men were still on the Golan Heights and surely wanted home leave as badly as I did.

Despite the cease-fire the Golan Heights was as tense as ever. Our formations stationed in the Syrian enclave continued to engage the enemy. The relative quiet was calm before a storm; everyone believed another confrontation was imminent.

When I reached home I found the telephone working overtime; I was to return to the battalion at once. My family contemplated me inquisitively as I prepared silently for the trip.

Returning to my men and finding the columns of tanks redeployed for battle, I recovered my confidence. I loved the enlisted men and the junior commanders. I loved to wander among the tanks and see men packing gear, loading ammunition, and attending devotedly to each and every piece of equipment. This time no one had to open the maintenance manuals to bring the machines up to par. Every crew knew its job to the last detail. Some things really matter and others matter less; war had taught the men to distinguish between the two. I sensed that the group of men under my command could meet any challenge, carry out any assignment. No changes were made in my tank crew, but the driver, Yuval, dug up some bazooka plates and mounted them to protect the hull from hits by the enemy. Gideon, the loader-radioman, had placed some spare ammo in the tank's cupola basket and rounded up another machine gun and an extra two-way radio. Kilyon, the gunner and assistant to the other two crewmen, recited his war experiences incessantly to anyone who cared to listen. Gidi Peled, the battalion operations officer, seemed suddenly older and more mature. The scars of war were perceptible.

Swiftly I jolted the battalion out of its tranquility and moved it to training grounds on the Heights. The companies and individual tanks trained as if war were about to erupt. There was no need to set up targets; plenty were scattered in the field-gutted Syrian tanks, damaged in the fighting and not yet hauled away. Among them we found undamaged tanks and personnel carriers. We quickly separated them from the others so as not to destroy them before the war salvage unit arrived.

The emergency depots were opened, and we found ourselves bundled up warmly and equipped with new gear. We packed the tanks' secret compartments with cigarettes and sweets. We began to recover the weight we had lost during the war. Most in demand were flak jackets, now available to us after having been lacking throughout the worst of the fighting.

The sensation of being on the threshold of a new war was felt by everyone because the political maneuverings seemed to hold little promise. Negotiations were under way on both the Egyptian and the Syrian fronts. Our triumph notwithstanding, the Syrians displayed the confidence one only associates with victors. I sometimes wondered where they summoned the strength to demonstrate such gall. Was it some secret, invisible weapon they had acquired? The Soviets, we knew, were filling their entire wish list and replacing everything they had lost in the war, including tanks. If to judge by the negotiations, our presence 20 miles from Damascus hardly troubled Syria.

At this stage I abruptly tore my thoughts away from grand geopolitics and redirected them to my paramount concern, my battalion. If my premonitions were true, we would shortly be returning to the enclave we had taken in the war, where we would have to dig in and defend our positions by force of arms. The Battalion 77 ("Oz") camp in Sinai was dismantled, equipment and all, and sent to us on the Golan Heights. With each passing day we were told of additional comrades who had fallen. I prayed with all my heart that those lists of names would reach their end. The IDF is built in such a way that those who spend years in the service get to know a large number of people, encountered at various junctures of their careers. I tried not to search those lists too carefully, perhaps trying to postpone the bitter news.

The media — talk shows, radio and TV news, newspaper headlines — reflected the new national sport: scapegoat-hunting. Israel had taken a blow that she was not built to withstand, a trauma in whose wake the country's citizens doubted their strength. Before the war we had perceived ourselves as being a strong country with secure borders. When the public wanted more butter and fewer guns, the IDF thinned its ranks without fear. Just before Yom Kippur it was announced that conscript service would be reduced to thirty months or so instead of thirty-six, and that reservists would put in thirty percent fewer days' duty each year. Preparations for dismantling one of the two conscript armor brigades in Sinai were launched. In retrospect, some of this seems to have been related to the approaching elections; the government was apprehensive about mobilizing the reserves at the first sign of imminent war. Such a step, the pundits said, was meant only to gain political capital just when the "man in the street" felt that Israel had reached safe waters at long last. After all, the Soviets were providing us with new immigrants, the Americans with weapons and grain, and the Arabs with convenient, cheap manpower. It was in this ambience of leisure and calm that the fateful decision to call up the reserves before fighting broke out had to be taken. Then, as now, Israel cannot be defended by its regular forces alone. To engage in a general war with all necessary deterrent and offensive might, the IDF needs its reserves.

The end of the Yom Kippur War found the country choking on itself. Life did not return to normal, and the threshold-of-war sensation aggravated the controversies that wracked public opinion. The populace was overwhelmed with fatigue; all everyone wanted was a bit of peace and quiet. Admittedly, our bargaining position on the Egyptian front was good: we had surrounded the Egyptian Third Army, and Egypt appealed to the superpowers for help and protection. In his book on the crossings of the Suez Canal, Gen. Shazli, Egyptian Chief of Staff during the war, admits frankly that Israel could have twisted his country by the arm at the time. The Syrians, by contrast, remained obdurate, refusing to discuss the repatriation of POWs and conditioned any negotiations on our removing our threat against Damascus. The bitterly cold winter chilled the morale of the soldiers on the Golan Heights, thus keeping pressure on the political echelon as well.

Post-War Days

The fighters of Battalion "Oz" 77 began to live double lives, returning to routine training while maintaining alert for continued fighting. Many of the men requested permission to let their wartime beards grow. I refused unless they promised, in writing, to keep them for half a year. They got the hint: we were returning to prewar discipline and order.

Officers and men had begun checking in their Uzis and replacing them with captured enemy weapons. Handguns and Kalashnikov assault rifles could be seen everywhere. This booty, however, endangered the men: the battalion did not have ammunition of the right kind and quantity, and nobody knew how to maintain the weapons. Thus I put an end to this practice, too, and we went back to our own Uzis.

The tanks looked different. Bundles of spare gear had been strapped to the hulls and fenders, as if the soldiers had compensated themselves for everything they had missed during the war. External compartments were filled with ammo, turning an enemy hit into a potential disaster. I ordered the men to store the ammo where it belonged. Spare parts tied to the tanks' outer plates were a different matter. Apart from permitting the men to solve mechanical problems in a pinch, the extra gear was good for added protection. The bazooka plates that ordinarily protected the tanks had disappeared during the fighting. The crews set out for the Vale of Tears and returned with the missing plates to make sure nobody "borrowed" them...

To counter the fierce Golan chill,, the men donned multicolored overgarments that made them look like gypsies. It was hard in those early post-war days to impose leadership on fighters who had so recently emerged from hellfire. By any delay in knocking them back into the military framework would only make things harder later on. A commander has got to learn lessons and apply them in his unit at the first possible opportunity. When a tank is encumbered with super-fluous gear, its gun cannot complete its 360-degree swing and is therefore vulnerable. Spare ammunition endangers the crew and the surroundings; "custom" white markings enable the enemy to identify the tank at a distance.

Soldiers' inclinations to let their hair down acquire legitimacy when their thoughts turn to their comrades who did not return from the battlefield. Suddenly they consider themselves lucky for having survived. Indeed, this may have been the result of good fortune, not necessarily of wisdom. In this frame of mind, soldiers tend to make light of conventions, of doing things by the book. The "me-first" attitude can swamp the emotions of any fighter who wishes to ready himself for the hardest act of all without relying on others.

At this point the Adjutant department sent me a computer printout explaining the whereabouts of my men who had been wounded in action. So dispersed were they among Israel's hospitals that I could not have located them any other way. The idea that some-body might simply vanish always troubled me. Thank God, my battalion had no one missing in action. During the war I was concerned that my battalion's casu-alties might not be identified, and I made sure that the evacuation teams kept the men's dogtags with the bodies. On the second day of the war, as we retreated from part of our sector, one of my tank commanders was killed by an artillery shell. The crew abandoned the stricken vehicle and we soon found ourselves holding a new line, far from where the commander had fallen. We could not return to our previous positions because enemy forces were circulating there. As soon as I got the go-ahead, however, I attacked the area in order to recover the commander's body and bring it to the rear. Under Syrian machine gun and artillery fire we reached the tank; the commander was removed and brought to Israel for burial. I shuddered at the thought that I might have to face parents whose son had not returned from the battlefield — an MIA.

Missing in Action

The concept "missing in action" — MIA — makes my skin crawl. Few in the IDF have gone through that terrible ordeal. I'm happy to say that I know of it only through the experience of other commanders.

The IDF defines MIA as a soldier who is alive unless proven otherwise. A distinction is drawn between an MIA, who may still be found alive, and casualties whose place of burial is unknown. A soldier who was evidently killed in battle but whose body has not been found is called PBU — "Place of Burial Unknown". The authority to determine — on the basis of testimony and battlefield evidence — that a missing man is PBU and not MIA is entrusted to one man and one alone: the Chief Rabbi of the IDF. His verdict is crucial. The wife of an MIA, under the religious law that governs personal status in Israel, is an "aguna", ie., an "abandoned wife" who may not remarry. It is also very important to dispel relatives' doubts about their son's fate. Since 1948 the IDF has listed 58 soldiers as PBU. To them one should add the

69 crewmen of the submarine Dakar, which disappeared at sea in 1968.

A special department handles MIA affairs; its hierarchy is headed by the chief of the General Staff Manpower division. In the aftermath of the Yom Kippur War, much was done to formalize the handling of MIAs; the Air Force set up its own MIA branch, and the IDF established its own all-service agency for the sole purpose of locating MIAs, with representatives in every regional command down to the division level.

At the end of the Yom Kippur War, approximately 1,200 men were recorded as MIA. Obviously, most of them were defined as such because of recording problems; some, too, had been taken POW and their names had not yet come in. After comparing the POW rosters and solving the recording problems, we found about 300 genuine MIAs. The special MIA agency, in concert with the Army Rabbinate, labored long and hard to resolve the dismal affair. Some of Israel's top professionals were assigned to help the teams in the field. Innumerable inquiries and reconnaissance behind our lines and in enemy territory brought the number of MIAs down to nineteen. The Chief Rabbi of the IDF confirmed that all of them had fallen in action, thus facilitating their reclassification as PBUs. Five of them had belonged to the Air Force, two to the Navy, and twelve to tank crews in the Armored Corps.

At the end of Operation Peace for Galilee, 43 soldiers were listed as MIAs. At the present writing, the IDF cannot verify the whereabouts of seven men: three tank crewmen who are presumably being held by the Syrians after having been ambushed in the battle for Sultan Yacoub; a Druze soldier kidnaped in

Lebanon; two soldiers kidnaped by Hizbollah on Lebanese soil in February, 1986, and an Air Force navigator who has been held by Amal since October, 1986.

As a commander who has taken part in several wars, I can say for sure that the number of MIAs can be reduced to a minimum. The MIA phenomenon contains several interrelated problems that one has to resolve. First, every IDF commander should be taught how to cope with the problem and prevent it. He ought to familiarize himself with the human story behind one of the MIAs; in particular, he should get to know an MIA's family. The record-keeping problems are solvable; the IDF has given thought to some of them. Soldiers fill out special forms before they head for battle. License numbers are welded or embossed onto tanks and other vehicles. Soldiers carry extra dogtags in their boots, apart from the ordinary ones around their necks. Infractions of discipline in these matters should be treated with special severity. The preliminary record-keeping is obviously no problem, with the IDF's computer system.

Once the matter is brought to commanders' attention, no soldier will be found anywhere, even in the midst of combat, without I.D. The fallen soldier is evacuated to the rear, where a team from the medical corps or the Army Rabbinate takes over. The body goes from one unit to another, none of which know the casualty. Thus the moment he is evacuated from the battlefield, his comrades ought to attach to his body anything that might help identify him. Yes, it's hard to do under fire. But remember that we're handing him over to his comrades or the medical team attached to the unit; they and they alone will get him off the battlefield. Sensitive commanders would even bring the men to a halt and order some of them to remove a casualty from an area that our forces may no longer control at a later time.

At the end of a battle or war, a commander with MIAs in his unit faces court martial or a commission of inquiry. Such a blunder as leaving an MIA behind cannot be treated lightly. The court martial has exclusive power to rule on the commander's innocence or guilt. The IDF gives commanders a great privilege when it lets them lead soldiers into war. The men follow their commander through fire and water, trusting him to lead them to victory. They follow his orders, sometimes assuming blindly that they are right and that his judgment is trustworthy. Soldiers who entrust their bodies and souls to their commanders have got to know that they will not be abandoned if wounded or killed in battle. In all times and situations the IDF derives its might from its fighters' unqualified belief that they will not be abandoned come what may.

I had to visit the bereaved families promptly, and I was apprehensive about it. I built a file on each soldier, including any details I considered important: exactly how and when he fell, the men who witnessed his death, those who could meet with the family and tell them more about their son's last moments. Commanders wrote their accounts about those final seconds; these, too, went into the file, as did the names of the crewmen who evacuated the casualty. I refrained from being overly vivid or gory. In short, the information I placed in the casualty files included everything I wanted to know about my brother Emmanuel, who fell in Sinai.

A computer print-out provided me with the names of additional men from my battalion of whose death I was unaware. They had remained in Sinai to safeguard the battalion. My tanks had gone over to a different unit, which integrated the men into its own forces. When they fell they officially belonged to the 77th Battalion in Sinai. They were Eitan Lochenberg, Eli Ben-Simon, Sashi Zak, Eli Ivri, and K. Terrence. Ben-Simon's body was found two months after the war. Eitan was an MIA too. They found his body in the dunes of Sinai eight months after the war.

This fact placed me under a new kind of stress. Who was responsible for these corpses? Who was to report their death to the army authorities? Who would visit the parents? How would the families be cared for, and who would tell them about the battle in which their loved ones had fallen? These questions disturbed my peace of mind. I saw these war casualties as my men in every respect.

Visits with bereaved families were the sort of experiences I have never forgotten.

I made sure to let the families know in advance that I was coming, and in most of the meetings the whole family was present. I was anxious about questions to which I had no clear answer. One factor, however, made me "part of the family" from the moment I entered the home: my unshaven face attested to my own situation as a mourner. No one was hostile to me. I tried to convince the men to visit, also. I made sure to emphasize the importance of the battle in which their sons had fallen. It was small consolation, but every family was give to understand that its son had not fallen in vain, that he had died a hero's death in defense of the homeland.

Families of the 77th Battalion became one great

clan. Subsequently they met twice a year at the monument built by battalion members, overlooking the Vale of Tears on the Golan Heights. The battalion consecrated the memory of its fighters; every new commander studies the episode in detail. The battle heritage imbues the soldiers with strength, just as their certainty that the battalion will not leave their families to cope for themselves imbues them with confidence.

Slowly I learned how to handle the difficulty of meeting with a bereaved family. The tag of "unapproachable" that marked some of these families vanished. Conversation with such a family, I learned, should have nothing to do with the weather or politics, even though it tends to gravitate to such topics to avoid mentioning the fallen son, husband or father. Conversation should be allowed to flow as the family wants it to. Fear of inflicting pain causes people to venture on to tangents. For mourners, shared concern and sorrow mitigate the pain.

Bereaved parents never get over their anguish. Everything reminds them of their son; they do not need Memorial Day, when all Israelis express their identification with bereaved families. The Rehabilitation Division of the Defense Ministry cares for families in areas where commanders and comrades-in-arms cannot. It is the function and duty of the latter to stay in touch with the family as best they can. A wreath embellished with the unit's emblem, laid on the son's grave on Memorial Day, consoles the parents more than almost anything else. If we learn to cope with these problems, we may perhaps alleviate, in some small measure, this incurable agony.

After days of organizing and of endless alerts on t he Syrian front, the battalion was hastily ordered into the enclave to check a possible Syrian offensive. The battalion was at that point at Khan Arinba, east of Nafah. Now we began to understand the broad outline of the war and with it the immensity of the blow we had received. It is many times more complicated to command a unit after a war than before one. However, I quickly adjusted to the new reality, not letting up for a moment.

To leave or not to leave

Thirty days after my brother Emmanuel died, I went home for the tombstone unveiling. Late that night, Haggai Regev, still with the 7th Brigade as liaison, called me frantically: I was to return to the Golan at once. My absence from the memorial ceremony, I knew, would hurt my family deeply. For them, too, this would be the first encounter with Emmanuel's grave. However uncomfortable I felt about it, I requested — and received — permission to return after the ceremony. Hanging up, I could no longer close my eyes. I understood from what Haggai had said that my unit was being transferred without the presence of a commander. True, the brigade command was in contact with Ami, a company commander with the battalion, who I had placed in charge during my absence. The usual doubts flashed through my head: Where was the unit going? Had I the right to stay home while everyone headed for the new positions? Then I stopped myself: no one asked me to get into the car and drive to the Golan Heights in the middle of the night.

The unveiling of the tombstone was one of the harshest experiences of my life. Whole families ran about at the provisional cemetery at Mishmar

Hanegev, looking for their loved one's grave among the many. I beheld my family at one of its most difficult moments.

I went back to the battalion, unable to forget the sight of my family. The days passed; still I was troubled by the way I had treated my family. Go home, my father said before I left, even for just a little while. He knew I had been sent to the Syrian enclave, and was afraid that I would come under fire again. My mother just cried. My wife Dalia tried to refrain from pressuring me. She agreed with my father but understood what I was going through. Her eyes, however, had lost their luster, as if they had recessed into their sockets.

"I can't leave the battalion today," I repeated each time they tried to change my mind.

Back with the battalion, I felt my confidence return. It was hard to be away from the group of men with whom I had fought. The war machines all around us had become parts of our bodies. The tanks, cold as they were, had provided us with warmth when we were in them. Inside me the struggle, to stay or not to stay, went on. I tried to repress the thoughts, but they surfaced time and again. Alone in my room I knew I was going home. Outside, mingling with my men, I knew I was staying.

My vacillation drove me back to 1967, to the hospital, where I lay after having been wounded in the Six-Day War. It was then that I first felt the power of family. I had many visitors, but each went his way and left me alone with my pain. Only my family stayed with me. I admit it: I never reciprocated for the warmth they had given me. They gave me everything.

Front-line soldiers usually come home once a week,

and those few hours do not permit them to be a real part of their families. Quickly their wives and children learn to do without them. When they get longer furloughs, embarrassing things can happen. Suddenly you discover you don't know very much about your children, what they want, how they think. Your influence over their behavior diminishes. Still, I always knew that somebody at home knew how to fill my shoes. However far away I might be, the home remained intact. As I argued with myself, I kept this in mind. But this time, I felt, I would lose it all.

I made up my mind, fearing the moment when I would present the brigade commander, Yanush, with my decision.

It was late one night, in the village of Khan Arinba in the Syrian enclave. The men were elsewhere, attending to their personal affairs. I stuck my head into Yanush's car.

"I'd like... . I need to consult with you," I began. I said something about how nicely arranged, how comfortable his car was. Then I got to the subject.

"I've got a problem: my family. I feel I'm going to lose them. I feel my family is collapsing. I know I belong here and nowhere else, but things are bad back there." I looked into Yanush's eyes, trying to read his response. "I've been carrying this in my gut for a long time. It's damned hard."

"I knew it was going to happen one day," answered Yanush, confirming that my cause was real. "I remember how they called me every day during the war so I'd let you go home. I couldn't. You understand why: your deputy was wounded, and I'd handed the main burden of holding the enclave to your battalion. I just had to rely on you and your company commanders." Then Yanush apologized for not having told me about my brother's death until the war was over. That was dangerous, he admitted, but it was hard for him.

"Yanush, I already told you back then, in the jeep, that I'm glad you did what you did and didn't force me to make up my mind. In your shoes I would have done just the same, and maybe it was for the best. I'm sure I would not have left the battalion. You would have just made things hard for me, trying to cope with the battalion in the middle of the war." I had decided to go, and it appeared that Yanush would agree to it.

"In any case, I'm glad nothing happened to you since I got word of it," Yanush smiled.

The conversation lasted well into the night. Hot coffee and soup were brought to the car, and one subject followed another. Yanush asked me to wait until he had a chance to speak with Raful. Raful, the division commander during the war, was the one who approved the replacement of battalion commanders.

As for the man who would replace me, I knew there was only one candidate. Lt. Col. Yoss Eldar was just back from the hospital; he was available and had not duties. Yoss had been wounded twice during the war. On the second occasion he had taken shrapnel from a shell that had fallen near his tank. He returned to the brigade limping, insisting that he could function nevertheless. By that time, however, his second-in-command, Yossi Melamed, had taken over his battalion, the third battalion of the seventh brigade. Yoss demanded his battalion back, but it was no use; the battalion had a new commander.

Yanush and I agreed that Yoss was indeed a viable candidate; he could take over at once. When presented with this, however, Yoss himself resisted vigorously. Yossi Melamed should take my battalion, he said, and he would return to his own. Some time later, Raful approved the arrangement as Yanush and I recommended. Then I let my battalion know I was leaving, although not officially. I floated the rumor. That way the men would not be taken totally by surprise when they heard it from me personally. I gathered the company commanders and, concealing nothing, told them what I had decided and why...

However, my hand-picked replacement continued to balk. The three of us met for what proved to be a tough conversation. As I kept my silence, Yanush, short tempered, tore into Yoss:

"I know some of your problem is real. You don't want the battalion because you're afraid of stepping into Kahalani's shoes. You know how the battalion relates to him. That's what you're afraid of."

Yoss was embarrassed and I was even more so. The atmosphere was electric. Even though I really wanted to get out of the car, I broke into the conversation, trying to steer it in gentler directions. I talked about how one had to help out, how I had no second-in-command just then, how dangerous the situation was. Summing up, we decided to transfer command the next day. Yoss admitted his apprehension to me:

"First of all, I want my battalion back. Besides, I don't think your battalion will accept me so easily!"

I did everything I could to alleviate the difficulty of his new duty:

"Yoss, it's a top-notch battalion. I still mean to tell the boys why I'm leaving, and believe me, that's more complicated than taking over the battalion. Let's not make it hard on them. It'll be easier and simpler than you think."

Then, with no further ado, I began drawing up a schedule of meetings with all elements of the battalion scattered across the Syrian enclave and the Nafah area.

In my parting talk I chose not to review the path we had trudged together in the war. Rather, I focused on why I was leaving. A glint in the listeners' eyes told me that they knew why and may even have thought my action justified. To make my talk go over easier, I started out with a few cracks at my own expense and the men's, "getting even" with those whom I could not have touched previously. I introduced Yoss as my good friend and hand-picked replacement, adding that there couldn't be a better man for the job. Yoss and I had much in common, and I left it to the men to figure out what those traits were. For another reason, too, the battalion would not suffer from the change of commanders: both of us were graduates of the same "finishing school" — armored officers' training.

I did have one request, which I explained at length:

"Visit the wounded men. Visit the bereaved families. That's a must. Do it for the sake of our friends whom we fought with and who are no longer with us. Don't put it off. It's more important that going home on short leave. Go to them and tell them about their sons' last moments. I know it's scary, but I'll make you swear to it: talk with them, and look 'em in the eye when you do it. Don't put it off. Later it'll be more unpleasant, and then you may never do it! And something else: get yourselves together and put up a monument over the "Vale of Tears". In the future we'll go there and look into the valley and remember those who are gone."

All this brought tears to my eyes. My throat choked.

I seated myself on the only bench in the area, trying to suppress my emotions. I listened to Yoss.

"I promise you, Avi," he said at the end of his remarks, "that you'll hear only good things about us!" I packed my gear and went home.

2. A MATTER OF HOME AND ROOTS

Nes Ziona, originally a little farming town, is my home.

My father Moshe was born in 1923 in Aden, at the very bottom of the Arabian Peninsula. His family had fled to Aden from San'a, then capital of Yemen and today of North Yemen, lest the Muslims convert the orphaned nephews of my grandfather, Saadia Kahalani. It was in Aden that my grandfather met and married my grandmother. A few years later they decided to resettle in Israel, then Palestine, making the trip by ship via the Suez Canal. My father was one year old at the time. On the way, my mother gave birth to twin daughters, one of whom died later.

After some searching, the family found a little shack in Tel Aviv, in the Sheloush neighborhood next to Neve Tzedek. Three years later they moved to Kerem Ha-Teimanim, Hebrew for "Yemenites' Vineyard." Times were hard; my father fed his family by making the rounds of the grocery stores, picking up leftovers. In the Arab riots of 1929 my family, like all the Jews in the area, shut themselves up at home and prepared their self-defense with all available weapons: sticks and stones.

My father attended an Orthodox boys' school in the Mahane Yosef neighborhood south of Kerem Ha-

Teimanim. My grandfather could not afford to buy
him shoes. Sometimes my father, barefoot, would
cross the sizzling sand dunes between our home and
the school, only to be kept out of class for being
shoeless. When the teachers deigned to admit him, he
was often on the receiving end of their rod; the "peda-
gogues" were wont to whack pupils on their legs. To
walk home, the shoeless ones had to collaborate with
their more fortunate classmates: the sand was so hot
that the latter would carry the former on their backs.

In the early 1930s the Kahalani family moved to
Manshiyya, next to Arab-populated Jaffa. In the Arab
uprising of 1936 they became refugees; several months
later, in 1937, they made their way 15 kilometers
southeast to Nes Ziona.

At this point my grandfather fell ill and became
bedridden. My father left school to help support the
family by picking and packing oranges in the orchards of Nes Ziona. During World War II sources of
livelihood in our village dwindled, and my father
migrated to Tel Aviv in search of work.

It was there, in Kerem Ha-Teimanim, that he met
my mother, Sarah, whose family, the Sianis, had
settled there after reaching the country from San'a in
1933. At an early age she had had to leave school and
go to work. Education was not compulsory then, and
the family, due to its background, was not aware of
the need for it. At that time, girls did not study as
boys did. This had no subsequent effect on my
mother's credentials as a fine homemaker and an
exemplary parent.

Sarah and Moshe married in 1943, and their firstborn son came along exactly nine months later. Their
prayers had been answered. Eight days later, at the
circumcision ceremony in the Yemenite Quarter syna-

gogue, a serious argument broke out: "Call him Saadia," the congregants instructed my father. "Name him after your late father; that'll guarantee him long life."

"No! Not Saadia, and not Zecharia! We're in Eretz Israel; he needs a name that fits the times and the country. We'll call him Avigdor," my father proclaimed, standing firm against his critics.

"What! An Ashkenazi name!" came the rejoinder. How could a proud Yemenite Hebrew give his firstborn a name typically chosen by the effete Jews of northern and central Europe? My father stubbornly held his ground. He was highly impressed by this name, which belonged to two men he respected: the late poet and author Avigdor Hameiri and Avigdor Yosifon, the legendary watchman from the neighboring village of Beit-Oved. The dispute was resolved by the rabbi, who inserted the name of choice in the prayer following the circumcision: "Avigdor, son of Moshe Kahalani, this little one, may he grow... ."

In 1944, after serving as an auxiliary policeman in the British Army during World War II, my father enlisted in the Hagana — the Palestinian Jewish community's main militia — and was posted as a guard in our town. After the Hagana went over to field operations, my father and his friends were left behind to protect the neighborhood. Displeased with their duties, they quit the Hagana and joined the Irgun, one of two rival militias, and participated in some of its operations. In the 1948-49 War of Independence, when the underground militias were disbanded in favor of the newly established Israel Defense Forces, my father was demobilized because his work was considered vital for the economy. Dissatisfied with these priorities, he quit his job a few months later and reenlisted. This new-old soldier, the father of two, was assigned to the "Portzim" ("Burglars") Battalion of the Harel-Palmach Brigade under Yitzhak Rabin. He spent the War of Independence in its ranks. Many sites in Jerusalem and the land corridor approaching it from the west are named for this battalion. One of the actions in which my father took part was the capture of the Hartuv police station and the Arab villages of Deir Ban and Deir al-Hawa near Beit Shemesh, 20 kilometers southwest of Jerusalem.

Our home in Nes Ziona was the last in a row of houses bordering the Arab neighborhood of Wadi Hanin, or "Rose Valley." The house was made of reinforced concrete so it would withstand the bursts of gunfire that emanated from the Arab quarter. Even so, our Arab neighbor Mahmud, a few years older than me, was a regular playmate of mine; our favorite haunt was the area near the fence between our yard and his. The toilet and shower were out in the yard, as was a security shelter of the sort commonly used in those days. Our house opened onto a court shared by the homes of my grandmother and two uncles.

Some time later, displeased with the cramped quarters, my father obtained some land and built his own home far from the neighborhood where he grew up and where I was born. He built it himself, from foundation to shingles, and it was my duty to bring his lunch to the construction site each and every day. He reinforced the slabs of concrete with metal poles lifted from Arab houses that had been abandoned and demolished. Since then the house has not changed, but

the neighborhood is quite different. During my childhood it was repopulated with immigrants from Po-
land. Yiddish became the neighborhood vernacular,
and in order to understand our new neighbors we too
had to learn it quickly.

This is not to say my family broke relations with
the Yemenite quarter; we continued to pray in the
neighborhood synagogue and visit friends who had
stayed there.

Today Nes Ziona is an urbanized suburb of Tel
Aviv, but in the 1940s and 1950s it was a little town
divided in two. The town's agricultural founders
("peasants," they called themselves) lived west of the
main street, and later arrivals ("workers") had their
own neighborhood east of it. The workers, my family
among them, labored in the farmers' citrus groves.
When it came time to enroll me in kindergarten, my
parents sent me to the "wrong" side. To this day I do
not know why, and cannot understand where my
parents marshaled the audacity to consign me to three
years among the offspring of the town's aristocracy....

How well I remember the tension and dread that
gripped me every morning as I crossed the main street
from east to west. It wasn't the busy traffic that frightened me, but rather the clusters of Arabs along the
main road, especially near the mosque, whose minaret
was later downed and the entire structure converted
into a synagogue. I remember the bonfires the Arabs
of Nes Ziona used to light in their neighborhoods, and
I recall very clearly how they left, packing their be-
longings and heading southward toward the Gaza
Strip. I watched them through my window, and when
I asked what would become of them, I was told:
"They'll come back when the war's over."

For first grade I was sent to a new school in the workers' quarter. Dividing the pupils into classes, the administration placed me among recent immigrants who did not know Hebrew. My father made inquiries and was told:

"We decided to put all the kids who didn't go to kindergarten and have learning problems in one class," the teacher explained. "That way they'll get special care."

My father, quick to anger in any case, trembled with rage. Only upon further inquiry did the administration discover to its surprise that I had three years of kindergarten behind me.

The family grew, Emmanuel and Arnon following my sister Ilana. We all had a happy childhood. My mother met our every need, and our house was a model of cleanliness and order. My father had gone back to his regular work at the nearby experimental farm and took on odd jobs for spare cash. In the evenings he plowed fields with a tractor he had bought, and I would join him. By the time I was eleven, I could handle the plowing alone.

Aware of my father's wish that I acquire a trade, I went on from elementary school to an ORT vocational school and studied precision mechanics. Since tuition was high, they sent me to the school in Jaffa, where fees were covered by the "combined method": half a day of study and half a day of factory labor, the wages credited to the school.

I loved to work, I loved to study, and I loved... my father's motorcycle. At night, my tender age notwithstanding, I would drag it out of the yard and ply the streets of Nes Ziona. It was a big bike and I could hardly control it. Impatiently I waited for my sixteenth birthday, when I could get a license. My mother threatened to leave home the day that happened, so my father and I sneaked out of the house when my turn to take the test came up. I put the family bike through its paces without the benefit of a single "official" driving lesson. I passed, and even my mother, her threats aside, could not conceal a smile at the sight of her beaming son.

3. INTO UNIFORM

Then I reached induction age. My natural objective was the Ordinance Corps. From the outset I had no intention of spending my army service practicing the trade I had learned: I was fiercely eager to change, to do something different. To my delight they first sent me for pilot's training, and the more I thought about it the more I wanted it. There was a problem, I knew: the hearing in my right ear was impaired, the result of some faulty treatment in my childhood. I got past the doctors in the induction center, where the checkup was simple: a technician told me to stick a finger in one ear and repeat the sentence he whispered behind my back. I left my good ear half-unplugged and heard every word. The Air Force, by contrast, referred me to an audiologist. The examination was professional this time; I had to respond to every buzz emitted by a machine and couldn't lie.

Back I went for reassignment. "Paratroops," I barked to the placement officer who asked what I wanted. A few minutes later I found myself running with a group of recruits who had the same goal in mind. The doctor who checked me afterward, himself a "red beret," pointed to the soles of my feet. "You've got very flat feet. You won't be able to walk long distances; it'll hurt like hell. You shouldn't be a foot soldier. You ought to go on wheels!" His verdict was clear enough: forget about infantry.

In those days inductees were given no advance information about army life, so I spent many days agitated and beset with unanswered questions. People you've never met are going to seal your fate, and no one guarantees that you'll have a chance to tell them what you want. Where am I heading? I asked myself again and again, as I gradually decided on Ordinance.

The very next day they attached me to a group of recruits marked "destination unknown." Every morning they marched us to a vacant lot on the base, ordered us to sit on the ground, and called out our names by group, each group slated for a different base. We called this the "slave market." A few members of my group, recalling the preferences they presented to the placement officer, hypothesized that we were headed for Armor. Once called, we were given five minutes to organize all our gear and return to our positions on the base, ready to board a truck destined for parts unknown. Now they told us, tersely and to-the-point, what the verdict was: "Armor. Camp Hassa."

Just what I always feared had happened. One thing I would not do in the army: I would not go to closed-in places. My father had made me swear: "Avi," he had said, "I don't butt into your affairs. Use your head and do what you want. But one thing I ask: do everything not to be a "tankist"!"

Nor did I have to ask him why he felt that way. He had described his daily ordeals in the War of Independence and the 1956 Sinai Campaign. As a tractor driver in the Engineering Corps, it was his duty to drag stricken tanks off the battlefield; he had been present when the charred bodies had been extracted from them. To his last day he could neither forget nor overcome the sights he had seen.

"It'll be all right, Dad. I'll be a pilot and fly over the house and dip my wings for you," I had promised him.

I still did not know which path I would tread, but I knew for sure it would not be a tank tread. They wouldn't shut me up in a tin can, breathing through a little pipe!

On the way to Hassa I planned my next moves. I'd put in a written request for reassignment. I'd go AWOL. Come hell or high water, they'd never find me in a tank!

Induction

IDF induction is planned by the General Staff Manpower Branch and implemented by an induction administration headed by a colonel. The administration's task is to make civilian teenagers into soldiers, utilizing all their potential for the IDF's benefit. The future soldier's first stop is the reception and classification base east of metropolitan Tel Aviv, where he is classified and assigned to the unit deemed best for him, as long as it fills the army's needs.

There are four rounds of conscription— May, August, November and February— with thousands of men and women in each group. Aiming to send those with combat predisposition to the fighting units, the administration tries to determine each inductee's potential before he or she is drafted, using various methods to determine who will head for command training, OCS, or other areas. The administration also attempts to spot those suited to special units: air crews, naval crews, rescue teams, intelligence, paratroops. Placement with these latter formations entails a try-out period, held before or after induction, that is meant to filter out all but the best. These are volunteer units, and it is the system's task to identify the most suitable candidates.

A conscript spends about four days at the reception base. On the first day he is introduced to the IDF's constituent corps, each tempting him with multimedia displays. On the second day they are interviewed by placement officers and given their first opportunity to state their own wishes. On the third day, the general decision on their placement already made, recruits are sent to the corps of choice for a pre-boot-camp medical checkup. This lowers the medical profiles of several dozen conscripts in every group. Some conceal their problems at the induction station checkup. Others come down with new conditions in the intervening months. Still others begin to harbor doubts upon induction and ask to be reexamined. Soldiers are allowed to undergo any test before assignment; many are referred to specialists upon induction, and these specialists rule on their state of health.

The induction system at the reception base is polished and efficient. The soldiers are interviewed and reinterviewed by highly experienced placement specialists, reserve officers with many years of such service behind them. Soldiers may specify three choices in order of preference. Before reporting to the formation, they are checked again. Every night the reception base staff checks their details, comparing the data collected in the various stages of induction, confirming that they were indeed posted to the formation requested. Thus soldiers are kept from falling between the stools, usually reaching their units of choice, without misgivings, on the fourth day.

The medical profile is a matter of great significance in placing soldiers. The healthiest, those with profiles of 97, are assigned to the IDF's spearhead formations. Infantry does not admit anyone with a profile under 80. Armor, Artillery, and Anti-Aircraft units accept profiles down to 72.

More than half of the conscripts— 80 percent of those in a recent group— asked for field units. Many graduates of technological high schools apply for technical trades, but some of them, too, are assigned to field formations as the army sees fit. Those with electronics training may commit themselves upon induction to an additional year's service in the standing army.

Some soldiers refuse to accept the system's decision and are called "refuseniks". The system doesn't yield; there's always a way to force conscripts to knuckle under.

Soldiers' conditions of service, including social welfare problems, are usually handled within their own formations. Even so, the reception base makes every effort to station soldiers with genuine problems close to home.

The administration also determines every soldier's "quality group ranking". Much debate goes on in the IDF about how to classify soldiers, count them, and assess their caliber. Naturally, the corps vie for quality recruits who can be molded into the next generation of commanders. When all is said and done, most soldiers go where they want— within certain limits, of course. Even those assigned to units not to their liking usually integrate within a few days. Comradeship and shared experiences evoke identification. Social pressure does its share, too, and almost every soldier acquires a sense of pride in his or her unit. Cases of soldiers assigned against their will who subsequently become their formations' greatest boosters are by no means rare.

To be a fighter, to be a "tankist"

The truck rumbled into Camp Hassa and headed straight for the recruits' tents. "Welcome to the 82nd Battalion," a dazzling sign affixed to one of the structures greeted us. Camp Hassa, a facility in southern Israel built in part on the ruins of a British camp, was not far from Camp Julis, site of the Armored Corps School, three kilometers north of Hodaya Junction. The 82nd was the IDF's first armored battalion. It had been set up as part of the 8th Brigade under Yitzhak Sadeh, the legendary "old man" who organized the army's first armored brigade. The 82nd was transferred to the 7th Brigade at the end of the War of Independence.

Within the battalion I was assigned to Company 7. The tent cluster bustled with fresh recruits, their heads small after brutal boot-camp haircuts. They were not completely bald; the barbers had left some stubble. Apprehensive, I lined up with the others for this experience. I had not had a haircut in several months. Within minutes my hair was shorn, and my head, like the others', looked small and ugly. Recruits raced around the tents frantically, by order of commanders with ranks of corporal and sergeant, who evidently enjoyed their duty.

Stepping into my tent, I was greeted affectionately by my new comrades. They taught me my first bit of army wisdom: how to "square" a pack. All the packs had to look like boxes, their sides perfectly straight, their canvas flaps down and their many clips and straps gleaming. I caught on right away: you line the sides with bits of plasterboard and cardboard, making your pack look straight and taut, ready for any inspection.

I sailed through basic training with unexpected ease. On Saturdays we would sneak into the tank shelter, peering curiously at the intimidating metal monsters. Later, in the "occupational" stage of bootcamp, we came into daily contact with them. Each of us was given a certain function to master, called our "occupation." I was trained as the gunner in a Centurion tank. The more I learned about the tank, the less I resisted and feared it. Slowly I even began to enjoy the drills. It was amazing to watch teenage soldiers move this great, cumbersome behemoth effortlessly, observe the heavy turret swinging around in search of a target, its facade mysterious and frightening. I performed well in all areas, operating the equipment dexterously, firing quickly and accurately, and retaining every bit of subject matter they packed into my head.

After the "occupational" training, the battalion prepared for field maneuvers on the crew, platoon, and company levels. To my surprise, I was assigned to the company commander's tank as its loader and radio man, not as the gunner. That was a blow. Everyone knew that the best men were chosen to be the gunners; loader-radioman was for the weak and the less fit. My protestations were of no use. The company commander, Maj. Meshullam Rattas, chose me as his loader-radioman precisely because of my quickness; he wanted his crew to out-fire everyone else. I accepted the verdict, but wrote home without pride about my role in the tank. The job I wanted had gone to my good friend Ovad Noma, and the driver was Yohanan Evioni, whom I had just met for the first time.

The company commander lit a fire under all of us. Rattas, whom we had previously known, stationed himself in front of us with his top shirt button open — deliberately, it seemed. His uniform was crisply ironed and tailored to his rugged body.

"You're gonna be the best crew in this company, and if not, I'm gonna bust your asses. Is that clear!?"

We nodded, our forced smiles concealing a measure of fear. What else could we have said? We were in for it now.

We moved to the Revivim area south of Beersheba and plunged into harsh, bone-wrenching maneuvers. We were in the middle of the Negev, surrounded by a barren landscape; the intense heat and dryness added to our ordeal. At night, while normal people slept, we watered down and raked the tent area. We lugged jerricans of water and fuel from faraway depots until our hands nearly came out of their sockets. We hauled heavy artillery shells in their crates, two men apiece, until our backs ached. But the whole ordeal — the difficult maneuvers, intensive upkeep of the tanks, the pressures — was meant to turn us into real soldiers. It worked too, and we were proud of it.

One evening I came down with a terrible stomach ache and was taken to the battalion clinic. It was Saturday, the Sabbath, and no one was around but a duty medic. As I writhed in agony, I heard the medic inform the duty commander that he had a faker on his hands. He picked two pills out of a little box, told me to take them, and sat down to wait for my pain to pass. I continued to complain until the medic had no choice but to summon the duty commander for permission to send me to the hospital in Beersheba. Capt. Menahem Razon set his eyes on the "faker" and immediately called me to attention. He was known as a good-hearted, fatherly type, supportive and helpful, but short of patience with incompetents. I had once seen him kick an ordinance man who had damaged an engine during maintenance. No one begrudged him his temper, since he fully believed in the justice of his cause. At times you could almost see his heart ache as he rebuked laggards and reported loafers.

Menahem Razon stepped over to my bed and began to check me out. I had been inducted in May — one of the "Mau-maus", as they called us, a problematic group who included high school drop-outs and others who were difficult to integrate into the army. Many of these conscripts routinely tried to evade hard work and tough drills, if not the service altogether.

"Get 'im out of here," Razon ordered after interrogating me. Now there was no doubt. Indeed, no sooner was I evacuated to Beersheba than I went under the surgeon's scalpel. My appendix was about to burst. I spend two weeks in the hospital and another two at home on sick leave.

I returned to the battalion knowing nothing about what it was up to. In my absence, no one had visited or taken the slightest concern for me. I took this for standard procedure and assumed it was the way things should be. Knowing what I know today, I can hardly believe it.

Upon my return I found the camp deserted. "They've gone out on final maneuvers and won't be back for a few days." I found my personal gear with the quartermaster's and had nothing to do but wait in my tent until my comrades returned. The reunion was pleasurable and exciting, but inside I felt bad: I had missed out on my comrades' ordeal and therefore was less of a tank crewman— if I'd be certified at all. I was swamped with feelings of isolation and dread.

With good reason. Company Commander Rattas pronounced judgment tersely: "Send him to the quartermaster." Second Lt. Eliashiv Shimshi, commander of the platoon to which Rattas' tank had belonged, tried to talk him out of it, but no go. His unequivocal ruling filled me with guilt, as if I had bluffed my way to the hospital. I refused to accept this bitter fate. As a disciplined soldier, however, I reported to the quartermaster for my new duty. My buddies, handing over laundry or exchanging work uniforms at my counter, commiserated with me but joked at my expense. The worst blow of all was my disqualification for tank commander's training; the rest of my group would go without me.

The maneuvers over, we packed our gear and returned to our home base, Hassa. The men restored the equipment to condition and began to organize for the course. Again Shimshi intervened with Rattas on my behalf, and again he failed. They turned in their gear the morning of their departure and it was I, behind the quartermaster's counter, who had to take it from them. By this time I'd been presented with a workable compromise: I would participate in the field maneuvers of the August conscript group, after which I would head for the course.

Then Shimshi burst into the quartermaster's room, a triumphant smile on his face.

"Kahalani, turn in your gear fast and get ready to join the tank commander group!"

Surely he was teasing.

"No joke," he insisted, noting my astonishment. "You've got more luck than brains. We gotta send a certain number of men to the course and didn't have enough. But so what! Turn in your gear."

I wasted no time. Elated beyond words, I jumped aboard the truck to Camp Julis, where the Armored Corps had its school. I was on the way to becoming a tank commander.

Parts of the course were held in Julis; maneuvers were conducted in the hilly area to the northeast and in the desert south of Beersheba. I tried to conceal the fact that I was recovering from surgery. The incision in my abdomen was rather wide and long, and I felt as if my belly was about to rip open again at any moment. Every small effort was a strain. But I knew I had to make good.

The 82nd Battalion trained on the Centurion, a British tank. Because this model was in short supply in the IDF, we worked with the Sherman tank during the course. We retrained for the old tank, which had seen service at the end of World War II. My platoon commander was 2nd Lt. David Yellin, who was killed ten years later in the Yom Kippur War.

As the course proceeded, I felt more and more like a part of the tank. I knew I could control it. At the end of the course I was named its outstanding trainee: while my comrades were promoted to the rank of lance corporal, as was the practice in those days, I was given sergeant's stripes by Maj. Gen. David "Dado" Elazar, commander of the Armored Corps at the time.

A chapter in my life had come to an end. I was a commander in the IDF; I had crossed the divide. From that point on I would have to act like a commander and develop a manner of behavior and thinking with which I could cope with soldiers. Any young man who turns overnight from a boot soldier into a commander is gripped with a sense of excitement. Leading a formation of fighting men is clearly a reason for apprehension. How would it be to stand there and give orders for the first time?

At the end of the inspection we paraded the tanks past the audience and saluted in the direction of the dignitaries' platform. Next to Dado sat Col. Avraham Aden (Bren), commander of the school. I wanted very badly to signal to my family, somewhere in the crowd, but I controlled myself firmly. I saved my excitement for our post-inspection reunion; I could sense their pride.

"What about officer's training, Avi?" my father asked, just to make sure that this was not the end.

"It's OK. I'll go right after furlough."

"Great. Keep it up! That way you'll know how to take care of yourself." My father patted me on the shoulder, and my little brothers lined up for a photograph with the brand new commander.

4. OFFICER CANDIDATE
SCHOOL

In the spring of 1963, after a short furlough, we were
sent to Training Base 1 at Camp Syrkin near Petah
Tikva, where the IDF had its officer candidate school
at the time. We pulled off our enlisted men's "sar-
dines" and affixed white plastic bands to our epaulets and a round white lining under the brim of our
caps. The transition was sharp and inexplicable. We
were tank crewmen no longer; we had to change our
ways of thinking, our habits, and our behavior. By
command, we were to be full-fledged infantrymen.
Our antibodies went on the offensive. We found it
hard to get used to the idea that every stone and
every lump of mud in the field was a matter of life or
death. We were out of our element.

My platoon commander was Maj. Yaakov Ben-
Yaakov, a.k.a. "Double Jack." He was an ethnic Bul-
garian; his accent and enunciation left no doubt about
it. The course instructors, I felt, were more interested
in verifying whether we were able to be officers than
in teaching how to be officers. An atmosphere of
tension and imminent expulsion reigned. Every few
days a couple of us were thrown out, for reasons that
I did not always consider right and fair. Fear of being
"kicked out" impaired our performance, leaving most
of us tentative and confused in our behavior.

I felt from the start that Double Jack was checking me out and trying to get under my skin. Did he know I had been outstanding trainee in the tank commanders' course? I asked myself. Perhaps it mattered to him that I was Yemenite, an "odd man out." Because he continued to single me out, I continued to wonder. There was no question about it: he was after me. My fear of him grew with each passing day, and his snide comments to and about me became more pointed and numerous. By treating me with derision when telling me to order the men into the field or to sum up a lesson, he merely added fuel to the flame. He never conversed with me on a personal level, never told me where I stood, never explained his feelings about me. All this came to a boil one day when he sent the platoon into the field for maneuvers and ordered me to stay behind to guard the tent encampment. When this happened the next day, too, I understood that Double Jack had no intention of investing his energy in me. I was more efficiently used as a guard.

One morning I was told to report to the company commander, Lt. Col. Barashi. He climbed with me to the top of a hill and began to ask me tactical questions about the problems this terrain presented.

"You've got an enemy squad on the second hill, and you're the commander of your own squad. What do you do?"

I felt I had been threatened. I did not know why he had summoned me. I studied his eyes, trying to deduce from them whether the decision to eject me from the course had already been taken. I answered his question. He said nothing in reply, and I did not know if my solution was correct and feasible. He left me there, pensive and eaten up with doubt.

The next day, the school commander, Col. Aviv Barzilai, called me in for a talk. I reported and waited for my turn with several other cadets, ignorant of what was going on behind the door. No one said a word. When I entered the commander's office, I was stunned to find no fewer than eight officers, including Barashi and Double Jack, arrayed around the table. Later I learned that an expulsion committee might comprise any number of officers, depending on the different functions involved. At the head of the table sat Col. Barzilai.

"Your name Kahalani?" he barked.

I nodded.

"We want to ask you a few questions, and I'd like you to answer." He signaled to one of the officers.

"You're commanding a platoon that's got to set up an ambush across the border," said one of the officers seated at the table. "Give a preliminary order for the operation."

All eyes were on me. I decided I had nothing to lose; there was no need to get overwrought.

I answered according to what I had learned, sticking to all the rules, sure that I had given an excellent reply.

"You've reached the area, and you have to choose a site for the ambush. Sketch for us your deployment and method," another officer continued.

I stepped to the blackboard, sketching the proper position of the ambush and marking the distances between the different squads. I knew the material well. They threw me another two questions of the same nature, and these, too, I fielded adroitly.

"I've got another question for you," said someone who looked to me like an education officer or somebody with similar duties. "Can you tell us how many states there are in the Republic of South Africa?"

Dead silence.

"I don't know," I answered.

"Don't you read newspapers?" snapped the officer.

Since I had been inducted, in view of the pressure of work and maneuvers, no one in my circle had time for anything. I do not remember seeing any of my comrades reading a newspaper. I was on the defensive, aware that in fact I did not read newspapers enough. I tried, in my few moments of leisure to sleep. Besides, our company had not been getting any newspapers at that time.

"Would you perhaps tell me who's the king of Yemen right now?" the officer continued to press.

Now I had a question for him: why Yemen, of all places? Instead, I struggled to remember.

"I think his name is Salal," I replied hesitantly.

"Make up your mind. Salal or not Salal." The pressure mounted.

"I think it's Salal. I'm not sure." My answer was correct — I could see it in their eyes — but my interrogator did not respond.

"Anyone have more questions?" asked the school commander.

"Sir," Double Jack broke in, "I want to say something. This cadet has not had any discipline problems, and I think he can become a good tank commander. From our standpoint he's weak on the subject matter, and that's why he's here. I believe Kahalani agrees with me." He sent me an inquiring gaze, but I did not reply. I knew that my answers had embarrassed those around and placed them in a situation for which they had not prepared themselves. "Wait outside and we'll tell you."

I saluted and stepped out, as the group of officers continued to debate my fate. They went at it interminably. Finally Double Jack came out and ordered me to report to the Adjutant. There was no doubt about it: I was out.

I returned my gear to the quartermaster's and the Adjutant handed me a reassignment form: Armor. A glance at the ejection form made it clear why I was expelled: "Poor familiarity with the subject matter. No command and leadership ability. Unfit to be an officer in the IDF." That was an insult. I could argue about my familiarity with the subject matter, if anyone was willing to hear me out. But that unequivocal ruling about "no command and leadership ability" was a real smack in the face. With that in my file, how could I go back to Armor and command a tank?

I lugged my kitbag home and swiftly reattached my sergeant's stripes to my sleeve. So I won't be an officer, I told myself. But how would I explain to my family and neighborhood friends that I'd been tossed out of the course? I had been the pride of the neighborhood. Even in synagogue, during the Sabbath services, they talked about me! I reached Nes Ziona in the afternoon, but only after nightfall did I head for my part of town.

My father heard the sad story and reached his own verdict: "It's not the end of the world! It's a pity, but there's nothing to do about it." I was distressed about having let down my family, but the warmth with which they greeted me assuaged the insult.

Another seven cadets from Armor had been ejected from the course— a real "bumper crop" that infuriated "Dado", the Corps commander. After lengthy arguments between Armor headquarters and OCS about the nature of the course and the number of ejectees, Dado decided to summon the ex-cadets to get to know them personally and assess at first hand the reason for their dismissal.

The closer our date with Dado came, the more excited we grew. When it was my turn, I stepped in, trying to evade Dado's glare.

"Kahalani, I don't understand what you're doing here," Dado began in a puzzled tone. "Just one month ago, I promoted you to sergeant as the outstanding trainee!" Around the table sat Col. Herzl Shafir, commander of the 7th Brigade at the time; Col. Avraham ("Bren") Aden, commander of the Armor School; Gideon Altshuler, the Corps' Chief Instruction Officer; and Pinny Lahav, the adjutant officer.

"They say I'm not suitable for it. That's all I can tell you," I replied tersely.

The officers looked me over, sizing me up from all angles like doctors trying to diagnose a naked patient.

"We want to ask you a few questions about the material. No objection, right?" Dado continued. When I nodded, the officers began firing questions from every direction: everything one could possibly want to know about tanks, followed by a test on the subject matter taught at OCS. I could hardly complete the answer to one question before someone threw me the next one. Heatedly I fired the answers back, demonstrating everything I knew. Then, silence. "So why the hell did they kick you out?" Dado shouted into the void.

"I told you I don't know," I answered, perplexed, "I admit there was one question I didn't know: how many states there are in the Republic of South Africa."

The officers smiled.

"I don't know that either," someone blurted.

"Kahalani, you're still gonna hear from me. Don't give up. It'll be OK!"

Dado sounded optimistic and sympathetic, and I stepped out of his office with a feeling of victory. But what decision could they take about me? Return me to OCS? That did not sound logical. Put me in the next course? I would not object. In any case, I felt I had come home, to Armor, where I had a warm and concerned family who would take care of me.

Armored officer training

One day I was handed a surprise, the nature of which became clear only some time later. Dado had asked Yitzhak Rabin, Chief of General Staff at the time, to approve my admission to armored officer's training even though I had not completed OCS. The point of this to examine how Armor cadets were being ejected from OCS. Rabin's acquiescence to this procedure knocked the OCS commander for a loop; he considered it both a personal insult and a circumvention of the IDF's major training ground for officers. Others, including the commanders of Training and Manpower, voiced strenuous objections of their own. Still, Rabin's decision stood. Surprised and happy, I joined my comrades for the first day of armored officers' training. Even though I alone lacked the platoon commander's insignia issued at OCS, I was obviously welcome in their midst.

This time, I had not a moment's fear of failure. AOT was my "home court," where I felt secure. As soon as we mounted the tanks I was appointed as tank commander, and I felt fully in control of the tank's every accessory. I might as well have been born in a tank; everything — crewmen, systems — responded at the pace and with the motions that I dictated. I earned high marks throughout, enjoying the course, bone-crushing though it was, and broadening my horizons.

The site was Shivta, in the bleakest part of the Negev. Night and day ran into one another. We were filthy with grease, oil, soot, and mud. We forgot the meaning of sleep. I saw fellow cadets slumber on their feet. On nighttime guard duty, I, too, would whack myself, run this way and that, wash my face, tell myself stories — anything to stay awake. Not that the guard duty stints were very long. Three cadets divided up such nighttime hours as remained after we locked up the tank, and once we set a record: each of us had 15 minutes of guard duty until reveille.

For the last week of the course we went back to Julis and began preparing for the final inspection and parade. Because I did not have a platoon commander's pin, I did not know what insignia to put on my epaulet. This was important, because the procedure was to cover the insignia and have it exposed at the inspection. The question was brought to my platoon commander, Capt. Shatz, on the very day of the parade. He answered without hesitation: "Second Lieutenant."

"I think that's strange," I answered. "They'll never approve it. You know I never finished OCS!"

"That's news to me? As long as no one tells you otherwise, put on Second Lieutenant."

Before he had time to reconsider, I rushed to my room and pinned the metal bars to my epaulet. Deep down I knew it wouldn't work.

About two hours before the inspection, while we were cleaning up the parade grounds, I was ordered to report to the course commander. I knew why.

"I know. They don't approve the rank," I asserted upon stepping into the office.

"Look, I just got a phone call and I'm really sorry, but they say you can't get second lieutenant without a platoon commander's pin. I'm sorry we misled you."

"You didn't mislead me. I told Shatz it would happen. I'm not surprised. I'm happy I finished the course, and I don't care about the rest of it."

"Today they're giving you Substitute Officer, and I believe they'll up it to second lieutenant sometime later."

"I don't want Substitute Officer. Give me First Sergeant. That's more respectable. I won't go around with Substitute Officer on my sleeve."

"Substitute Officer is better!"

"I won't go around with Substitute Officer. It's an embarrassment. It's for men who barely got through the course. And me — as far as you're concerned, could I command a tank platoon?" I pressed.

"For sure. You're one of our best men, and you scored high on the finals."

"So give me First Sergeant. At least you won't embarrass me in front of the whole audience. It might even be better to keep me out of the parade, on the sidelines."

Time was pressing. The parade and inspection would begin in a few hours, and in headquarters, Lt. Col. Yarkoni and his appointed replacement, Lt. Col. Oshri, were turning the screws to make me agree to take part and accept the grade of Substitute Officer. I was personally insulting them and all the course instructors, they said. I had done well, and they were proud that I had finished the course with a good write-up. Substitute Officer was better than First Sergeant, because with it I could shortly be promoted to Second Lieutenant. I could not withstand the two officers' entreaties. After all, my family, too, would be stunned if I were not among the graduates!

So I took my place in the parade. A platoon instructor removed the covering from my epaulets, revealing my Substitute Officer's bars to one and all. As soon as the parade was over I took them off. I wore neither a platoon commander's pin nor officer's bars. I was a private.

5. BACK TO THE 82ND BATTALION

I found the 82nd Battalion gearing up for brigade-level maneuvers in the Negev. Brigade Commander Lt. Col. Kalman Magen interviewed me the moment I arrived. I was issued a jeep and, as platoon commander of reconnaissance, I was sent out that very day to lead the brigade's supply convoys into mountainous terrain.

The brigade maintenance officer was glad to see me; now he had someone to navigate his vehicles. I went out to examine the convoy and almost fainted. There were about eighty vehicles, including water and fuel tankers, food and ammo trucks, and anything else one might need. The whole formation was to meet up with the brigade after several hours of simulated combat. At age 19, I pretended to be an experienced navigator and gave the maintenance officer a feeling of reassurance that I did not share. What if I made a navigational blunder in the vast, arid Negev? How do you make a U-turn with such a convoy? How do you make sure everyone is following, down to the last tanker? An inspector, Major Joe, had been sent along to assess my performance, but I could expect no help from him. He was a grizzled veteran who seemed to be offended by seeing a greenhorn like me assigned to this task. Along with the dozens of drivers and commanders, I attended a briefing for the night-time march. "The recon platoon commander will lead us to the brigade," the maintenance officer ruled confidently, pointing at me. Then, turning back to the men, he said, "You've got nothing to worry about!" As I watched him, I realized that he had no intention of enhancing his explanations with a map. The route was a difficult one, made the more so by the fact that I had never visited the area before.

It worked out anyway. To my great relief the convoy indeed met the brigade at dawn the next day. I assembled the recon platoon and, for the first time, faced soldiers to brief them on their duties. They were reservists, some as old as my father. One of them patted me lightly on the head — as if to put me in my place and to say, "You know your job, but don't forget you're the same age as our children..."

I still remember my first encounter with young tank crewmen. Facing my platoon — my men peered at me in bewilderment.

"Yes, I'm your platoon commander," I asserted, attempting to wipe the astonished looks off their faces. "I imagine you're looking for my bars."

Everyone nodded.

"They're in the laundry. And I imagine I'll stay this way until they come back."

The first hurdle vaulted, I immediately went on to the rest of the day's agenda. I never ran into trouble when commanding enlisted men with no officer's bars on my epaulets. The real problem was how to get into the officers' mess hall...

The battalion was sent to the Negev for maneuvers on the tank crew, platoon, and company levels. The platoon commanders vied for the honor of being the best. At the end of each drill a final exam was given.

We sensed that the maneuver had been dictated by the battalion echelon with brigade — level involvement in its particulars. As the tank crews went through their paces, we spotted the brigade commander, Herzl Shafir, and we realized that he was testing the crews himself. Mine was graded "excellent". I was proud.

The company was shot through with disciplinary problems, and it was up to us, the young commanders, to contend with them. Some officers simply reported misbehaving soldiers to the higher echelon; others devised their own penal code. I was one of the latter. I was not at ease with the possibility of handing a member of my platoon who had stepped out of line to the company commander for judgment. It was my own leadership problem, I believed, and I would have to solve it within my own restricted framework.

As the commander, I knew I had to be the best tank driver, the best loader, and the best gunner, so as never to put the platoon and the company to shame. I quickly realized that soldiers appreciated their commanders — with whom they are in contact every day, every hour — on the basis of their professional abilities alone. I worked overtime to make my men understand that "Platoon C always goes first". Even then I pounded them with lengthy briefings well into the night, every night. After taps, the junior commanders would gather in the company commander's tent and go over the next day's material by candlelight — at the cost of our sleep. We were more tired than our men.

After the maneuvers, we sent the best men to tank commanders' training. A few days later I again rode a tank carrier to the Negev for another round of maneuvers. As the platoons vied for supremacy, we, their commanders, became a close-knit, impenetrable group, a little family. Adam Weiler was in charge of Platoon A, Ben-Hayil Yefet of Platoon B, Kahalani of Platoon C, and Eliezer Marcushammer of Platoon D. We called ourselves the "quadruplets".

Every night we headed for the training area, far from the tent encampment, and picked out a deep furrow left by one of the tanks as the site of an improvised platoon commanders' latrine. The term "looking for a furrow" became part of our lexicon.

Adam was a chronically uncertain navigator. He had convinced himself that he would never learn to use a map to master the territory and joked that by the time we would become battalion commanders, he would still be commander of Platoon A. Yefet, of Yemenite extraction like me, often brought Yemenite delicacies from home. To his credit, it should be said that he always kept his cool. Eliezer Marcushammer, a member of my OCS group, had immigrated to Israel from Mexico several months before his induction. He was a soldier through and through, completing most of his courses as an outstanding trainee. Over the company wireless we were wont to imitate his heavy Spanish accent, to the amusement of every man in the company...

About this time battalion commander Kalman summoned me for a talk. There was no chance that I would get second lieutenant, he said; I would have to repeat OCS. I refused. I was satisfied with my platoon commander duties and had every intention of staying with the battalion.

Some time after this interview we were informed that Col. Shmuel ("Shmulik") Ayal, the head of IDF

Staff Administration, was about to pay the company a visit. I did not appreciate the significance of this. All I knew was that Ayal was responsible for the IDF officer corps. He reached us in an entourage, sandwiched between brigade commander Herzl Shafir and Magen.

With no advance notice the visitors began climbing on my tank. Within seconds Shmulik stepped into the gunner's nest and ordered me to teach him how to fire. Kalman ran a finger along my shoulders, as if indicating something. I did not get the hint, but my "pupil" scored good hits and clambered out of the tank to the sound of applause, smiling from ear to ear. Now the head of Staff Administration asked the officers to join him for a talk in the mess tent.

Every such meeting is organized along a fixed pattern: the officers present problems, and the commanders, around the main table, talk about their signing on for career service. Indeed, after a lengthy speech about how the officers' corps was developing, Shmulik Ayal let us ask questions. Suddenly Adam stood straight up and asked for the floor.

"Sir, you spoke to us about signing on for standing army duty, but there are some very basic things that you haven't solved." Everyone tensed. No one knew what Adam had in mind and where it might lead.

"Here in the battalion we have a platoon commander who we all think is the best in the company, and I've got no doubt that he's the best in the battalion. So I wouldn't be exaggerating if I said I believed there aren't many like him in the brigade."

What was the point of all this? I wondered.

"The platoon commander I'm talking about is Avigdor Kahalani, and his rank is substitute officer. How can an army in the mid-1960s behave this way?"

I felt myself blushing and bent over to conceal my embarrassment. Shmulik Ayal ordered Adam to sit down. "It's all right, it's all right," he called.

"What's all right? Don't cut me off. It's high time somebody brought this matter up. It's been going on and on for who knows how long!"

I wanted to bury myself but did not know where. Adam was finally assured. The matter was being dealt with; the head of Administration knew about it.

At the end of the talk, Adam and I were summoned to the battalion commander's tent at the top of the hill. I was ordered in first, certain that I would face yet another attempt to talk me into returning to OCS. I would refuse.

There in the tent was Shmulik Ayal. "You've got good friends, Kahalani," he said.

"I didn't ask him to talk about it."

"Look, I made a decision today and I hope Manpower won't kill me for it. Starting today, you're a second lieutenant."

His last words came out abruptly and took me by surprise. I responded by clarifying that if this was meant to solve the problem of a "social case" soldier, I would do without.

Furthermore, I would not let Ayal get into trouble on my account. Shmulik dismissed the social-case connection out of hand. Then, of course, he asked me how I felt about signing on for career service.

"What if I have to go back to OCS to get full lieutenant?" I persisted.

"From now on everything will be OK," Shmulik asserted, concluding the matter. Promising nothing, I stepped out of the tent perplexed, surprised, but smiling. Observing me, Adam, Yefet and Marcus understood that the matter had been dealt with. Now all I had to do was show my new present to my platoon and, on the upcoming Sabbath furlough, my proud family.

The day the maneuver ended I took my platoon back to the battalion at Camp Hassa. The moment I unloaded my tank from its carrier, however, I was ordered to report to battalion commander Magen.

"Bad news. You're going back to the field."

"When?"

"Tonight."

"What happened?"

"Tomorrow morning Dado's visiting, and I want you to do a tank crew test with him watching."

"What about my own crew?" I asked, playing the innocent.

"They stay here. I talked with Company Commander Shammai, and he'll put together a crew for you."

For months I had been waiting for an opportunity to sleep in a real room. Now, instead of this, I was to head back to the Negev in a truck reserved just for me. I reached Shammai's company before dawn. At daybreak I pieced together a tank crew, briefed the men, and headed for the testing area to put them through their paces under the Armored Corps commander's gaze. The round of tests completed, Shammai informed me that I was to remain with the company as reinforcement. The commanders were all new, Shammai said, and he needed my experience. Thus I joined a new group of platoon commanders: Avigdor Liebman, Haggai Regev, and Shalom Angel.

Capt. Shammai Kaplan was a familiar face in the 82nd Battalion, a towering, handsome man with a carefully trimmed beard, who looked as if God had granted him everything a man of his age might ask for. One of the gifts with which he was saddled was a problematic, under-achieving company. In one of his briefings he asserted, "There's only one man in the company on whose shoulders responsibility rests, and he is answerable for the whole company's caliber." At first I did not understand who he meant; later I realized it was himself. I was surprised by Shammai's candor with the young officers. My commanders knew how to point the finger at everyone but themselves. Shammai won me over. When we got to know each other better, I found that he was so easy on the commanders and men that he impaired the company's performance. Everyone, however, wished to help him succeed and to let him derive some pleasure from his job. For many years his example served me as the model of a commander's behavior.

Shammai was always the last man to go to sleep and the first to wake up. His red eyes revealed his lack of sleep. He loved to take chances, loved to be "naughty". He obeyed some of the rules — those he set for himself — and totally ignored others.

Now and then we drove to Beersheba for supper. We shoved our way into the jeep, loading more men aboard than regulations permitted, and sang Israeli songs at the top of our lungs all the way. The trip back was different. Yossi, the company sergeant-major, and Shammai would down a few shots of cognac during the meal, and that changed everything. We young platoon commanders distanced ourselves from the very smell of it...

On Alert in the North

One day during maneuvers in the hills near Sde Boqer, a kibbutz in the central Negev, my tank tipped over at a very steep angle. As I tried to set it aright, a special courier approached me:

"Drop everything and go back to the road with your platoon. The battalion bus is waiting for you. You're all going north."

This I had not expected. Was I supposed to abandon my tank and let it topple over? Hadn't we signed out the tank and the gear? I had no time to think. We threw the dust-covered gear into the bus and headed north.

En route, a few kilometers from Safed, we met with our new battalion commander, Lt. Col. Binyamin Oshri. He launched at once into a briefing:

"You'll meet up with your tanks farther on. Those are the new tanks, with 105 mm cannons, that were unloaded from the emergency depot just yesterday. Your task is to take them up to Kibbutz Dan. North of there in Nahal Dan (the River Dan) are our water sources. A bunch of Syrian tanks are threatening them. Your job is to smash them."

Proud at having been chosen for the task, but anxious about the responsibility, I pursued my tanks as they rolled northward on their carriers. Near the carriers I ran into my friend Avigdor Liebman. As he turned the tanks over to me, I could sense his disappointment. He had hoped to be the platoon commander assigned to this mission. Avigdor and his men had packed and loaded the tanks, thus inadvertently readying them for us. I felt uncomfortable watching Avigdor climb aboard the bus that would take him back to the Negev.

The mountains of Safed were too much for the old tank carriers. We had to unload the tanks and drive them on the highway. Their tracks scarred the asphalt. To conceal our movements from the Syrians, we entered Safed from the west, moving only by night and with our lights turned off.

Stopping one night at Kibbutz Sde Eliezer in the Hula Valley, about 20 kilometers south of Dan, far out of sight, I climbed into one of our three new tanks for the first time. I was awed. They had white interiors and equipment boxes arrayed in new compartments — everything factory fresh. Some of the tools were still covered with the oil and grease that had been applied to them when placed in the emergency depots. The ammunition either stood upright or lay horizontal in turret compartments, and the alert instruments had all been assembled. However, the gun had not been calibrated for the instruments. We would have to spend the next day adjusting the sights.

The 105 mm gun was impressive. Our possession of it was a secret at the time. Inside we found a new type of shell, armed with a charge of plastic explosives. We had heard stories about this shell, which did not penetrate the enemy tank but detonated outside it, shattering the enemy's armor with devastating effect. As was customary at the time, we fired a few rounds to calibrate the barrel. To our delight, the very first one hit the target. Thus far we had fired nothing but 20-liter, 84 mm guns, and the transition to heavy artillery was abrupt.

The three tanks were ready for war. At nightfall we loaded them onto carriers and headed for Dan. Every settlement that we passed gave us a tumultuous welcome. It was the first time in Israel's history that tanks had entered the area. The Armistice Agree-

ment signed with Syria after the War of Independence permitted weapons of only 9 mm into this
zone. That made the Uzi submachine gun the heavi-
est weapon we could use there. Indeed, we constantly
feared that the U.N. observers would spot us and
declare our entry into the area a violation of the
Agreement.

As we advanced up the Galilee panhandle, the
bridges threatened to buckle under the weight of the
tanks and carriers. We unloaded the tanks and took
them through the gullies. This was no easy task, since
we were traveling in pitch darkness without lights. A
veritable entourage of soldiers, civilian police, MPs
and miscellaneous visitors escorted us all the way.
From the turret I felt like a VIP for whom all routes
are cleared.

Plunging into the water of the Hasbani, one of the
Jordan River tributaries, my tank mounted a boulder
and its tracks spun freely. I could not continue. Men
shouted from all directions, advising my driver how
to extricate himself. The driver, suddenly surrounded
by so many officers, began to listen to them and not
to his own commander, positioned in the cupola of
his own tank. One roar from me reminded him of the
fact that he had one and only commander..In the
meantime, the driver's compartment had begun to
take on water. We were in danger of drowning. The
crew went into emergency mode. Ordering the driver
to back up slowly and gingerly, I succeeded in getting the tank off the boulder and across the river in
one piece. We sighed in relief.

At this point I indulged in a bit of mischief. I
advanced with the tank until it nearly touched the
row of parked cars whose drivers waited for the OK
to continue. The drivers' frightened faces, their terri-

fied reaction to the black monster bearing down on them, were my "reward". As the mammoth hunk of metal rumbled toward the vehicles, the passengers could only have thought that the machine was out of control.

Covering the last stretch of road we caught sight of Tel Azaziyya, a hill in Syrian territory. We were apprehensive: what if the Syrians had detected our movements? We rushed to the nearest kibbutz and, before dawn, concealed the tanks among the eucalyptus trees. We spent the day in huts that had accommodated Nahal (paramilitary agriculture) soldiers once stationed there. In the race against time and daybreak, we had won. Indeed, at dawn we spotted a U.N. car on the road a few meters from us, its passengers unsuccessfully trying to figure out what was going on. When battalion commander Oshri arrived later that morning, he too asked where the tanks were. "Next to you," we answered. The men had done wonders with camouflage nets and eucalyptus branches.

At sunup, after shutting down the tank engines, I saw a wondrous sight, of a kind I had never seen: lush, green vegetation everywhere, and channels of deliciously fresh, gurgling water running between the tanks. The sound of it robbed me of my sleep. My head was still stationed in the arid Negev, which I had left only two days previously.

Now it was time for a briefing from Oshri: "Your task is to hit two Lebanese tanks at Tel Nukhila, north of Kibbutz Dan. You also have to be ready to smash tanks or tractors on the Syrian side." Oshri was a blunt speaker. I was still not thoroughly familiar with him, and could not help but compare him with his predecessor, Kalman Magen.

"Why are we doing this now?" I asked. "Is there a special reason?" This front was far from my "home turf", and I found it odd that we suddenly had to use tanks here.

"The Syrians are trying to divert the water from Tel Dan. If they get away with it, the Jordan will lose a lot of water. We're going to defend our water, even if it means heating up the border."

Oshri reemphasized the importance of reconnaissance, in order to gain familiarity with every path on our side and the enemy territory into which we would be firing. A special excitement filled the air. For the first time we were facing a real enemy who could return our fire, rather than stationary targets and harmless barrels scattered across a hill. The Syrians had started digging a canal that would divert the Dan and Banias Rivers and carry the water the full length of the Golan Heights for local Syrian use. That would deplete the Jordan River of water that normally flowed into the Sea of Galilee, Israel's vital natural reservoir, located to the south. Only a few months previously Israel had dedicated the National Water Carrier, through which water from the Sea of Galilee had begun to flow to central and southern Israel. It was clear to everyone that Israel could not allow anyone to divert water from this area, and that for us it was a *casus belli*.

We engaged in reconnaissance for some three weeks, mastering every trail and visiting every firing position. We filled out cards specifying the range of every landmark on the Syrian and Lebanese sides. We were not battle-hungry, but we did wish to gain some operational experience. The time passed, however, and for reasons unknown we were not put into action.

In the meantime, I took the opportunity to enjoy the magnificent scenery. It was my first encounter with Tel Dan and the magnificent verdant area surrounding the Dan River. I was enchanted. I had been shamefully unaware that Israel possessed such a corner of pristine beauty. I waded in the frigid streams that ran alongside our tanks. As we climbed by foot to the lookout posts, we pushed paths through thickets of foliage as the sound of trickling water tempted our ears. We were troubled by the awareness that our heavy tanks would eventually savage this splendid nature reserve.

Local kibbutzniks, Northern Command personnel, and members of our battalion spoiled us incessantly. We were obviously a main attraction. Never had I been asked so many questions about our problems, needs, convenience and comfort. Oshri himself recorded in his ledger that we were to be brought a coffee maker, cooking equipment, and other luxury items. We take these things for granted today, but then — in October, 1964 — IDF soldiers were repeatedly told that the provision of such amenities was their responsibility. Rudimentary comforts were deemed the equivalent of pampering, and a pampered soldier was not so "good", not so "tough", and therefore not so operationally effective.

On one of his visits, Battalion Commander Oshri informed me that Maj. Jackie Even asked to interview me. Jackie was assembling a group of officers to join him on a secret mission abroad. I vacillated; I was up for demobilization in about two months and had not decided to sign on for career service.

Oshri tried to tempt me with promotion to deputy commander. That would make me second-in-command to Ori Orr, who trained raw recruits and later took them into the field. I liked the idea but was still disinclined to make a career in the military. In fact, I considered it self-evident that I would leave the service. A job was waiting for me at home. My father had opened a garage in Nes Ziona and called it "Avi": the idea being that I would run it after leaving the service.

In the end I turned over command to my comrade Avigdor and headed for my interview. There, in the Armored Corps building, I met Jackie, a blond young man exuding vigor and self-confidence.

After asking me a few personal and career questions, Jackie got to the point: "I can't tell you where we're going, but I promise it'll be a personal experience. It's important for Israel too."

"For how long?"

"About two months."

"Look, I'm not about to sign on extra time. I'm supposed to go home at the end of December, and it's already October. Can you tell me who else is going on this trip?"

Jackie listed a few of the names. I knew the men well; one of them was my friend Adam. He too had agreed? Well, my answer was still "No."

"Think it over for a few days," Jackie insisted. "Then give me your answer."

I talked the matter over at home, but I was still undecided. My father objected, of course. He was building me a cocoon. And what about the garage? I did not ask my mother; I merely updated her. I knew she wanted me at her side, and my personal challenges were not always consistent with her desires. Finally I made up my mind: I would go with Jackie.

A few days later the group was given the good

news: we were headed for West Germany, and the mission was to train with some new tanks and bring them to Israel. They were Pattons, which Israel would receive from the Americans through NATO via Germany. Because Israel had no diplomatic relations with Germany at the time, the trip was classified Top Secret. We were allowed to mention it to our parents but no one else, disclosing only that our destination was Germany. The arrangements were such that our cover would be blown neither in West Germany nor anywhere else in Europe.

As I packed my bags, a radio bulletin informed me of a serious exchange of fire in the area of Kibbutz Dan. From the details I understood that my platoon — under my comrade and replacement, Avigdor, had fired on two Lebanese tanks at Nukhila. In their excitement, they had missed the targets. That hurt, but there was nothing I could do. I was intensely envious of their mission. About two days before the trip, in early November, 1964, I was called to the 82nd battalion to bid farewell. It was customary to give every departing officer a key-ring engraved with the battalion's emblem, the officer's name, and best wishes. I received a key-ring without my name. The omission, it turned out, was by order of Battalion Commander Oshri. He considered me a "traitor" and would not speak to me. I was surprised. Not for a moment had I felt a traitor to the battalion that I loved so much, to which I was so connected. I could not help but disclose my feelings to Jackie. He exploded. Within a few hours I was summoned to the Armored Corps building for a meeting with the new Corps Commander, Col. Israel Tal. "Talik", as they called him, opened a notebook, seized a pen, and began to interrogate me. I answered his blunt questions sincerely, astonished to see him energetically jotting down my answers.

"I'll take care of this. You've got nothing to worry about; I'll let you know what comes of it," he promised.

If truth be told, I expected nothing to come of it and bore no grudges. I understood Oshri's feelings and treated his anguish at my departure as a compliment. Not wishing to hurt him, I began to regret having reported the episode. Indeed, a few months later I heard that Oshri had been reprimanded by the Chief of General Staff for his behavior.

In a subsequent incident in the north, Oshri, under Talik, commanded a tank that opened fire into Syrian territory. In the resulting exchange he was seriously wounded in the head by shrapnel. He spent many days in a coma. Even after regaining consciousness he was beset with amnesia for some time.

6. THE FIRST PATTON BATTALION

In the briefing before our departure I made my first acquaintance with the group of officers that would bring the Patton tank to Israel, under Lt. Col. Shmuel Gorodish and battalion commander-designate Jackie Even. The group included Adam Weiler, my friend and brother in arms; Shalom Angel, my fellow platoon commander in Shammai's company; Amos Katz, operations officer of the 87th Battalion; Haim Erez, company commander in the same battalion, Nattke Nir, former platoon commander in the same battalion; Maj. Ehud Elad; Yom Tov Tamir, Amnon Giladi and others. This was my first acquaintance with them; later we became good friends. Several career noncoms were added to the group; they were in charge of maintaining the tanks.

We were given some money and ordered to buy suits, ties, and funny-looking hats. Circumspection became a virtual end in itself. We were even given a cover: a group of students on a sightseeing visit. But when we stood at the Paris train station en route to Germany, anyone who eyed us would have known at once that we were soldiers. We stood about in little clusters, all wearing identical blue raincoats and carrying bulging suitcases.

Excited, we reached our destination: Muensterlager armor camp in northern Germany. Within a few hours we had been issued German army uniforms and looked like German soldiers in every respect — a harsh experience for several of us. All I knew of the Holocaust was what I had read and heard from others. I was ill at ease, feeling like a worm compared with those in our group whose parents had experienced the Holocaust and its agonies on German soil.

Each of us was given a separate room and excellent conditions. Studies were in German, translated into Hebrew by Israeli interpreters. Never did we tell anyone in the camp where we came from. We assumed some of them knew and imagined the others did not. The Germans called us "niggers" because we were swarthy. They saluted upon seeing our officers' ranks, marked on a patch above our lapels. We greeted them in English, but under our breaths we answered with a juicy expression — in Hebrew, of course.

By night, we assembled study kits from the subject matter. The academic material was fascinating, but most impressive was the tank itself. We marveled at the way it drove. Its automatic transmission made it like an American car. The brakes, too, were profoundly satisfying. Our veteran Centurion tanks constantly collided with each other because their brakes were so bad. My tank had gone through eleven such encounters, several of which endangered life and limb. The Patton's turret was easy and simple to operate. One little switch swiveled it in any direction. Zeroing in on targets, likewise, was childplay.

During the driving lessons, Adam and I would dispatch the instructor to warm himself up in the heated shack as we put the tank through its paces like a couple of lunatics. We ran through giant puddles just to get each other wet; sideswiped trees, trying to lop off the head of the man in the turret; and knocked over rowed of trees, ever astonished at the tank's capabilities. We showed the Germans how fast we Israelis could make the tank fire.

Adam looked like one of the locals. One day, as the tank was down for maintenance, a German officer turned to him:

"Why are you helping the niggers?"

"I'm one of them," Adam smiled.

The officer almost fainted with embarassment. "How can it be that in one country you've got a nigger like him" — he pointed at me — "and a blond like you?"

Wihthout hesitation Adam answered that he belonged to the northeast part of Israel, whereas I came from the south, thus explaining the difference in our color...

We had been warned not to start up with German girls nor rent cars when on furlough. This was meant to prevent unpleasant altercations with the locals. Our commanders disregarded the ban on rented cars and explored Germany, as if it were only natural that this was OK for them and *verboten* for us. Even so, we spent our weekends geing acquainted — if superficially — with Germany. Shalom Angel and I shared hotel rooms on these occasions and became the best of friends.

We returned excitedly to Israel to set up the first Patton battalion under the 7th brigade — the 79th Battalion under Jackie Even and his deputy, Nattke Nir. The new formation was stationed in Campt Natan near Beersheva, under a thick cloak of secrecy.

We were the most cohesive and idealistic group around. We worked without letup into the dead of night, demanding more of ourselves than our commanders demanded of us. Jackie regarded the new tank as a complex instrument, hard to operate, requiring above-average crewmen. It may have looked that way, but in fact of all the tanks in Israel's armed forces the Patton was the easiest to use.

The maneuvers were kept as secret as we could make them... until we began to get greetings from Radio Cairo's "Voice of Thunder", including mention of our exact location. Still we continued to be circumspect. Who were we, after all, to believe that the "Voice of Thunder" really knew?

I was appointed commander of the battalion's artillery group and Adam headed the drivers' section. We were like brothers. "Black god" and "white god", they called us. Later I became deputy commander in Yoel Gorodish's comapny, and finally I was named the battalion's operations officer.

About a year before going abroad, I met a very distant relative named Dalia at a family wedding. I was taken with her slight figure and was the first person who had not told her she was too thin. That very evening — I found out later — Dalia decided at the sight of my smiling advance that I would be her husband... Our love blossomed during my brief weekend furloughs and midweek nights off ("afters", we call them), when I would cover vast distances to spend just a few hours with her. In mid-1966 we decided to marry. With no money for a wedding hall, we thought we'd stage the wedding in a synagogue. Battalion commander Jackie, who had heard of our plans, immediately suggested the battalion camp as the site of our nuptials. The surroundings would be exceptional and quite far from the center of the country, but what of it?

Thus, amidst four gleaming Pattons, we were hoisted skyward in a giant cage. The wobbling box scared Rabbi Zimmel half to death; our parents, too, lost something of their swarthy complexion. But my fellow officers greeted us with a salute, and in the middle of the unforgettable experience I slipped the ring onto Dalia's finger. Our operations officer, Yom Tov Tamir, read the order of Operation Bride and Groom. Later he married Mira, the clerk who had typed it....

Once we had organized battalion operations and established a routine, Ehud Elad, an armored corps man, replaced Jackie Even as battalion commander. The fact that the two officers were not on speaking terms spread tension among everyone around them. Hardly had command been handed over when Jackie left the battalion, leaving Ehud with the task of learning the battalions functions and habits. As operations officer, I found myself instructing the new battalion commander.

A Tank Company of My Own

A few months later I was summoned to the office of 7th Brigade Commander Shmuel Gorodish.

"We're relieving you of your duties as operations officer and appointing you Commander of Company A in the battalion", he announced. Nor did he forget to remind me that in view of my tender age, the weight of this assignment and the responsibility he was vesting in me was of special significance. Yes, I was a young officer, but like everyone else I had been waiting impatiently to be named commander of a tank company.

In 1966, a tank company meant 14 tanks with side boxes and equipment, a technical squad, a parts warehouse, and a giant tank shelter — a veritable kingdom. And yes, a new, shining jeep next to the office!

My predecessor had been issued a relatively new jeep, and my comrades, the veteran company commanders, did not wait long before demanding the same as their due. Haim Erez, the deputy battalion commander, appreciated the difficulties this would entail and let the matter slide. Thus the jeep — No. 576 — became my home away from home. At night, my company in the field, I would bundle up in the back seat and close my eyes.

A commander's personal vehicle is an important aid at all times. I cannot imagine a commander without one. Only one who gets his first jeep as company commander can fathom the experience... .

My new formation, Arnon company, went through maneuvers on the crew, platoon, and company levels. When it was dissolved later on, most of its men went on to tank commanders' training.

After Arnon, I took over Buna Company for my friend Yom Tov Tamir. In April, 1967, our air force downed seven Syrian aircraft near the northern border, and I took Buna north to secure the suddenly hot front between Dan and Hulata. It was Passover, and we held the Seder and spent the festival night in the Hula Valley Nature Reserve. Dalia came along for the holiday vacation, joining me in a little tent I set up near the camp. Although we were so close to the Syrian border, we nevertheless felt at home. Still, our concern for the residents of nearby Yesud Hamaala and Hulata gave us any number of good reasons to remain alert through most of the night... .

7. THE SIX DAY WAR

On May 15, 1967, as the Independence Day celebrations subsided, we were called at home and ordered to return to the battalion. Egypt had moved several divisions into the Sinai Peninsula, and the IDF had gone on general alert. Fear of war was rife, as was the sense of surprise; the Egyptian border was considered quiet in those days. The reserves were called up and the entire country was paralyzed. Civilians leaped into uniform, waiting for developments on the Egyptian side. Egypt ordered the UN truce supervision force to evacuate the Gaza Strip and then blockaded the Straits of Tiran. The country was swamped with a sense of suffocation and imminent war. Levi Eshkol's vacillating government compounded the tension. Even kids like ourselves could sense that the leadership was confused.

Indeed, when Eshkol visited my company and sat with me under the camouflage net, he looked like someone who was not overly familiar with anything pertaining to an army... . Nevertheless, his paternal aura was evident to one and all. He asked me some questions in Yiddish that I could not answer. I told him only that we were ready for the order to move, invoking the simile of a coiled spring. Statements like that, I felt, encouraged him and strengthened his spirit. Proud as a groom on his wedding day, brigade commander Gorodish escorted Eshkol and Chief of

General Staff Yitzhak Rabin around the training area.

We stopped near Kibbutz Gvulot and then headed for the Gaza Strip. One morning during that period of limbo, Gorodish addressed the battalion and started out by blurting: "Tomorrow is war". His remarks were forceful and threatening, leaving us agape.

"I want you to empty your machine guns on them. Leave no one alive. Run 'em over with your tank treads. Don't hesitate! If you want to live, wipe 'em out. They're your enemy — you're not gonna be shooting at barrels anymore. If you don't fire at them, they're gonna hit you! They hate us. We should have gone into Egypt long ago and given 'em the smashing they deserve! It's a historical moment; let's exploit it!

The atmosphere was electric. Gorodish asked the battalion sergeant major, Benzi, to lead us in our traditional battle cry: "*alei krav*!!" (To War). Benzi shouted with all his might, and we answered in kind. But war did not break out the next day. Thus we roared the battle cry reserved for that kind of occasion "*alei shchav*!" (To Snore) thereupon climbing onto the tanks and laying down for a snooze... .

One day they brought us some anti-gas kits, which we mounted temporarily in the tanks. That was smart: we'd learned from what the Egyptians had done in Yemen, and knew the chances were they would use such weapons against us, too. Without giving the matter much thought, we rushed out for some quick drills in attaching and breathing with the system. It's not fair, I thought. We cannot compete with such a weapon. Face us like men. Make it a contest between equals. Don't gas us from a distance!

We used the time to ready ourselves for the unknown. A letter from my father indicated that he was with his unit several kilometers from my position near Kibbutz Gvulot. Dalia, eight months pregnant, had left our home in Beersheba and settled in with her parents in Jerusalem. We went on waiting, seemingly without end.

The battalion was ready in every way. The last series of orders was read in the tent next to that of the battalion commander, Ehud Elad. Ehud, grave-faced in any case, looked even grimmer this time.

"Tomorrow is it. This time its serious."

We passed around a bottle of champagne, each of us signing it. Ehud's deputy, Haim Erez, gave each company commander a puppy: his dog had given birth to quintuplets. Only Gil'ad, commander of Platoon C, turned down the gift. Thus I got one puppy and another for the third tank company commander, Benzi Carmeli, an old battle fox who had resumed career service after several years of civilian life. Hagag was with us, too, commanding an armored infantry company made up of reservists, who went about in armored personnel carriers.

Before nightfall we gave our soldiers a final briefing. This time let's not shout alei krav (to battle!), I suggested, my thoughts already straying to the next morning. The battalion sergeant major, whose false-alarm battle cry had turned into a joke, concurred with a pensive smile.

Before turning in I glanced at the map once again, making sure I remembered all the details and directions. The 7th Brigade belonged to the "Steel Division", under Armor Corps Commander Maj. Gen. Israel Tal. To me the division echelon seemed tremendous and distant. The brigade's task was to enter Khan Yunis, in the middle of the Gaza Strip, with the 79th Battalion while the 82nd Battalion moved south of Khan Yunis. The two formations would then move southward toward Rafah, at the southern end of the Gaza Strip, with intent to circumvent the town and capture the positions south of it with a brigade-strength offensive. The Egyptian 7th Division was deployed around a crossroads south of Rafah, and two mechanized brigades were arrayed at the junction, waiting for us. There our brigades armored infantry battalion, the 9th, was to join up somewhat later, while the conscript paratroop brigade under Lt. Col. Rafael Eitan Raful would enter the area from the south, via Kerem Shalom. From Rafah junction we would progress south, capturing Sheikh Zawid and advancing to Jirdi, ten kilometers north of El Arish. An armored reserve brigade under Mann (Menahem) Abiran would join the two conscript brigades in that vicinity. El Arish seemed far away, and at that moment I did not think much about the city and the enemy it harbored. In general, all the forces shared one mission: occupy Sinai and reach the Suez Canal.

Monday, June 5, 1967

We woke up to a predawn alert. While it was still dark we readied the vehicles and tied our personal gear to their flanks. We started the engines, warmed up the systems, and waited in radio silence. The sun rose. It was 0700 hours and still no sign of the beginning of a war.

I took off my overalls and sat down on the tank to rest. My sunrise briefing to the company had been terse. I did not want to make the men jittery, giving them the impression of my being the hard-pressed-commander type, always bustling about at the last moment to solve this or that problem and nail down this or that point. I sat on the tank and waited for the radio news. Maybe the situation had changed.

At 0800 on the button the radio emitted a siren. Surely a reception problem! I shook and pounded the radio, hoping to silence the racket. It didn't work. The war had begun.

A pair of Fuga aircraft passed low *en route* to the Gaza Strip. Soldiers began to shout in all directions: "Red Sheet! Red Sheet!" I wondered briefly who had disclosed the code. In any case there was no doubt: this was it, the point of no return.

My company had 14 tanks. All the crewmen, including their commanders, were under 20 years of age. My deputy was Lt. Daniel Tzafoni of Kibbutz Beit Alfa. The platoon commanders were Nuri, Shlomo, Amir, and Egozi. The company staff sergeant, Avraham David, rode in the command car, while my driver, Haim Shaar, drove the jeep. The technical squad, commanded by Arieh Rosenblum, occupied two personnel carriers. Among the tank commanders (mostly lance corporals) and platoon sergeants were Davidovich, Avraham Shalom, Moshe Shakrazi, Yisrael Mizrahi, Tuvia Ben-Ari, Ephraim Liba, Yair Geled, Leon Rothmensch, Arieh Zelig, and Noam Rotem. The company clerk was Dagan, and the medic was Grushka.

Our 90 mm Patton tanks lurched forward, roaring wildly out of the eucalyptus groves that had concealed them along the highway. We lined up on the shoulder, facing west. Excited soldiers along the road waved to us, wishing us good luck. Several even applauded. I felt a surge of pride: here I am, leading my company into war. Suddenly everyone was watching me, following my actions. Even the tank commanders did not conceal their excitement. Their answers on the two-way radio were terse and to the point. Everyone responded to my call. Not a single tank failed to start up; the metal monsters were cooperating. "Can we load the machine guns? Can we load the cannon?" — the radio network crackled with questions. To the commanders, it might have been just another drill.

I was troubled about the possibility of getting lost with my company as we headed for Gaza. Our orders were to approach the border in two columns. We headed south to Kibbutz Nir Oz and entered the kibbutz's farmland. I had some idea of the way, having made an observation from the kibbutz grain elevator. I had also flown along the Gaza Strip border in a light reconnaissance craft. The left column was headed by Battalion commander Ehud Elad, supported by his deputy, Haim Erez, and two companies under Benzi Carmeli and Gil'ad Aviram. Behind me was the battalion's reserve armored infantry company, known as "Dveika".

Ehud, leading the column, suddenly took a left turn instead of heading toward the entrance to the Gaza Strip. I had the unpleasant duty of alerting him to this over the radio. I groped for the right words.

"Ehud, this is Kahalani. I can see the entrance very clearly. Its 500 meters from me. We've got to take a sharp right."

He got the hint and pulled to the right. Several hundred meters later, Ehud's column disappeared, and I found myself heading the force that was racing toward the frontier.

There it was: a white dirt road. Just that. No minefields, no fence, no anti-tank ditches. Just a dirt road. It was 0848 hours.

"Buna stations, this is Buna," I called into the microphone. "Attention. It is 0848 hours, June 5, 1967. At this moment I am crossing the border. We are making history. Good luck to all of us."

The tank commanders signaled with their flags that they had received my announcement. Looking back again, I made sure none of the commanders was visible in the turrets. In maneuvers I had had to order those cocksure commanders time and again to get their heads down lest they be blown off. Now they got the message.

Trailing my tank was Nuri Conforti, commander of Platoon 1. As we had agreed before the war began — conventional practice then and now — Nuri was to pass me and proceed in front. I could not tell Nuri to do this; I could not send him into enemy fire ahead of me. I continued along the route previously learned, machine guns and main gun loaded and ready to fire. Both sides of the path were strewn with profuse prickly pear cacti and sundry obstacles.

Plunging into the cacti, I came under machine gun fire. At first I did not hear it; the engine was thundering and I was wearing earplugs. I did wonder why chips of paint had begun dancing around the turret and hull, and realized only a few seconds later that they came from my tank, loosed by enemy machine gun rounds. I returned machine gun fire in the direction of some houses from which the fire seemed to originate. I saw no enemy gunners' I fired merely to reassure myself that I was in control. The tanks behind me also began firing past my flanks. They followed the sound of my gun, which played the tune I appreciated so much: an uninterrupted rat-a-tat-tat.

Suddenly the dirt road narrowed; the prickly pears closed in until the path would not accommodate the

tank, three-and-a-half meters wide. We could not back
up. I decided to take the tank into the cacti until the
road widened. The vehicle stopped atop one of the
cacti with a deafening roar. A quick look at the front
end told me why. The chain had come off. I couldn't
believe my eyes. Now what? The tank was still under
fire; I had to get my head inside. Repairs were out of
the question. I had to switch tanks fast. I issued a
string of orders. First, the men behind me were to
cover my tank. Then Nuri leaped into the tank behind him, and I into his.

Now I ordered the column to back up carefully
until I found an opening in the prickly pear fence. At
least that curse was behind us. I let the tank blaze a
new trail, relieved that I had not failed in my first
challenge of the war. I had no doubt about where I
was heading. I took the column through back yards
in the village of Abasan Alkabir, *en route* to the next
village, Bani Suheila. After Bani Suheila came the
first objective: Khan Yunis, at the southern end of the
Gaza Strip. I advanced from yard to yard, occasionally firing at suspect houses and groves of trees. Then
my tank engine emitted a kind of deafening roar I
had heard before. The motor was spinning freely.
Again, the chain had come off. I was beside myself.

They had relied on me, a young commander, sending me out on my own axis, and this is what they got.
Israel would lose the war and I'd be the major cul-
prit! I could already see myself facing a commission
of inquiry. In the meantime, the whole column was
stalled behind me, commiserating with the bungler
up front who had caused the traffic jam. Again my
men covered my tail, and my second-in-command,
Tzafoni, volunteered to get me out. He passed several tanks until he was directly behind. I parted with

my crew. "Take care of yourselves," I ordered. After all, I was abandoning them in enemy territory!

To this day I do not know why the chain came off. In any event, Tzafoni hopped into the loader-radioman's compartment and I into the command cupola. We returned to the cactus path that led to the objective. We knew the village approaches were mined but not exactly where. Indeed, two of my tanks, trying to pass other vehicles rather than following mine, set off mines and were abandoned in the field.

"Buna stations, this is Buna," I shouted into the wireless."I warned you to follow me only!"

Now I ran into a barricade of branches, stones, and metal containers. One shell blasted everything away, and we moved on. There was no enemy resistance, although we occasionally heard shots of uncertain origin. Then two little children jumped in front of my tank from the prickly pear thicket. They fled, frightened and bawling, occasionally looking back at the monster a few meters behind them. I silenced the machine guns. Now I saw their mother. She stood there down the path, howling, wailing, waving her hands. I wanted to assure her that I would not injure her children, but of course I could not. The kids continued to run, my tank following them. Reaching their mother, they leaped into her arms; she caressed them vigorously, shaking her head at me in gratitude, and got herself out of there. Only then did I open fire on some Egyptian soldiers I had noticed.

As for my route of progress, I relied on intuition rather than a map. In Bani Suheila I advanced slowly and cautiously toward one of the crossroads. There, in a back yard encased in a tall concrete wall, an old Arab woman was hanging laundry. I felt insulted; she was behaving as if tanks parked next to her house every day.... From a nearby gully an Egyptian soldier suddenly materialized and began to march toward me, dragging his rifle, evidently confused. About five meters from the tank he stopped and stared, as if trying to identify a former schoolmate. Get out of my way, I motioned to him. It was no use. I could not gun down this pitiful clod just like that. Had he thought, at the sight of my swarthy complexion, that a Saudi or Yemenite force had come to Egypt's help? I fired a few rounds from my Uzi at his legs. Realizing that we were not comrades, he spun and raced madly toward one of the houses, cringing behind it, looking back threateningly, pointing his weapon at me. I returned the gesture.

Then, from an alley to my right, the barrel of a tank cannon appeared. I tensed, ready to fire. A few seconds later I identified the tank and its commander: Gil'ad, commander of Platoon C. He was alone and nervous. Right behind him was the commander of Platoon A in Benzi Carmeli's company. In the turret was Berko, firing in every direction. As he passed me I asked him where the company commander was. In the tank, Berko motioned with his hand. I was astonished. Then Berko gestured again: Benzi was sleeping or otherwise prostrate. Later I found that Benzi Carmeli had been seriously wounded. A sniper had hit him in the right eye, the bullet exiting near the right ear. At that moment Benzi was lying in the turret unconscious, his courageous platoon commander trying to take him to safety.

I circumvented Berko and Gil'ad, wondering where the battalion was. The first two tanks of the battalion commander's column were nearby, but where was the battalion commander? Even so, I was not overly concerned. I had not heard him over the radio, but my intuition said he was looking for me. According to the plan, we were to join up in the Rafah area.

We advanced toward the major crossroads of Khan Yunis, scattering uninterrupted machine gun fire every which way. I fired two shells at the junction, terrifying civilians in the houses all around. If anyone had harbored doubts about the Israeli presence in Khan Yunis, this dispelled them... .

The shoulders of the road were lined with trenches. We fired into them indiscriminately.

"Buna stations, this is Buna," I ordered. "Cover each other even if you have to shoot over the fenders."

Indeed, the only way to protect my tank was to have the vehicles behind it fire right over its rear flanks. I led the convoy down the road, only my head protruding from the turret. I wanted to get out of town; I was not made for combat in an urban setting. For one thing, I had no armored infantry to call on. That's a must in urban territory, and its absence among the tanks was sorely felt. Only armored infantry gives you a large number of "eyes" on the enemy. Only with it can one train many weapons on every window and alley with no limitations of angle and elevation.

Reaching the crossroads in the center of town I turned left, south, still navigating by intuition alone. There as a large building opposite the junction; a police station, maybe a school. Its yard was full of Egyptian army vehicles. Positions in the compound opened fire at my tank commanders' heads. Mercilessly I fired at the building. The enemy's attempt to kill me was intimidating, true, but infuriating as well. I fight best when I'm angry.

Rapidly we advanced south. I gave the driver no

directions and the gunner no instructions. Tzafoni and I operated the machine gun and spattered Uzi fire into the trenches on either side of the road. I also tossed all the grenades we had in the turret into the trenches; not since boot-camp had I had a chance to lob so many. Detonating in the trenches, the grenades sounded weaker and less effective than I had expected. I wanted to see them wipe out every enemy lying there, and I was not getting my wish.

Then a courageous Egyptian soldier rose from one of the trenches and threw a grenade at my turret. It stopped there, just in front of the hatch at which Tzafoni stood. Frantically we ducked inside, waiting, every second an eternity. The grenade went off literally over our heads. We were unharmed. "Step on it," I shouted at the driver, Siani, who was meandering down the streets of Khan Yunis as if he were sightseeing. The gunners in the tanks behind me fired like lunatics. How would I stop them if I had to? They fired for two purposes: to hit the real threat, there in front of them, and to gain the confidence every fighter gets from hearing his booming cannon, clattering machine gun, and roaring tank engine: the sounds of battle.

Little by little the houses thinned out. We were leaving town. A convoy of trucks was making its way in the opposite direction, from Rafah towards Khan Yunis. I stood up in the turret and flagged them off the road. My signal was received with mixed reactions. Several approaching Arabs fled for their lives; others came down to the highway, applauding or gesturing "good luck" in other ways. Evidently they too thought they were witnessing an Egyptian force that was about to smash the Jews...

A U.N. truck approached, about ten soldiers seated

tensely inside. I stood up in the turret and flagged the truck off the road, which was too narrow to permit both of us to pass at once. My gunner, Rafi Bertrand, gazed at the truck without really paying attention to it. In doing so, he swiveled the man gun to the left. Suddenly I noticed the protruding muzzle and returned to the turret quickly to move it back to the right. As I grasped the swivel control, I felt a sharp jolt. The gun had struck the U.N. vehicle so hard that it "shaved" everything in its path. For a moment I was stunned, hardly able to climb to my feet. Recovering my bearings, I returned then to the front as the tank continued to move. The truck, however, was disabled and immobile in the road. We passed it carefully.

Afraid that the gun had been damaged, I wanted to stop, but time was too precious to waste, and I had to link up with the battalion. I was out of radio contact with Battalion Commander Ehud, and felt it necessary to re-integrate into the battalion framework. I tried to contact him several times; no one answered. Might I be on the wrong road to Rafah? I pulled over and checked the map. Sure enough; there were two roads to Rafah. I should have taken the western one, presumably overlooking the Mediterranean, whereas my present route was some distance to the east. I decided to turn right and cross the dunes in the direction of the coast.

In the middle of this action I stopped again to pinpoint my location. Yes, I was on course now. I called Oved, Benzi's second-in-command, and asked him to report to my tank. Oved brought me up to date: Benzi had been evacuated to the rear. (I learned later that he was left in a personnel carrier that remained behind in Khan Yunis.) I ordered Oved to follow me with his company. He became the *de facto* commander of Benzi's company. Even though he continued to identify himself on the air as his deputy, everyone knew Benzi would not be back.

We found several enemy trucks crossing the dunes, heading, like us, for the western highway. I ordered Rafi to open fire. Strange noises emanated from the turret. Making inquiries with the men up there, I found that the firing system had been damaged. I examined the turret and the firing mechanism but could not figure out a thing. Leon, a tank commander serving as loader-radioman for the war, knew what the problem was and informed me that we had no chance of overcoming it.

A tank without a gun is like a hunter without a rifle. The cannon is the tank's major weapon, without which the tank has no *raison d'etre*. Compounding our distress, the 0.5 machine gun in the commander's cupola had problems of its own. The weapon was so hard to operate that I had ignored it thus far. So all we had now, in this mighty, terrifying tank that led the formation, was one machine gun operated by the gunner. We had a little Uzi ammo left, and on my hip was a handgun that I had never fired. I repressed the thought of switching tanks again. I would brook no further delay; I had to proceed quickly to Rafah junction and meet up with the battalion. "Let's keep going and figure out what to do", I ruled, putting an end to the crew's deliberations. A few hundred meters farther on we reached the second road to Rafah, the correct one. I turned left and advanced toward the town at top speed, the column in train.

White flags fluttered on the humble houses at the outskirts of Rafah, begging us not to fire. I was as tense as a spring, loosing bursts of machine gun fire at any suspicious movement. I was afraid of being hit. Machine gun fire was all around, and all of it, I knew, was aimed at me. The racket was deafening and audible even inside the tank. I ducked inside, raising my head only after the fire died down. Now, I saw, we were moving deeper into town. I looked for a way out. Combat in an urban theater was not for me! It was a trap from which we would not escape intact. We could not call on outside artillery and air support; even my tank's artillery was out of order. Rafah was a sprawling, densely populated city, and those who entered it found themselves increasingly entangled and lost. Staying there meant spending several days in combat at close quarters. But where was the way out?

Suddenly I remembered the railroad. It would lead me out of town! I returned to it and followed the tracks, recalling a half-joking, half-serious order we had received before the war: "Don't destroy the railroad; we'll need it to bring back the booty." Who cared about the booty, or at that moment, about the track itself? What mattered was to return to wide open spaces. The tank's tracks rattled on either side of the rails; the more distance we put between ourselves and the city, heading south, the less intense the fire was.

Just out of town I spotted a UN camp and several tanks on a hill to its west. With the binoculars I identified the Pattons and the red panels we had affixed to them before the war.

"There's the battalion!" I told my second-in-command, Tzafoni, urging the driver to advance toward the hill.

The closer I got to the battalion, the more puzzled I

became. Who was fighting whom? Several of our
tanks had been damaged, and pillars of smoke rose
over the area. I approached Ehud's tank, looking forward to an emotional reunion, but he was preoccupied with his two-way radio and had no time for me.
To his left, in the loader-radioman's position, was the
operations officer, Amram Mitzna, wearing women's
sunglasses. I grinned despite myself: where had he
found such a sense of humor in the middle of the
war? Taking a second look, I noticed that the tank
had been damaged, evidently by artillery, and Mitzna
had taken several bits of shrapnel in the face. The
tank's antennas had been damaged, thus explaining
why I had not been able to make radio contact with
Battalion Commander Ehud. As I waited for Ehud,
the brigade commander approached him and signaled me with both hands, leaning over the top of his
personnel carrier, showing me the direction in which
we were to begin storming the enemy. Once I understood what he wanted, Oved and I began to advance
in the direction shown.

I arrayed my company in a straight line and told
Oved to deploy his to my right. Then we began to
race across the vast dune area (on which the town of
Yamit was later erected) in a full-fledged operation
whose target I still did not know. A few minutes later
we reached the crossroads and encountered the first
trench, from which hundreds of Arab heads pro-
truded. The enemy soldiers, frightened, burst into
flight with ourselves in pursuit. Slowly we advanced
in their wake, machine guns rattling without letup.

A shell exploded two meters in front of me. To my
left was an enemy T-34 tank dug into a position, its
turret protruding, its muzzle pointed directly at my
tank. I ducked into my turret. My own main gun was

dead, making my tank easy prey for the Egyptian machine. My driver raced forward. I looked for a furrow of land in which to hide, but the terrain was flat and exposed. I waited for the next shell, which should have been fired several seconds after the first. It was clear to me that I would not escape this situation in one piece. I radioed my company's tanks.

"T-34 to my left. Hit it fast!"

One of our tanks pinpointed the enemy machine within a few seconds and sent it up in flames, its barrel still trained on me. Ever since, I have drilled the lesson into my students' heads: "Whoever shoots quicker and better lives longer."

Now we encountered the second trench in the Egyptian compound. In it were anti-tank guns and positions, meant to put up a tougher defense. Without stopping, my men shelled the positions, atomizing them and their human contents. The Egyptians went into a panic, ducking into the remaining trenches and cowering. We had to wipe them out, I knew. Otherwise they would reclaim their positions and inflict losses on our forces. I stopped my tank at the edge of the second trench, swiveled the cannon, and sprayed into the trench with my machine gun. I had assumed a dangerous angle. I was afraid to stop, and my main gun was pointing right, not forward where the enemy was. I tossed several grenades into the trench, but sensed that they accomplished little. So I kept moving, chasing after a group of Egyptian soldiers.

One of them fell in front of my tank and looked up pitifully. "Swerve left," I ordered my driver. Yet I did not trust the Egyptian. As we rushed past I looked back cautiously. Sure enough, he was firing his weapon at me. I ducked behind the command cupola and continued my headlong rush in the hope that someone behind me would take care of the ingrate. The machine gun in the command cupola was out of order, leaving me with the machine gun in the turret and nothing more. That would not do.

At all stages of the fighting I maintained radio contact with the company, transmitting orders down to individual tank level. I kept one eye on the road and the enemy in front of me, and the other on my flanks, trying to note the positions and progress of all my tanks. Most of my messages were meant either to spur stragglers or to update gunners on the changing positions of targets they were missing. The tank commanders fought vigorously; even in mid-battle they continued to wave their pennants to indicate that they had received my orders. My driver kept the pedal floored. More than once I found myself speeding several dozen meters ahead of the company's line. When storming an objective, the point is to advance as fast as possible. With the enemy in stationary firing positions, a tank commander wants to minimize the period of exposure. Worse still is the situation of one who pushes ahead of the company or battalion line; he is a conspicuous target that attracts fire. So, as I continued to control the tanks in mid-combat, I tried to slow down. Tzafoni intervened from time to time, directing our gunner toward targets and spattering Uzi sub-machine gun fire at Egyptian soldiers nearby. Once I whipped out my handgun and fired from the command cupola at an Egyptian soldier in his trench. It sounded like a cap gun in the din of battle. I missed, of course.

Deputy Battalion Commander Haim Erez joined us as we stormed the junction area. Later, when we drew to a halt on one of the area's low hills, I found, to my surprise, that my company had acquired additional partners: four tanks from Gil'ad Aviram's company, which had lost radio contact with their commander. I attached them to my network.

"We're naming you Platoon E," I informed the platoon commander, who was pleased to have found a new "father".

Another tank approached us a few minutes later.

"Where's Gil'ad's company?" its commander asked; he was Sergeant Alon and had formerly been under my command.

"I don't know. Join us, " I ordered. Alon agreed. I plugged him into our network, assigning him a code name that coincided with his own. By waving his flag, he signaled his understanding of the new arrangement.

"Now listen, Alon," I continued, "you drive next to my tank. My cannon is busted. When I tell you I've got a target, I want you to hit it. In other words, from now on, you are my gun."

Alon signaled in the affirmative. With that my confidence returned. Several times when I reached a position and spotted a clear target up ahead, I radioed Alon. He advanced, lined up to my right, and destroyed the enemy. Then we advanced together.

Still I resolved to switch tanks the first time we stopped. I wasn't looking forward to that ordeal. In a new tank I would have to retune all the radios for my networks; and that would take time. I would also have to switch crews — another unpleasant chore. After crossing the second trench we found the enemy forces thinner. We came across some anti-aircraft guns concealed in piles of dead bushes, and wiped them out down to the last nut and bolt. The fleeing Egyptian soldiers knew they had to reach the coast rather

than the dangerous inland to the southwest; thus
they all headed for the dunes to our northwest. As
they ran, many of them stopped to take their boots
off and throw aside their weapons, and so, barefoot
and defenseless, they raced toward the Suez Canal.
They were heading for terrain that was virtually impassable from our standpoint; we kept away from it
in any event because it was not part of our task. But I
shall never forget the sight of hundreds of Egyptians
scampering across the dunes.

The Egyptians had no idea how the IDF would
treat them if they were taken prisoner. Only after we
had taken our first POWs did the rumor spread among
them that Israeli captivity was a better deal than a
life-threatening marathon across the dunes. Taking
prisoners is hard to do when storming an objective;
one wants to leave them with infantry, of which we
had none. In one case I had to assign a tank to stay
behind and baby-sit a large group of enemy who had
put their hands up. It was a tradeoff: I had lost a tank
that could have gone on fighting, but gained the dis-
arming of enemy fighting men who could have attacked the defenseless logistical systems that followed
in our tracks. When one storms and captures one
objective after another, one always risks being unable
to leave forces behind to make sure the enemy, down
to the last man, is either out of commission or taken
POW. It has often been known to happen to the IDF
and to other armies that combat forces continue to
advance while the enemy reclaims its positions. We
had to set up special forces to cleanse and secure
objectives after their capture.

Just as we believed we had wiped out the enemy
arrayed at the crossroads, we stumbled into an area

crisscrossed with trenches, each concealing a truck bearing ammo, water, food, and other gear — everything an army needed in wartime. We were so astonished that we began to attack them so fiercely as to endanger ourselves in the tanks. I ordered the men to stop firing at once and make sure none of our soldiers or drivers were near the trucks. Later we appropriated the booty and turned it in the opposite direction of that intended.

Alon performed brilliantly. I was amazed by his agility, valor, and ability to stay at my side. Time after time he destroyed, at ranges of 150 meters or more, enemy tanks I had located. I still remember how they went up in flames upon being hit, plumes of black smoke rising skyward. We had overused our machine guns and were running out of ammo. By contrast, we had ample artillery shells, at least at that stage.

We were still out of touch with the battalion commander, Ehud. After the Rafah junction area had fallen, I saw him charging ahead to my left and plotted my course on the basis of his. Today I can say with certainty that I stayed informed only by virtue of the briefings and orders given us before the war. I understood the task and the goal, and knew which way to go and what I had to do even when the battalion commander was unable to instruct me.

Throughout the campaign I found the sandy landscape particularly impressive. How could a large army dig in amidst the dunes? Where would an army get the manpower to keep the positions in shape, bailing out the sand that poured into them relentlessly? The Egyptian uniforms were lighter than ours; thus the enemy was better camouflaged.

I hoped my present onslaught would end with a

general lull. With hours of combat behind us, my men and I felt we had to stop and learn lessons. I wanted to sit with the tank crews and their commanders, hear them describe their experiences, and make sure they knew their tasks. Obviously this would have to wait. Fortunately, I had the radio at my disposal. What a wonderful tool. All I had to do was issue an order, listen and repeat the sequence. I could run almost everything that way.

As I radioed orders, I had to make sure they were in the same tone I used before the war. As company commander, I was heard by every tank, every driver, every gunner in the company. Every man would detect any trace of anxiety or excitement in my voice. Everyone knew my location: a large red panel had been affixed to my turret to permit our aircraft to identify us and to distinguish the company commander's tank from the others. I have always believed the panel does more harm than good. With it, the enemy too can identify the command tank, making it a prime target.

When Israeli A2C Pattons were hit, we found, they were consumed at tremendous speed. The flames sped to the turret, where the ammo was stored. Thus whenever a turret was hit, the ammo blew up and the crewmen perished. More than once I saw turrets fly off their moorings when the explosives were ignited. We called the Pattons "goznikim" — Hebrew slang for the primitive torches we used to mark targets and paths at night. Neither were we enthusiastic about the Patton's 90 mm gun; the Centurions fielded a 105 mm piece.

This war was my first face-to-face encounter with Egyptian soldiers. I always knew they were swarthy, but found to my surprise that I was swarthier than many of them. From afar they all looked alike, but up close their features and reactions were different. They all looked scared; once their initial obduracy fell through they fled for their lives, turning their backs to us. Apart from the one group that raced across the dunes, they did not drop their weapons. At most they dragged them behind, glancing back beseechingly from time to time.

That's not how I wanted to wage war. The enemy should have looked me in the eye and fought me head-on. I would rather have seen their fingers on the trigger as I pulled mine, despite the danger. I attacked no one who did not imperil me. On the battlefield it is hard to know where the real danger lies; when you stop firing in one direction, you get hit from another.

As I could gauge from the radio chatter, my fighters were agitated and tense. The tank commanders displayed greater agility than I had known them capable of. When they were not firing the command machine gun they generally stayed in the turret, safe, only their eyes peering out. We treated the tanks like rolling bomb shelters, aware that our chances of staying alive were greater behind armor.

Tanks damaged during the assault ground to a halt. The crewmen jumped out, eyes toward me. "Don't forget us," those eyes said. Stopping in the middle of a charge is a dangerous matter. I could only look back quickly and signal them to stay where they were. I gestured to them: "I see you, I know, I'll make sure somebody returns to pick you up." Then I went on.

Young, green soldiers expect to hear their commander's voice at all times. More important, they

need to know where he is. The most important thing
of all is to see him. Indeed, my tank was visible from
afar. Many tanks circulated around me, and I was the
one who dictated the direction, speed and targets. I
made a half left turn to indicate a change in the
direction of advance; immediately, as if it were self-
evident, the tanks to the left decelerated and those to
the right accelerated.

The desert had a clean beige complexion. Apart
from the occasional pillars of smoke, it seemed like a
fine place for large-scale maneuvers. As Armored
Corps men, we always looked for broad, open spaces.
Formations were always encouraged to deploy as
wide apart as the territory permitted, and here in
Sinai they could. In mid-battle, however, the tank
crews wanted to crowd together, togetherness spawn-
ing greater confidence. I wouldn't have it. I roared
into the radio to spread out, and they redeployed.
Confidence aside, tanks defend each other more easily when they are further apart.

The pell-mell advance ended in Sheikh Zawid, 15 km
southwest of Rafah. For the first time we could stop,
look around, and try to understand what had happened thus far. I peered at my crews from the top of
the turret. They did not rush to kiss and hug. Nor did
they burst into animated conversation. They just
stretched. Reflexively the tank drivers hurried to check
their treads and drive trains.

Fighters do not share experiences in mid-combat,
preferring to keep their stories to themselves until
the tension ebbs. As I moved among the tanks, asking
the men how they were and taking stock of the remaining ammunition, the men tried to make light of
their stress with a smile or a gesture signifying

"everything's OK." Quickly, however, they fell back into their state of edgy readiness. We knew we still had much work ahead, and that the next battle was waiting for us over the hills. I decided to switch tanks. I called on Tzafoni to find us another tank.

At long last I met up with the battalion. Brigade commander Gorodish and Battalion Commander Ehud huddled together, exhausted even though it was only early afternoon. Shammai was a few meters from me. Shammai had shaved his beard in case it became necessary to use the gas mask; I could hardly recognize him. I hopped into his tank and gave him a friendly embrace. Comrades at arms. I overheard the rasp of a transistor radio in one of the tanks. The Voice of Israel had nothing to say about us; everything was still secret. "Our forces in the south have gone out to repel an Egyptian offensive," the announcer asserted. I smiled. Repel? Why not say The government of Israel has ordered the IDF to push the Egyptian army back to the other side of the Suez Canal?

"The Jordanians are attacking in Jerusalem," the newscaster went on. "They have occupied the High Commissioner's residence and are showering many parts of Jerusalem with artillery." Now I was taken aback. Never had I imagined that the enemy would open a second front. I knew we did not have enough forces in Jerusalem to defend it. Then I remembered that Dalia had gone there, to her parents home. I pictured her scampering frantically in search of shelter amidst the artillery shells. Suddenly I sensed that the real war was just about to begin. Now it was serious. I knew one piece of information the radio would not broadcast: permission to go home... .

Then I noticed battalion commander Ehud racing

to his tank and signaling me to do the same.

"Buna stations, this is Buna," I radioed to my subordinates. "We are going on into the heart of Sinai. I want to tell you that the Jordanians are attacking Jerusalem, and you know what this means. Load your guns and follow me."

" Buna, this is Ehud," the battalion commander called me. "Follow me. I'll explain as we go."

Ehud put his tank through a U-turn. I followed, my company in train. I had not had time to change tanks.

"We're gonna help the reds; they have problems," Ehud continued, referring to the paratroopers red berets. "Nobody really knows what's happening. Start pulling toward Kafr Shen. Get to your positions fast so you don't bump into any reds."

I passed Ehud and advanced with several of my tanks. The terrain permitted us to spread out. Later I understood that the conscript paratroop brigade under Raful, which had penetrated Sinai about four kilometers south of Kerem Shalom, had run into trouble and was finding it hard to link up with us in Sheikh Zawid. We passed Kafr Shen and went on to Kerem Abu Sharif, three kilometers to the east. I strained my eyes to avoid hitting Israeli forces or being hit by our own artillery. We did not accomplish much.

Then we were ordered to turn back. Tzafoni and I spread out our map to figure out how to do this. Engrossed in this endeavor, our trunks and heads out of the tank, we suddenly heard a lengthy burst of gunfire behind us. The shells spattered the tank several millimeters from the map. We leaped inside. A stain of blood spread on Danny's shirt. I glanced back. A group of Egyptians was hiding in the bushes;

one of them had fired the burst. We were alive only because the command shelf was in its vertical position and therefore stopped the bullets. I backed up and wiped out the enemy. Danny took off his shirt: a bullet to the right hip had perforated the flesh. Aryeh, the loader-radioman, dressed the wound and I went back to searching for the route to Sheikh Zawid.

We returned to Sheikh Zawid, climbed onto the highway and headed south toward El Arish. Traffic was quiet, allowing me to enjoy the scenery. The sun was no longer fierce and the wind dried the sweat off my face. I donned safety glasses to protect my eyes from the sand. At the head of the convoy rode the brigade commander's advance command group in several personnel carriers, followed by Ehud. About eight kilometers south of Sheikh Zawid, where the railroad crosses the highway, I was ordered to pass the brigade and battalion commanders. I was to lead the brigade. No one had briefed me about the enemy and positions I would encounter on the way. My map, too, offered no details about the enemy forces.

"Move toward El Arish. Fast!" Ehud ordered. I passed him and we exchanged grins. Brigade Commander Gorodish gestured thumbs-up, wishing me good luck, as did Yossi Ben Hanan, the brigade operations officer. I was in the lead, just where I like to be. Mine would be the first Israeli tanks to reach El Arish. Good.

It was nearly 1800 hours, almost sunset. My company tail-gated me as we moved on. Directly behind me was Alon. He had become redundant, it seemed; in the past few hours we had fired at nothing. Siani, my driver, kept his foot to the floorboard, and the tank roared ahead with youthful vigor.

Suddenly I spotted three soldiers lying in the

bushes on the right side of the road. I turned my cannon aside and ordered my gunner, Rafi, to prepare for machine-gun fire. The three jumped out of their place of concealment and motioned me frantically to slow down. To my astonishment, they were Israelis.

"Watch out. Egyptian tanks nearby!" one of them yelled at me.

" Where!?" I shouted back.

The soldier pointed down the road. As we continued to advance, we found a burnt-out personnel carrier blocking the road. I was not surprised. Along the way I had passed many gutted Egyptian vehicles, some hit by our air force. Looking again, however, I noticed an IDF license number under the wreckage. I ordered my driver to slow down and pull onto the left shoulder.

Mounting a low ridge in front of me, I stopped the tank and tried to look south and west with the binoculars. Perversely the sun struck the lenses. I couldn't see a thing. I retreated into the tank and leaned on Rafi's shoulder, asking him to try to identify enemy tanks through his sight.

"All I can see are trenches. No tanks," answered my gunner.

Up in Flames

Then, without warning, my tank shuddered. I heard an explosion and felt what seemed to be a knife plunged into my back. What happened? For a moment I was paralyzed. Then I fell back into the tank, driven by fierce pain. I understood.

"We've been hit. Jump out," I shouted.

The turret was engulfed in flame. I tried to force

my hands and legs to push my body to the hatch overhead. My strength failed; I fell inward. I was in shock, like a drunk who had lost control of his body. "Don't howl," I ordered myself.

"You're the commander; all eyes and ears are on you." But I felt I could hold it back no longer. The stench of cordite and slime filled the tank, as if the vehicle and its passengers had been shoved into a furnace. I closed my eyes, again straining my limbs to reach the hatch. This time I made some progress but fell back again. Shouts emanated from the turret, but I could not focus on them. I fell on the turret floor, utterly spent.

"That's it," I said to myself. My life is over. Thoughts tripped over each other. I felt like a drowning man whose last hopes had faded. Alone. I tried to part with my loved ones. They flashed past my eyes like a motion picture, their features crystal clear: father, mother, wife Dalia, my sister Ilana, my brothers Emmanuel and Arnon, friends, home, neighborhood.

Just as I managed to bid them farewell, I was gripped with a fierce will to live. I strained every muscle I had. The hatch was more than a meter overhead. I drew up my last reserves and found myself standing on the commander's seat. I shouted with all my strength:

"Mother, I'm burned, I'm burned, I'm burned..."

I ripped away the radio cord attached to my helmet. I leaned over the command hatch and lurched downward, toward the tank engine. From the hull I leaped into the sand behind the tank. I fell, climbed to my feet, and ran with whatever strength I had. This only aggravated the flames, turning me into a human torch. Quickly realizing this, I flopped onto the ground, enveloping my body in sand, leaving only my head exposed. It was soothing, enfolding. For a moment I wanted to stay there. Artillery shells were falling everywhere, and tanks from my company scrambled this way and that. We had fallen into an ambush.

One of our tanks moved threateningly toward my cocoon. I could not see its commander in the turret. I wriggled away before it could crush me. My tanks were scattered in the field, shifting about nervously as they fought to break through the ambush. Several tank commanders did notice me and stare in puzzlement. Apart from my shoes, I was almost naked. I burst into motion again, distancing myself from the fire-spitting tanks. As I ran, the battalion commander's tank pulled up beside me. Ehud leaned out of the turret:

"Kahalani, what happened?!"

I shrugged helplessly.

"Watch out. Enemy tanks out there," I answered.

Ehud's eyes had the expression of a father worrying about his son and sharing his pain. I continued to run, motioning Ehud to move on ahead of me. This was no place for me to stand. The sand that had stuck to my body began to come off. Shreds of skin dangled from my palms; I tried to remove them as I ran. I felt defeated. I had abandoned my soldiers and fled the battlefield. No one, it seemed, was interested in me at all in those every-man-for-himself moments. I knew I had to find someone, quickly, who would get me to the rear.

One of the tanks was still behind me. I spotted its commander, Lt. Ilan Maoz, and flagged him down. "Let me come aboard," I signaled. Artillery shells began to rain down on the clustered tanks. The vehicle stopped. I summoned the strength to climb aboard. Balancing my legs on the track, I hopped onto the hull and thence into the loader-radioman's position in the turret.

"Ilan, get me out of here fast," I ordered in a tone that left no room for misunderstanding.

"OK, Kahalani. Don't worry," Ilan said soothingly. The loader-radioman, making room for me to rest in his domain, seemed to be in shock, words stuck in his throat. Ilan tried to turn the tank around. I heard the tracks screaming, about to slip off their wheels. "Don't break the chain," I tried to tell Ilan. "Be careful. Don't leave me stranded with the tank." I was still alert and attentive to everything around me. The radio chatter gave me the feeling that I was still in a command position.

Suddenly I felt fire in my shoes. The loader-radioman helped pry off the soles and the few bits of clothing that still clung to my body. My socks were burning slowly, penetrating the shoes. He ripped my shoes off. Now I was totally naked. All I had was my wristwatch.

The tank stopped beside the brigade commander's vehicle. Ilan and the loader helped me climb down. Brigade commander Gorodish and some officers around him gazed at me, unable to believe their eyes. Surely they were marveling at my physique, seen for the first time without the camouflage of a uniform... .

"Get him to the rear. Now!" Ilan ordered the driver of the brigade commander's recon jeep. "It's Kahalani, a platoon commander. Move!"

The driver propped me up in the passenger seat, made a U-turn, and raced north on the highway. He careened in and out amidst the heavy traffic of tanks and personnel carriers. I sat naked on the commander's seat, clutching the handle so as not to fall out of the open jeep. As we passed the tanks, I saw my comrades gesturing at me. First came smiles and waves at the unexpected encounter. But as I came closer, the hands came down and the smiles gave way to sad, astonished stares. Theirs was the last column of tanks waiting to enter the Jirdi position. Most of them were Pattons. I knew all the crewmen, including my good friend Shalom Angel and his second-in-command, Amatzia Atlas. Both had finished their conscript service a few months before the war and returned to civilian life. Their battalion, that of the 105 mm Pattons, was commanded by Lt. Uri Bar On, who subsequently founded the first Patton reserve brigade.

The shreds of skin on my palms flapped in the breeze as I held on in stinging cold and fierce pain. When we reached Mussa's armored infantry company, the driver screeched to a halt. "Give the man some morphine," I heard him say.

Protecting the Troops

A tank formation has five attributes: firepower, armor, mobility, strike capability, and communications. A tank's steel, we always knew, could not withstand the firepower of a tank's gun. That is, the ammo would always be one step ahead of the metal. I had briefly thought that the Egyptians' Stalin would prove me wrong. Surely no tank shell could penetrate such a monster. In the Six Day War, however, the Stalins turned out to be as penetrable as anything else. Today we have reached a new era in troop protection systems. The major device is a single-layer steel that defies most attempts at penetration. Israel may be the world's most advanced country in this regard. Its

Merkava tank represents a quantum leap forward in crew protection technology. Maj. Gen. Israel Tal, assistant to the Minister of Defense for the manufacture of the Merkava, spared no effort to develop steel or steel alloys that would protect tank crews. Protection is every tank developer's sacred goal. It taxes the intellect and the drains the defense budget. When it comes to saving human life, however, the price is never too high. Today I am quite sure that had I fought the Six Day War in the turret of a Merkava, I would have ended the war on the bank of the Suez Canal, not in the hospital.

The new protection systems mandated a redesign of the tank's interior. They made the tank heavier, thereby requiring a more powerful engine. As the tanks grew, their contours changed significantly as well.

In the Merkava, the ammo is stored so that it can neither explode immediately nor injure the crew if the tank burns. The interior systems are coated with non-flammable materials that also minimize shrapnel. The gun alignment and elevation systems are electronic, not mechanical, thus keeping flammable lubricating oil out of the turret. The exterior of the turret and its steel housing are angled so as to prevent the penetration of tank shells through the Merkava front end flanks. The engine is in the front, providing yet another layer of protection between the enemy shell and the turret. The tank has a back door. Ordinarily used to load equipment, ammo, and additional fighters, it facilitates escape when necessary. Finally, the crewmen wear fire-resistant overalls and fireproof gloves at all times.

It is important for every family to know that the army spares no mental or physical effort to protect crewmen. Nor has cost ever been an impediment. We apply the advanced technology we have developed in this area toward the protection of other vehicles, too. Thus everyone — infantry, engineering, and other corps — comes out ahead.

To the hospital

"Morphine, morphine! Medic, medic!"
People were running everywhere. A medic rushed to my side, injecting morphine. Instant relief. For my comfort they placed me on a stretcher and loaded me into the rear of a jeep, my legs sticking out over the side. The driver careened down the road, maneuvering agilely in the heavy traffic. Occasionally my stretcher bumped into obstacles; each time I was sure I would tumble onto the highway and fall under someone's wheel... My blanket whipped in the breeze, striking me like a tent flap come loose. I gripped the blanket, the stretcher, and the driver's seat. My strength was running out.

One moment I begged the driver to speed up, for I could hold on no longer. A moment later I asked him to slow down, for I could hold on no longer. I entrusted myself to man and god, suspended between heaven and earth, given to the mercies of those around me.

We stopped at a casualty station. I was immediately removed from the jeep. That was a relief. I felt professional hands examining me, inserting an IV.

"Don't give him morphine, " somebody yelled. "He already got some."

No one asked me anything. It seemed as if the

medical team saw not point in asking some very basic questions: What happened to you? Where were you hit? How do you feel? How long ago did it happen? Who was wounded with you?

Now that I had reached the aid station, I expected my saviors to provide a little warmth along with the needles they stuck into me. Today I understand that the doctors get straight to the point because they are afraid to lose time. They quickly pinpoint the source of the injury and work systematically, going by the numbers. The doctors also seem to believe — correctly, perhaps — that the seriously injured cannot function, think logically, or express themselves. If so, their disregard would appear to be legitimate. In any case, the combat casualty needs more than immediate medical care. He needs to be calmed and told briefly about his condition. He is anxious about his fate and, at times, cannot analyze matters correctly and accommodate himself to the possibility of imminent death or lifelong disability.

My stretcher was placed under a tree with two others, and the IV pouch was slung over a branch. I said nothing, but my eyes took in everything. I was surprised at the speed at which the medical crew worked. Like a well-oiled machine, the team tended to me and the other casualties. Did they know me? Did that really matter? Maybe it did. If I were to die, I wanted them to know who I was, so they could describe my last moments to my loved ones. I did not ruminate about death but kept the possibility in mind. My train of thought meandered. Slowly I felt my body becoming rigid. I was beginning to dehydrate.

Nearby, two doctors were discussing personal affairs.

"I understand there's a serious battle going on

there. We were warned that other casualties are on the way," one of them asserted.

"We don't have enough IV. I think the evacuation from here to Rafah junction is a little too long," answered the other.

"These three right here" — they looked in our direction, as we lay on our stretchers — "the one to the right is X, the one in the middle, I think he's also X, and the one to the left got hit in the stomach and the hand, but he'll be OK." I strained to listen.

"So who do you think I should put in the first truck out?"

"You know what? Let's wait and see."

Who did "X" mean? On the stretcher to my left lay a body with a blanket over its head. I knew him: Globus, deputy commander of the 82nd battalion. To my right lay a sergeant major in the brigade recon unit, Haim Lavie, whom everyone knew as Etzioni. Suddenly I understood. "X" meant dead, and I was the one who would soon be "also X". I felt uncomfortable about lying so close to a corpse. Now, appreciating how badly off I was, I wanted to distance myself from him, as if "X" were a contagious disease.

Another medic approached. Totally agitated, he identified me at once. It was my company's medic, Grushka.

"What happened to you, sir?"

"See for yourself."

"Don't worry. I wont leave you!" Grushka's hand was bandaged.

At dusk the medical team and most of the other personnel departed for the front. Left behind were a few medics and several reservist drivers, who were to evacuate us to the rear in Willys trucks equipped with special stretchers for this purpose.

Suddenly I heard the sound of shooting close by.

"Egyptians attacking. Over there!"

Everyone broke into frantic running. "They've lost their wits," I said to myself. They might even lose their lives that way.

I mustered my courage and called out to a reservist passing me, "Disperse in the field. Lie down and open fire."

"Shut up," the man shouted, continuing to scamper in search of a place to hide. At that moment I understood my position and condition. It hurt badly to be unable to help, to be out of commission at precisely such a moment. I heard first a few isolated shots and then some nervous bursts of gunfire in the direction of the Egyptian soldiers. The Arabs evidently got the hint and fled the scene. The men around me calmed down a little and went back to work, loading us on the special truck to Rafah junction.

On the way, Grushka crouched beside me, making sure to rouse me whenever I closed my eyes.

"Don't sleep. Try to stay awake," he prodded. I was not thirsty, but again and again Grushka tried to force fluids into me. After traveling a short distance, we stopped. A vehicle coming the other way, from Rafah, pulled up beside us.

"How's the rest of the way?" our driver asked.

"I don't advise you to go there. There are Arabs there. I think they fired at me," the other driver replied.

"How did you get through!?"

"I don't know. I floored it and got out of there."

All this was clear enough. This time I didn't even think of giving advice. The other vehicle continued toward Sinai. Our driver sat there, looking for a way out. After consulting briefly with Grushka, he started the engine.

"Hold on tight," he shouted at us. "We're going!"

Indeed we did, at breakneck speed, expecting enemy gunfire all the while. We got through safe and sound. As soon as he saw IDF soldiers, our driver slowed down. Again I closed my eyes.

"Wake up, sir. We're almost there," said Grushka.

"I want to sleep a little. I didn't sleep enough last night," I replied.

"I'd rather you be awake when we arrive." Grushka didn't let up. He had set himself a goal and saw it through to the end.

Most of the casualties on the front, it transpired, were brought to Rafah junction. Considering the noise, commotion, and lights all around, no one seemed concerned about being attacked by Arabs who had not yet fled the area. Near the crossroads I met Yom Tov, a company commander in my battalion, now on loan to an armored infantry battalion *en route* to Jirdi. "I'll make 'em pay for what they did to you," he promised.

The field hospital, enveloped in a cacophony of helicopters, was staffed by a team of paratroopers, not one of whom I knew. A doctor approached me, pulled the IV out of my arm, and searched for a place to reinsert it. That was no simple matter because my palms, like the rest of my body, were burned. Then he discovered that the soles of my feet, protected by my shoes, had gone unscathed. Immediately I felt a sharp pain as the doctor went to work on one of my veins, cutting it open so it would admit the IV. Only after I acquired some expertise in medicine did I understand that he was administering the IV by running a little tube into my vein rather than a needle through my skin. I groaned in agony, eliciting a surprised look from the doctor. Of all the nerve, he seemed to be thinking. You're seriously wounded. Lie there quietly and accept my ministrations with love. You're halfway to your grave; why complain about such a pin prick?

"I'm almost done," he said encouragingly. In fact, he had no luck with my left foot and now went on with my right. It ended well enough; the IV was inserted.

Now they took me away from the illuminated area and set me down in the dark, to wait for a helicopter that would evacuate me to the hospital. A medic who circulated among the casualties called my name and offered me something to drink, noticing my state of dehydration. It tasted strange but good. It was booty, Coca-Cola from the UN camp at Rafah junction. Coke was unavailable in Israel at that time; afraid of the Arab boycott, the Coca-Cola company had not yet recognized the State of Israel.

A few minutes later another stretcher was placed alongside mine. On it lay a giant of a man, a black. He howled with pain and rocked to and fro on the stretcher, emitting groan punctuated with the kind of juicy Arab profanity every Israel child understands and knows. Quickly I identified my neighbor and the cause of his distress: he was an Egyptian officer who had taken a bullet in the posterior.

Fearing for my life, I feigned sleep and played dead. The fellow might attack me or try to rip out my IV. I expected someone from the medical team to come over, but perversely no one approached. I stared at the sky and began to count the starts that hovered like an ocean over my head. When I tired of this, my apprehension mounting, I began to compose a prayer to God in heaven, asking him to come to my rescue. I would resume observing the religious commandments as I had as a boy, I promised. "God, if You're watching, I've got one little request: please give me a moment of Your time, and do everything to get me to a hospital!"

Right then, as if my prayer had been heard, the Coca Cola medic came over and asked me how I felt. Whispering into his ear, I asked him to put me somewhere else. I could not speak loudly, so overtaken by weakness that I could not move a limb. Even my voice betrayed me.

"I'm not sure there's any room in the light. Let me check."

He returned several moments later, glowing with jubilation. After a drink I was carried to an area illuminated by the lights of cars and trucks all around. A little later some other casualties and I were loaded into a giant helicopter which, after a flight marked by ceaseless, embarrassing vomiting, landed at the central Negev hospital in Beersheba.

Combat Medicine

The many arms of the IDF Medical Corps touch upon almost all branches of medicine. White-frocked corps veterans practice in the country's general hospitals as doctors, nurses and auxiliaries; some owe all their training to the corps. Instruction ranges from first aid courses for rank-and-file soldiers to medical officer training.

Medical Corps men and women take part in combat formations on the squad, platoon, and company level. Combat medics are full-fledged members of the fighting force. Every battalion has a doctor who commands a medical department that meets battalion level needs. In wartime, this platoon staffs the battalion's casualty collection station.

Battalion medical platoons receive regular help from higher echelons. This may take the form of a brigade-level medical battalion, but it is usually a divisional medical brigade that assigns medical companies to the brigades, from which help is proffered to the battalions. Beyond the divisional level, casualties are sent to general hospitals around Israel.

The battalion-level doctor and medic are of paramount importance. The quality of our fighting men would be impaired if they were to sense, even for a moment, that there was no one around to help them if they were wounded. State-of-the-art technology aside, the very presence of doctors and medics at the fighting man's side permits him to devote greater concentration to combat and less to the time-consuming care of comrades. This way, also, he is less worried about his own future.

The will to live and survive is one of the fighter's major motives in battle. The Israeli soldier, for one, can be sure he will never be abandoned on the battlefield. If wounded, he knows he will be given medical care as expeditiously as possible.

Immediate primary care — the heart of combat medicine — saves many lives on the battlefield. The system's involvement, however, cannot stop there. After administering primary care it must evacuate the casualty to a safe place, tend to him there for whatever time necessary, and then get him to a hospital in the rear. It is indeed a complex mechanism, one that requires coordination, precision, and other means — sometimes the very best — to meet the task. As commander of a battalion, brigade, and division, I was well aware of this. I assigned my best motor vehicles and manpower to the battalion medical platoons. They repaid the investment many times over.

First-aid instruction is part of all IDF soldiers' basic training. A soldier who cannot care for his comrade-in-arms should remember that the latter may not be able to care for him! Teaching the troops first aid is as important as showing them how to hold their weapons. Optimally, however, the wounded are evacuated by the medical system alone, letting the fighting men get on with their work. A tank engaged in evacuating a casualty creates a void on the firing line; the absence of its gun may seal our fate for better or worse. By the same token, individual fighters who volunteer to extricate casualties not only risk their own lives but reduce the size of the fighting force and disrupt its continuous operation.

Commanders on any level who devote less than full attention to their medical teams should not be surprised to find their casualties helpless just when they need help the most. There is no way to describe a commander's anguish upon hearing of the death of a casualty who left the battlefield in reasonable condition but failed to reach the hospital alive. On the other hand, how pleasing it is to meet a soldier who seemed on the verge of death on the battlefield, now sunning himself on the hospital lawn, surrounded by doting relatives and recuperating.

8. IN THE HOSPITAL

We landed on the hospital lawn in Beersheba at 0100 hours. The helicopter doors were pulled open and dozens of people ran toward the craft, offering their help. Teenage volunteers vied for the honor of carrying the stretchers into the emergency room. After they arranged the matter among themselves, several of them carried me on the run, as if it were an event in their school's field day. I clutched the stretcher poles for dear life.

I made my first acquaintance with the central Negev hospital in Beersheba in 1962 on the occasion of my appendectomy. Now, I noticed, its spacious entrance lobby had been converted into an emergency room. The statue of Ben-Gurion which had once greeted visitors now contemplated dozens of hospital beds, among which scurried nurses and doctors in white — helping, examining and caring for the wounded with speed and devotion.

I was placed on a white bed. Safe at last.

It took only a few moments for a doctor to come and look me over. He identified the burns and determined their severity; a nurse alongside him wrote down the findings on a form. I listened too: burns on sixty percent of my body, mostly third-degree.

"How do you feel?" the doctor asked, resting a hand on my forehead.

"Just fine," I whispered.

"Does it hurt?"

"Not especially. I'm all right. Take care of the others," I said. I meant it: it was enough to have reached the hospital. For lack of space, the maternity ward had been converted into a burn ward under the Plastic Surgery Department. This was where I was taken.

With an IV and catheter attached and penicillin powder sprinkled all over my body, I lay on my back in a room occupied by several other burn victims. I wondered what was happening to the battalion and how the Jirdi compound had been captured. And what had become of my tank crew? I had not yet worked through my ordeal in the tank. I had convinced myself that only I had been wounded, that Tzafoni and the other crewmen had continued fighting in Sinai. Tzafoni must have taken over the company, just as Oved had assumed command of Benzi's company when he got hurt. I wished him well with all my heart. May he take the company into the heart of Sinai with no further casualties. Only a few days later did I hear what had happened to the 79th Battalion. Its commander, Ehud, who led the assault on Jirdi, was dead. Operations Officer Mitzna was wounded, and Deputy Battalion Commander Haim Erez replaced him. The remains of the battalion broke through on the main highway heading south to El Arish. Leading the force were Shalom Angel and Amatzia Atlas, of Uri Bar On's Patton Battalion; they had been transferred to the 79th for the duration. Nine tanks were hit and enemy positions remained uncaptured. Now the brigade commander threw additional forces into action. The first of these was a half-company of tanks under Amir Yaffe; behind him came the 9th Battalion, the brigade's armored infantry, which mopped up the area throughout the night.

I commiserated with Hava, Ehud's wife. We had always been welcome in their home, having lived in the same neighborhood of Beersheba. Sometimes Ehud and I went on home leave together and returned together.

With piercing anguish I heard of the death of Shammai Kaplan. Shammai had been hit by an Egyptian tank about 30 kilometers from the Suez Canal.

A regular visitor to my room was Maj. Benzi Carmeli, the company commander who had taken a bullet to the head. He had lost his right eye and part of his skull; his head was misshapen, too big for his body. On one of his visits, I suddenly realized that everyone to whom Haim Erez had given a puppy before the war had been either killed or wounded in battle! How odd the ways of fate are.

Benzi would fall on my neck and cry each time he visited.

"Pretty soon," he'd say, "we'll get better and go straight to the Sinai and fuck all the Arabs!"

Time and again Benzi begged my forgiveness — for what, I didn't know. Later his wife Frieda told me: he was sure it was he who had hit my tank. My explanations didn't help; neither did the facts, which attributed the strike to Egyptian artillery alone.

After recovering, Benzi insisted on returning to the tanks. Within two years he was appointed commander of a tank commander course in the Armored Corps school.

Adam Weiler, a comrade close as a brother, interrupted his studies in England to join the war effort. He literally elbowed his way onto a flight bound for Israel and refused to get off even when they told him it was for his own good. From Lod Airport he went straight to the battlefield in Sinai.

Eliezer Marcushammer, my friend from basic training until his demobilization, fell in the sands of Sinai, leaving his wife, Nurit, and a young daughter.

My friend Amnon Giladi, company commander in Uri Bar On's battalion, was killed leading his company into battle. For several years Uri and Shlomo Angel had been my roommates. After Amnon's death, his older brother Gideon reenlisted and demanded reassignment to Armor, in order to follow in his brother's footsteps. Gideon perished in a tank during the Yom Kippur War. He was posthumously awarded the Israeli equivalent of a Purple Heart.

My good friend Shalom Angel returned to IDF service as a career soldier, even though he had to leave his kibbutz, Ramat Hakovesh, as a result. On one of the last days of the Yom Kippur War, I received word of his death. He had been killed en route to the battlefield. I was thunder-struck.

After two days in the hospital I asked a nurse to write a postcard home for me, telling them everything was all right. It didn't work. My sister Ilana, who had just completed her army service in the medical corps under Southern Command, immediately identified the hospital's army post number. She was given leave from her reserve unit and rushed to the hospital for a reunion that proved as enervating for her as for me.

My father came the next day.

"Wounded, eh!?"

I actually felt guilty about it.

"How are you?" he asked, his voice choked.

"OK. Does Mother know?"

"No. I didn't come from home."

Then, for the first time, I saw my father, such a

tough man, cry. I was astonished. Tears flowing down his cheeks, he turned and left the room.

Several years later my father told me he had spoken with Dr. Irwin Kaplan, head of the plastic surgery department, before entering my room. Dr. Kaplan, a talented physician who saved many lives in the Six Day War, spoke Hebrew with an accent that betrayed his South African origin. Apart from being a superb surgeon, he was a good soul. He would stroll through the department day and night, instilling calm and confidence among the patients, never overlooking anyone. He never lied to us, never tried to fool us. He always explained the next stage of treatment, the next test on the agenda. Before every round of surgery he explained, in scientific detail, how he intended to operate, from where he would take the skin, and how and where he would implant it. We loved him, without exception and without reservation.

"His chances are very slim," Dr. Kaplan told my father. "If he comes through, it'll be a miracle."

My father stepped into my room having been prepared for it like that, and I did not know about it.

A few days later, Dalia came from Jerusalem. They told her I had been slightly wounded in the hand. Imagine her shock, then, at the sight of me. She almost burst into tears. I returned the favor with some tears of my own.... Dalia, her slender body carrying our first child, looked helpless. All she wanted to do was help, and this was out of the question.

The next visitors were my mother and brothers. Profoundly agitated, my mother stationed herself beside my bed, moving about silently and restlessly, studying me at length and carefully examining the parts of my body that were not covered. She was afraid her sensitivity might offend me.

A lengthy series of different treatments was my daily fare at the hospital. Each day, by order of Dr. Kaplan, I was placed in a warm bath in which several little bags of salt had been dissolved. It took eight male and female nurses to bring this about. Four of them positioned themselves on either side, picked me up sheet and all, and slipped me into the water. Once I'd been there for about 20 minutes, stage B of the therapy began. The objective was to separate the sheet that had stuck to my wounds. This was hell on earth. I would order everyone out of the room, put a towel between my teeth, and pull as hard as I could with the one hand on which the fingers worked. Sometimes the sheet was difficult, but what was a sheet against a strong, stubborn tank commander?... Now all that remained was stage C, the post-bath spreading of cream over my wounds. It was like being burned all over again. My whole body was aflame. They pointed fans at my shuddering body to alleviate the pain. As time passed, I learned to take a sedative before going into the bath, so it would begin to work as I came out.

Occasionally I received new roommates and wondered where the old ones had gone. Later I understood: they had died.

One day, not long after I had been hospitalized, they put someone new in the bed next to mine. He had been severely burned in the face; his head was so swollen that he could not be identified.

"Hi, Sir," he blurted at me.

"Hi," I answered hesitantly.

"How are you?"

"All right... Who are you?" I asked, embarrassed.

"Rafi."

"Rafi who?" I asked, still straining to identify him.

"Rafi Bertrand, your gunner!"

The words stuck in my throat. He looked terrible — nothing like the Rafi I had known.

"Ah, Rafi... How are you? I'm sorry, I'm a little under the weather and I didn't recognize you." I said nothing more to him; I was in shock.

On the few occasions when I asked what became of my crew, I received evasive answers and preferred to leave things that way. The uncertainty comforted me. One version of affairs had it that Tzafoni, my second-in-command, continued advancing with the company and was now its commander. It was convenient for me to believe this. Sometimes I demanded more specific information from visiting soldiers from the company and the battalion.

"What's happening with Tzafoni?" I would ask. "Why doesn't he visit me?"

The answers sounded rehearsed: "He stayed on alert in Sinai," "He doesn't even go home." And the clincher: "He'll visit you the day he comes out."

Seeing Rafi with his injury, I had begun to harbor some disturbing thoughts. Visitors and roommates took my mind off them, true, but they recurred whenever I was alone. The fate of my company gave me no rest.

More than a month later — I remember it as if it were yesterday — I came out of my daily bath, clean, shining and scrubbed. No particular pain that day. I had taken the bitter Optalgin pill before going in, and the drug had already worked its wonders.

Yoel Gorodish was waiting for me outside the shower room. First came some polite questions and mutual how-are-you's. Then...

"Avi, I've got some bad news for you." Silence. I

looked hard at Gorodish. He was fishing for a way out.

"Tzafoni's dead."

I flushed.

"When?!" I asked, astonished. Surely at the very end of the war, deep in Sinai, I told myself.

"Tzafoni was killed when you were wounded."

Then came the tears, flooding my eyes, choking my throat, compounding my weakness. After I calmed down, Yoel told me that Tzafoni too had been burned. He had leaped from the tank, and everyone believed he would be the one to survive and I the one to perish. He succumbed a few hours later. Now I asked about the rest of the crew. Leon Rothmensch, my loader-radioman, was seriously wounded and had not succeeded in extricating himself from the tank. Sinai, the driver, had escaped uninjured.

I spilled my soul freely. I felt close to Yoel ever since I had been the deputy commander of his company. At that time Yoel had undergone a series of medical treatments and sometimes had to leave the company in the middle of maneuvers. Out of sympathy I did his share of the work in his absence.

After our spending some time in the maternity ward, they transferred us, the "steak platoon", to a large, new hospital building where the entire plastic surgery department was later housed.

One night I felt terrible. The duty physician checked me out but could not reach a diagnosis and called over a colleague for consultation. The two of them looked into my eyes, squeezed my abdomen, and listened to my internal organs.

I could see the anxiety in their eyes, even though they tried to hide it. Even when they stepped away from me, I understood what they were saying by reading their lips and following the motions of their hands.

"Hepatitis. No doubt about it."

"When did he come down with it?"

"I don't know. I only got here an hour ago."

"He held on this long, but this'll wipe him out."

I forced myself to keep quiet. The wounded are not sick. Unless they have head injuries, they are capable of noticing even those minute matters that those around them are sure they cannot perceive. Constantly we reminded our nurses that we were injured, not ill, and that we should be treated accordingly.

I ran a 105-degree fever for quite awhile. I hallucinated, suffering flights of fantasy that to me were totally real. One night after parting with Dalia, I saw someone enter the room and tell me my wife had just stepped into the maternity ward and given birth to a son. I pressed the buzzer to call the duty nurse, Ada, a woman of Italian origin who did not know Hebrew well and therefore lost her temper easily. She argued as best she could that it was 2:00 a.m. and that no one had entered the ward.

"That can't be. He just walked out! Would you please check with maternity?"

"Avi, you got a high fever. I understand. No one come here," Ada persisted, her Italian accent thicker than usual.

"Maybe you didn't see him, but someone was here for sure. I'd like you to call maternity."

"I can't. They'll laugh at me."

"Then I will!"

Since being hospitalized, I had not climbed out of bed unassisted. Drawing all the strength I had, I raised the blanket and threw myself to one side. My bed had a metal frame over which the blankets had been spread tent-like so they would not touch my body.

"You crazy!" she yelled, referring to me in the Hebrew feminine in her panic. Then she surrendered: "OK, OK, I'll call." She raced out of the room and returned, panting, a few minutes later. Dalia was nowhere near the birthing area, of course... .

Because I had been separated from my men in mid-war and was troubled by not having finished the war with them, I hallucinated about resuming command of my company. And because my awareness of having been injured had penetrated my subconscious, I knew that I needed my men's help to climb into the tank. I imagined that they strapped me to a stretcher padded with sponges, and thus I could press a special switch and operate the radio. After my fever subsided, my roommates told me that they had heard me issuing orders and instructions as if they were all on the battlefield. A crash course in company commandership, as it were.

With Dalia truly on the verge of giving birth, my sister Ilana took over as my regular bedside aide. She cared for me day and night, handling tasks and treatments normally performed by nurses. She debrided my wounds, seated me on the toilet, and force-fed the nutrients I needed for my recovery but abhorred. Eggs and coffee — what an abominable cocktail! My sister, an exotic beauty, attracted all visitors' eyes until I sometimes wondered if they had come to visit me or her.

Many of my visitors were soldiers, stopping off by the dozen on their way home from Sinai. Even though I was constantly fatigued, I never asked them to let me sleep, and tried frequently with some effort to be good company for them until they left. My reunion with Adam Weiler, my comrade and brother, was unforgettable. For a long time we sat facing each other, sharing stories, experiences, and emotions. Adam had come straight from Sinai, dust-covered and wreathed with a thick beard. He refused to part with me until I insisted explicitly that he go home.

All kinds of visitors showed up. Some stood at the door, announced that they were looking for Kahalani, and scanned the occupants of the room one-by-one without identifying me. Despairing, they apologized and went on to the next room. Others turned away in nausea and rushed to the terrace. Tzvika Stern, my second-in-command until a few months before the war, engaged me in spirited conversation, sipping soup as I sat on the bed, slightly elevated. Then his eyes began to roll in their sockets and he slumped in a faint — but not before spilling his hot tea on me. Today Tzvika is a senior physician and director of Hadassah Hospital on Mt. Scopus in Jerusalem.

Some visitors used the occasion to engage in stormy bedside discussions to which I was only an incidental witness. Others stood alongside my bed, speechless because they did not know what to say. Finding them too embarrassed and upset to speak, I undertook the task of encouraging them. Sometimes the polite roles were reversed, making my work easy: "How are you?" I would ask, whereupon my visitor would begin to describe at length some slight injury he had sustained and miraculously recovered from.

Neither was there a shortage of curious souls who simply went from room to room observing the casualties, just to add another experience to the tapestry of their lives. The sweetest of all were children who had been sent in groups to the hospital to deliver flowers to the wounded men. Innocent, solemn and emotional, they came and went. We were never indifferent.

Few of them really knew what the wounded were going through. Quite often visitors commented: "We know you. You're strong; you'll get over it!" This may have been the silliest sentence of all to utter in circumstances like these. By contrast, I loved visitors who knew what to ask and took genuine interest in my well-being. Sometimes one should not hesitate to nudge the casualty and make him express his pain. An attentive ear is better than ten Optalgin capsules.

Whenever I could just find someone to listen, I was happy to describe the moments of my injury, down to the last detail. That relieved the pressure, and, I believe, prevented the accumulation of suppressed residues that might burst to the surface without warning. My sleep was never shattered by nightmares of the incident. I was aware of what was happening to me, and I was willing to accept it all.

Rather early on I knew that I was facing a nearly intolerable ordeal. Patience was the first order, I told myself. And even if that did not suffice, I would not give in. It would be a unique experience: not everyone merits it. A test of life. I had gone through several ordeals, and was curious to know how I would stand up to this one.

I set myself one inviolable rule: I would ride through without making those around me suffer. I would bear my pain quietly, inwardly. I did not summon the nurses for trivial matters. I tried not to hassle them, aware that they were overworked as it was. Sometimes I could not refrain from sobbing in response to pain, weakness or a moment of crisis. I would stuff my head under the sheet and let the tears flow. Only after they had dried and my state of mind improved did I pull the sheet away.

Night was the most terrible time of all. I gaped into the dark, unable to fall asleep — but also unable to read or talk. Hours on end I would lay motionless, staring at the ceiling, thoughts running wild. Night gave me unlimited time for thinking. I exploited those hours, half-listening to the nocturnal sounds of the hospital: bits of conversation as a casualty tried to start up with a nurse, calls for water from somebody like me who couldn't sleep and wanted attention, and cries of pain reverberating in the halls.

The casualties visited one another, of course; sometimes turning the ward into a wheelchair racetrack. The visits also helped strengthen the fraternity of the wounded and fostered the development of a special, morbid humor. It was a brutal brand of levity that only the wounded could understand. Only they could allow themselves to clown at each other's expense.

"I let my fingers do the walking," grinned a man who had lost his fingers.

"My leg?" answered an amputee. "I just forgot to bring it back from the war. That's OK — no more athlete's foot!"

Once an amputee named Ya'akov mounted his prosthetic leg and held the straps under his pajama pants. He sat up on the bed, two legs dangling, shoes on both, and waited for one of the student nurses to enter the room.

"Give me a little help," Ya'akov requested, as we looked on in anticipation. "Pull my legs a little, one at a time, so it won't hurt so much."

The trainee was eager to help. When she got to the

prosthesis, Ya'akov began to emit alternate groans of pain and sighs of relief. What a performance.

"Pull harder," he urged. When she complied, he released the straps and the girl fell backwards, fake foot and all. Frightened and hysterical, laughing and crying, she ran out of the room, her shouts echoing down the hall. We laughed ourselves crazy.

One day they gave us an evening at the movies. There the amputee waved his cane and threatened, "I'm gonna kill this fly that's climbing on my foot! "

The blow of the cane followed at once. At the sound of the thud, an old woman seated next to him almost fainted... .

The hardest cases of all were the facial burns. It was difficult — impossible, really — to look at these burned men. Only we were capable of contemplating the beauty of the ugliness, assessing the results of the latest operation, and informing the casualty with satisfaction, "Now you look much better!" Of course, the hospital staff — doctors, nurses, and auxiliaries — were equally profuse with words of encouragement.

Jeanette, a physiotherapist from South Africa, tried to bolster the men's morale at every opportunity and prodded us in every way possible to outperform ourselves. Unfazed, she induced one of the men to move his hands by letting him feel her breast. With her help and that of others we competed for unofficial prizes for walking or weightlifting.

Neither did we neglect the arts. That was our occupational therapy! I became an expert craftsman of bracelets, beads, and copper ornaments. Hardly a visitor came by who didn't ask me to fashion a pair of bracelets for his wife or copper trinkets to embellish his apartment. I took pride in my work, subsequently displaying it at a hobbyists' exhibition. I briefly considered vocational retraining, but on second thought decided to put it off a few years... .

There were hard times too, plenty of them. I underwent twelve rounds of plastic surgery. One treats third-degree burns by transplanting skin from undamaged parts of the body. Usually they took thin layers of healthy skin from my hands with a special vegetable peeler, and cut them into stamp-like squares that they would attach to the wounded area, a few millimeters apart. As they merged, the patches of skin would send little extensions to each other, thus forming a new layer of skin and closing the wound. This took time: about a week from the time of surgery until the bandages were taken off the implant area. It was always a period of tension and anxiety. Which of the stamps would take hold, and which would the body reject? Interestingly, the area of the surgery never hurt; the real pain came from the area from which the skin had been taken. It was a sharp kind of pain, which ebbed only many days later, when the wound had healed over and vanished.

The most difficult were the operations on my back, after which I had to lay on my abdomen — a painful and highly uncomfortable posture. For weeks I lived upside down. Just the thought of relieving oneself in this fashion makes ones skin crawl... .

Then I would sense a pungent odor emanating from my body.

"I'm rotting!" I told the doctors.

It was indeed the stench of rotting flesh. I couldn't stand it. Even the pleasant aromas around the room did not mitigate the stink that reached my nostrils.

The trip to the operating room, in my bed, became a routine matter. The more operations I had, the less upset I was before each of them. On the contrary, I loved the numbing anesthesia that made me indifferent to my surroundings. I have never been a drug user, but from what I hear, it seems that addicts go through much the same experience. I fought to stay awake and timed my ability to do so. When I woke up, I hurriedly felt the areas where skin had been taken and implanted, just to make sure there had indeed been an operation. Several times Dr. Kaplan decided in mid-surgery to clean me up and do no more.

The biggest problem of all was the contraction of the skin as it healed. It prevented motion of the joints in my hands and feet with a force no physiotherapy could overcome. Many of us had lost the function of our hands in the process; my ordeal afflicted two fingers of one hand and my left foot, where one joint had become so distended that I could not straighten it. I had to goose-step until the taut skin was removed and replaced. In each case as the new skin healed, it itched and caused cysts to develop. I would scratch both sides of my back like a monkey. I couldn't help it.

I'll never forget the first time I got back on my feet. A tremendous surge of blood struck me from below. I was overcome with dizziness. A black mask fell over my eyes and I tumbled back into bed.

To those lying in hospital it seems that everyone in the world is injured or sick. Everyone who's been hurt has their own personal nightmare. Mine was the catheter through which I urinated; of all things on earth, I hated and feared it the most. For days on end

I tried to convince Dr. Kaplan to take it off. A few hours after he agreed to this, I begged him to reattach it. Without it I couldn't urinate. They'd open all the faucets in the world in my honor, emitting the unmistakable sound of rushing water, but it didn't help. I summoned memories of those good days when we had lined up in the field, peeing onto the green grass — but this too was useless. Even a silly song I knew about a sprinkler didn't help. How does an action so simple and automatic become complicated and uncontrollable? So they put the catheter back, and with it, the pain. Much time passed before it was removed again. This time, perhaps because of my prayers, or perhaps just because of the fear that they'd reattach the abominable thing, the experiment worked out. It was one of the most beautiful and festive moments of my life... .

Another nightmare, one we all shared, was the bedpan. Imagine the preparation a wounded or sick patient needs to cope with a problem like this! At first I sought to deny myself the experience; I was stubborn as steel. But nature had its way; even steel cracks under enough stress.

My firstborn son, Dror, was born in the hospital. The ritual circumcision, organized by the Soldiers Welfare Committee in Beersheba, was held on the Sabbath in the hospital. Maj. Gen. Israel Tal — Talik — showed up in my room to help me come down to the party. I was excited and elated, in a wheelchair for the first time. I was given a royal welcome; the guests seemed more interested in the reborn than the newborn. I could not conceal my ecstasy. Only when I clutched my son for the first time did I become aware of how much I owed my family.

I felt like a little child in those days. I had lost so

much weight and most of my hair. Together with my son I grew and regained my fitness. Our ages were 23 years apart, but went through similar processes of development. People were amazed by both of us: Dror because he sat up, stood and walked; and I when I stood up, ate and showered without assistance.

Then a crisis of no small magnitude befell me. I discovered that the world had continued to turn in my absence, and that I was a mere onlooker. As I continued to recuperate, I refocused on my surroundings and my army comrades. All had been placed in key or other sought-after positions, and I had been left behind. Life was proceeding as before, I ruefully observed, but I had lost my influence. The world gets along without you. They've almost forgotten you. Today, more worldly and experienced, I accept the phenomenon and understand it. Then, however, I would have none of it. I insisted on going to work. I would not wait at home for the next operation, waking up late and shuffling around in pajamas until evening. My self-confidence began to wane. I wanted to prove that I could contribute, and demanded with all my strength to be assigned to something. So, still in bandages, I returned to the Armored Corps School and gradually worked my way back. Subsequently, I trained the motorized column that took part in the 1968 Independence Day parade.

After a brief period of life outside the hospital, I went back to the plastic surgery ward for some patching up. The skin behind my left knee had shriveled so badly that I could not straighten my leg, and no treatment or physiotherapy helped. While on the operating table I found that Dr. Kaplan had stepped out and that his assistant would do the operation. That didn't bother me. This was a simple operation; all they had to do was slice the skin behind the knee.

After coming around, I found a massive blood-stain on my bed. They changed the sheets, but another stain of fresh blood appeared a few hours later. It was evening. The surgeon had left the area; no one could find her. Nor did the duty physician dare to open my cast and find the source of the bleeding. I knew I was losing alot of blood. Slowly I lost sensation in my fingers; even a rush transfusion was of no use. Everyone was bustling around me, at a loss for what to do. Only after midnight did the surgeon turn up. She cut the cast open, and there it was: blood flowing from my leg in the rhythm of my heartbeat. She quickly plugged the slashed artery and everyone calmed down.

The operation, implants and all, had been for naught. I lay on my stomach and looked back, stunned, unable to believe my eyes. Suddenly I couldn't take it any more. Helpless and agonized, I felt I was about to crack. Having been "on the outside", it was much harder to return to the sheets and the smell of drugs. The latest incident was such a letdown that I almost gave up.

Dr. Kaplan rushed to the hospital and visited me the next morning. He tried to hide his shock, but I had learned to read his eyes and his mind. I said nothing. I knew my operation had become the talk of the day. I was part of the hospital landscape, a veritable expert on plastic surgery. I was well aware of the magnitude of the blunder. Still, I found it convenient to feign ignorance, pretending to believe that such things were bound to happen. As for the assistant surgeon, she heard nothing from me but words of understanding. Deep down, however, my emotions were in tumult. I had expected to spend two weeks in the hospital after the latest operation; now I faced several long months within its confines.

In retrospect, my injury clearly had a very positive impact on my life. This terrible ordeal, experienced in youth, did more to toughen me than anything I had undergone. I love my scars. I fostered them step by step, with pain and affliction. I am not ashamed of them. I have learned to live with them.

Disability

Disability isn't all in the mind but it starts there. Virtually all disabled can return to ordinary life, more or less, if they meet the first requisite of recuperation: conquering self-pity. Cripples who bear their pain with good cheer and refrain from using their handicaps as means of presenting demands and extracting favors are happier. That's because society is cruel: people are preoccupied with daily concerns and spare little affection for welfare cases. Here the family comes into its element. It has to learn to accept the cripple as he/she is. Its the family's job to shower its son or daughter with attention, love, and warmth, of which there can never be too much.

Even so, the disabled must help themselves by making a mental effort to bolster their own strength. No one will do this for them. In everything else, however, IDF casualties are treated to the best possible care by the Ministry of Defense. Comparison of casualties' care with civilians care is sometimes embarrassing. Almost all casualties are fated to return to the hospital time and again after their original discharge for recurrent operations and various treatments. At every stage they have access to the best physicians, all committed to restoring fitness and healing shattered limbs. It is a genuine labor of the intellect to restore wounded man to the best approximation of the health that we generally take for granted. How good life is for us with our scars as they are — and not as they could be... .

Upon discharge from the hospital, the disabled are happy, but not totally so. They are often beset with fear about resuming ordinary life. I personally saw many who prolonged their stay in the hospital with various excuses for no reason other than fear of coping with the outside world.

In this context it suffices to consider, for example, those handicapped men and women who take up sports and register world-class accomplishments. Mentally, for sure, they are absolutely healthy. They neither bewail the past nor lose hope. They contemplate only the future and aspire relentlessly to progress.

9. RECUPERATION

When they discharged me from hospital it was clear that I faced at least a year's recuperation and would have to spend it doing things that were far from my heart's desire. Moshe Nativ, the Armored Corps' Adjutant, suggested that I study in the Army's high school to prepare myself for matriculation. I jumped at the idea.

"You still can't serve in the field," Nativ ruled when I returned to him a year later, having finally received a secondary school diploma. "The corps commander thinks you ought to command a gunnery section in the Armored Corps School."

No objection. I had just undergone another operation. Slowly I had begun to get used to the scars on my body, and they to me. We were becoming one.

The Armored Corps School, a massive enterprise, trained armor officers, reconnaissance men, tank commanders, armored infantry squad commanders, company commanders, and tank crewmen in all positions. The school commander, Col. Motke Tzippori, a born educator, was a fine principal and teacher.

I considered my new assignment an important and challenging duty. I was in charge of thousands of armored corpsmen in the process of becoming members of tank crews. From my school they headed south to Sinai or north to the Golan Heights, for further maneuvers and operational activity. The War of Attrition (1969-1970) was on, and many of the trainees were tense. Hardly a day went by without bitter news about our dead and injured. I had to invest all my strength and powers of persuasion to instill these 18-year-old kids with confidence and minimize the number of them who dropped out when they found out that their destination was the front.

I spent the first days as gunnery group commander putting soldiers on trial. I was the only officer of my grade authorized to conduct these junior-scale court-martials, and every complaint — from infractions of discipline up to loss of equipment — was passed on to me. One day yet another young soldier was brought to me for judgment. His name: Emmanuel Kahalani. My brother. During one of his lessons he had answered a question without the instructor's permission. I had previously tried a friend of Emmanuel's for a similar offense and exonerated him. This was unquestionably a trivial matter, worthy of punishment on platoon level and no more. Court-martialing a soldier for it was simply wrong and malicious. Be that as it may, Emmanuel Kahalani was brought to Avigdor Kahalani for judgment. I threw the book at him, fining him five pounds — about one third of a month's pay — and warned him never to speak in class without raising his hand.

Again we were at war with Egypt at this time — 1969-1970 — a desultory exchange of gunfire and raids known in Israel as the War of Attrition. I did not take part. My brother came home on furlough with a full quiver of war stories, and I, now a nine-to-five "jobnik", with a guilty conscience about it, imbibed every word. I was greatly worried about him. Intuition always told me that Emmanuel was liable to get hit. He never walked when he could run. Time and again I cautioned him; his commanders, too, tried to slow him down. Was it raw courage or rash haste? How do you draw the line? A happy soul with a marvelous sense of humor, Emmanuel nevertheless went about with sadness in his eyes, even when he was telling jokes or imitating the army comedy troupe that he loved so much.

I had always wanted to do some parachuting. Even after my injury that dream had not faded. I was about to take the field service test, and my medical profile was liable to be an obstacle. True, the IDF is customarily liberal in cases like these and leaves the decision to the officers themselves. But I needed further proof. My medical profile had been lowered to 31, making me eligible for discharge from the army. Now I changed the figure in my records to 97 — a sign of near-perfect health. Then I headed for paratroopers' training. As an officer with the rank of captain I was given a personal instructor; my friend Benda, a paratrooper himself, made sure of this. I cleared the first committee with no problems. But after a few days of bone-wrenching drills the school commander summoned me for a talk.

"Kahalani, you're not in shape to finish the course. Gorodish talked with me about you too, and he said I was crazy!"

I didn't budge. Two doctors volunteered to reexamine me. Their ruling was unequivocal: "No way."

I fumed. "You can't throw me out. My surgeon said I'm fit for anything!"

True enough. More than once Dr. Kaplan told me:

"Do as you think best. As much as you can. Ultimately you are your own best doctor."

So, as my own doctor, I made up my mind to go on, and talked them into approving it after lots of persuasion. While ordinary cadets made five jumps during the course, I made twelve happy, intoxicating descents from heaven to earth.

In the middle of the War of Attrition my friend Shalom Angel visited me in the armored corps school with some terrible news: Adam Weiler had been killed.

It was like a sledgehammer blow to the head. My senses went fuzzy. My friend Adam, my brother Adam, had fallen on the bank of the Suez Canal. Shalom and I carried Adam's coffin to Mount Herzl in Jerusalem and buried our comrade there. The armored corps had lost a commander and leader, who knew to storm his objective ahead of his men. I had lost a comrade-at-arms and a dear friend.

April 10, 1967
My dear brother Kahalani,
So what if I wrote that I don't care if you don't answer because you're busy? I want to hear from you. How's Dalia? How are you? How are Ilana and the whole family? You bastard, are we brothers or aren't we? So what if you're already "Buna" or "Golan" or someone? Just because you're a platoon commander No. 1 for all time, is it impossible to speak to you? I'll become a platoon commander with you in the battalion yet! Write to me, tell me how you are. I'm sure you're enjoying the position. I see you're succeeding. Look, I know you: you were born to command and lead men. That's because you're honest. When you get mad, you really get mad and screw the whole world. The fact

that you're a recon and so on, that's contrary to your nature. But tell me what it's like to work with officers and command so many soldiers on a regular basis? Do the officers work hard? How are the sergeants treated? Benny Inbar, Vanya, or Benny Yehuda and Yifrah?

I've just been on a tour of Norway. Hitchhiking. I left with IL 240 in my pocket and spent only IL 120 in three weeks. I ate bread, cheese and carrots! Once I got caught on the way to Norway and spent a night at -14 degrees centigrade, holed up in the snow. But I went skiing and spent a few days in the mountains with a rural family. I hadn't been so happy in a long time. When I came back, I also found that I'd passed all the important five-year tests.

I'm thinking about you working all those long weeks and hardly having time for a snooze, and I don't even know where you live.

Write to me, you maniac!

Adam

Young leaders

The progress of a war depends fatefully on those who carry it out — the fighting men and their commanders.

Among the latter, those on the company level are of supreme importance. These junior officers, in daily contact with the men, are by nature supposed to instill basic trust and confidence in leadership and lead the men into fire in such a way that each is willing to do as he is told, with complete faith.

Of course there are born leaders, Big Men on Campus, imbued with certain personal traits that give them the ability to lead groups and stand out among equals. Without such traits one would have to go to great lengths to achieve the same group motivation. It is a fact, however, that those placed in command positions by the IDF and by other armies are not put through a filter that admits only innate leaders. Even if not graced with classic leadership attributes, our commanders do not need to seek metaphysical nostrums. Rather, they lead and motivate with their insignia and experience. By virtue of the very hierarchical structure of the army, the place and status of everyone within its contours is clearly defined. Therefore the system is powered, more than anything else, by acceptance of higher authority. The insignia itself is nothing but a decoration on one's clothing, but it is given to those who have earned a level of command. That command carries with it power and responsibility which are the source of its strength and importance.

Platoon or company commanders, however, can be undermined by their youth and inexperience. The longer soldiers have been in uniform, the harder it is to force them to maintain discipline and carry out tasks. No younger than their platoon commanders, they are not daunted by the sight of officers bars. Thus the round-the-clock proximity of commanders and enlisted men elicits certain patterns of personal relations that certainly make the commander's work no easier. Squad and tank commanders find their work many times harder; they are often younger than their soldiers. In such cases, young commanders can impose their will only by wielding the powers vested in them. Those whose grade does not provide sufficiently broad power have to marshal all their talents — both the natural ones and those acquired during their military career — to get the job done. It is only natural that young commanders, charged with motivating soldiers every hour of every day, need — more than others — thorough instruction in the modalities of leadership and command.

Commanders on all levels choose a certain image that permits them to attain their goal more easily. Sheer pretense, however, is doomed to fail. Even commanders who do not come into direct contact with enlisted men cannot maintain a false front for long. All the more so junior commanders, whose true attributes are put to the test 24 hours a day. Being oneself is more convenient, too: how nice it is to wake up in the morning without having to remember what sort of image you projected yesterday!

But being yourself is no simple matter for the young leader. First of all, you have to be a pro in your own field. Professionalism bestows authority, and it is obtained only by hard work, thorough study, longevity, and experience. Subordinates appreciate professionals, acknowledge their superiority, and accept their command without hesitation.

Moreover, the soldier who naturally seeks a leader — especially at times of stress and anxiety — looks for an image that will sell him and motivate him to do anything. Thus young commanders have to compete successfully with their soldiers in just about anything: running, shooting, knowledge of the enemy, familiarity with the technical features of the weapons used. Many admiring eyes will follow the commander who is in better physical shape than his men and who can solve, matter-of-factly, problems on specific military themes. Even a commander not naturally endowed with the characteristics of a born leader can do much to overcome their absence by means of professional prowess.

Neither can the mutual influence between soldiers and commanders be disregarded. This interaction manifests itself mainly in the "test of courage" syndrome. Admittedly, how well one vanquishes fear is a personal matter, but all young commanders call out the IDF's famous "Follow me" order and display guts and cool in time of trial — if only to satisfy the soldiers whose eyes are always riveted on their backs and who expect them to behave in this fashion and no other. Perhaps the young commander feels no differently from his men, but by virtue of his position he must lead with confidence and self-assurance.

Nor is this enough. He must also lead conspicuously, making sure his men notice him without strain and ensuring that everyone hears and understands everything he says. His tone of voice over the radio in the middle of an emergency should be no different from the familiar tone used in drills. The content of what one says is less important in times of anxiety. It is the tone of voice that can convince men to storm an objective — or to refuse. Courageous commanders are those who induce their men to overcome their fear. Eyes riveted on him and ears attentive to his orders, enlisted men will be willing to jump at any moment. A prerequisite for this is to instill the feeling that the commander is level-headed, responsible, and above all a leader who accompanies the men as they charge.

Listen to the fighting men talk. When they keep saying "He said" as if this is reason enough to do something, you know "he" penetrated their minds and souls. These soldiers have the privilege of having a leader for a commander.

10. THE 77TH BATTALION — "OZ 77"

En route to the battalion

During my two years with the armored corps school I made a full recovery. Again I was fit for field duty in a command position in the battalion. Despite my attempt to speed up the process, however, I was not given what I wanted. Instead I became a rank-and-file cadet in the Command and Staff College.

Command and Staff is the army's highest institution. Here officers are trained for staff work and command positions. Its cadets — captains, majors, and lieutenant colonels — take the whole course along with general academic studies in one year. All this makes C&S an attractive facility, especially for the many officers who never graduated high school and are now given an opportunity to advance to university. It should be noted that despite the army's ambitions, studies at C&S are a prerequisite neither for the grade of lieutenant colonel nor for appointment as battalion commander. Circumstances often dictate other criteria.

The cadets are divided into study squads, twelve or so to a squad, under the command of an instructor with the grade of colonel who accompanies them for about three months. These instructors hold the key to the cadets' success. No matter how interesting and useful the subject matter is, the men must acquire an "oral law," i.e., the IDF's command and education heritage, handed down from one generation to the next.

Anyone in a scholastic environment, however exalted his rank may be, behaves like a pupil. The drive to achieve sometimes elicits behavior which is not always above board. Some cadets went to greater lengths to obtain the answers to previous years' tests than to cope with the current problems they were handed. Several men took a long-term perspective, making it their top priority to develop good relations with the instructor; others tinkered with their cars when they would have been better off studying. Toward the end of the course, I was amazed to witness tough officers who had gone through hair-raising ordeals on the battlefield, now trembling at the thought of report-card day...

As noted, however, final grades had no direct bearing on the placement of many officers after the course. When it came time for evaluation and placement, officers experience and background were given more consideration.

For the record, the methodology and modes of study invoked by the school's command and instructors were not my cup of tea. As time passed I increasingly felt that many cadets were being over-evaluated. The school eschewed tools that might have yielded an objective assessment of every cadet; too much emphasis was placed on impressions and emotions.

For my 28th birthday Dalia presented me with an original and special gift — our daughter, Vardit. This news was brought to me excitedly by the clerk of

Brig. Gen. Mussa Peled, commander of the school. She burst into my classroom to inform me that I had become the father of a "large family".... .

On the last day of the course I was summoned to Mussa Peled for my final grade and a short parting talk. Mussa stretched out in his chair, clutching a thick cigar that filled the room with a pungent stench. My file lay on his desk.

"Kahalani, you're a nice guy and your soldiers will love you. I think you're going to be a lieutenant colonel!"

"Thank you," I nodded. Mussa could only have meant that he considered lieutenant colonel the limit of my potential as an officer. Upset, I wanted to leave the room.

Mussa puffed on his cigar and resumed: "Where are you going from here?"

"Home."

"No. I mean, what's your next assignment?"

"Deputy commander of Battalion 77 in the 7th Brigade," I answered tersely and stepped out, trying to conceal the tempest that raged inside. Mussa had never made my acquaintance, I knew, and I was never the type to flaunt my knowledge for acclaim. If so, how could Peled assess my ability? Why did he have to speak his mind as he did, even if he was being sincere? What good did it do? Hadn't the man ever heard of tact?

I couldn't calm down. Sizzling with resentment I repeated his terse remark that had caused me so much pain. For appearances' sake I held it in and smiled at my classmates as they waited their turn on the grass.

My "assignment" at C&S was command of a tank battalion in a reserve brigade. During my studies I established the battalion and took it on extended maneuvers. Therefore I considered my real-life assignment as deputy commander of Battalion 77 in the 7th Brigade as something of a letdown, a step backward. True, Bren, commander of the armored corps, had promised that I would soon take full command of the battalion. That was encouraging. My dream, however, was to command the 82nd Battalion, the IDF's first tank battalion. It was with this formation, now under Mitzna, my comrade from the 79th, that I had done my basic training and later served as platoon commander. It was famous for its stories of valor and an impressive battle history, or "battle heritage" as we called it. That was just what I wanted: an opportunity to educate my men in view of a glorious battle heritage transmitted from one generation to the next. The 77th, by contrast, was only three years old and had not yet taken part in battles or incidents of any kind.

The 7th Brigade headquarters and two of its battalions were situated near Beersheba. The 77th Battalion was stationed in Sinai, housed entirely in tents with the exception of the commander's bureau, clinic, and mess hall. These central institutions were deemed worthy of a higher standard of accommodations: portable structures.

The battalion commander, Lt. Col. David Yisraeli, greeted me warmly and hurried to set up a bed for me alongside him in his sleeping quarters in the heart of Sinai. From the very first I noticed how sensitive he was to my performance in the battalion, so I went about carefully until I knew which matters were the battalion commander's exclusive province.

It took Yisraeli a few months to realize that I was not trying to lay claim to his turf. Trying not to forgo my own image and authority, I sought to assure him that he was ruler of the roost. Finally we became friends and made a productive working team of ourselves. Once this happened, it was enough for him to say "take over" whenever he went home on furlough and turned the battalion over to me. When we had begun working together, his briefings were as long as the furloughs themselves... .

Yisraeli ran the battalion in a highly centralized, perhaps over-centralized, manner. That was his nature. He wouldn't even let anyone help his children with their homework, rather "briefing" them by phone. His allegiance to his commanders and comrades knew no limit. He was an intellectual, who wrote poetry in order to articulate his sensitivities.

Second-in-command

Second-in-command — from deputy company commander to Deputy Chief of General Staff — is one of the least sought-after positions in the IDF. It has no precise definition. Traditionally the deputy replaces the commander in his absence, but because commanders are hardly ever absent under ordinary circumstances, the two have to draw lines of demarcation around different activities and stay out of each other's hair.

By the nature of things, the deputy tends to matters that the commander hasn't the time or the desire to handle. Most commanders tend to neglect organizational and administrative duties, and thus the deputy, toiling to tie up loose the ends his superior has left him, finds himself waist-deep in the problems of drivers, quartermaster clerks, and mess cooks. Those not endowed with initiative and ability to ride above the storm quickly find themselves perceived as having limited talent. Such officers do not acquire professional authority and cannot fill the commander's shoes when this is necessary.

Frustration and hardship are therefore part and parcel of a second-in-command's life. However exhausting and time-consuming his work may be, his superior always takes some — sometimes too much — credit for any achievements. On the whole, the deputy strives to display loyalty toward his commander, at the expense of his own uniqueness and personality. Therefore the deputy has to weigh every step from the very first, ever in quest of the golden mean along which he may operate.

The deputy has to engage in all matters entrusted to the commander, even though the decision-making authority remains with the superior. He must use this all-embracing involvement in the formation's affairs to make the men understand that he is in no way professionally inferior to his commander, and that his organizational and administrative responsibilities merely reflect the constraints of necessity and time.

The substance of relations between commander and deputy depends on both individuals. A deputy who takes no decision without consulting with the "boss" turns very quickly into a mere liaison whose input is unneeded. At the same time, the deputy must keep his superior abreast of his actions and decisions, including his motives, not only to abide by the prerogatives of command but also to foster harmony between them. In wartime the second-in-command should be in the field along with the "boss," amidst the front line forces. Sometimes he commands some of them and coordinates the units with his commander; on other occasions he merely stays on alert in case he needs to take over. In either instance he must be Johnny-on-the-spot, ready to intervene in the course of the battle. Neither does the deputy's presence on the front exempt him from handling matters that come within his competence — evacuating the wounded, repairing damaged equipment, and supplying fuel, ammo, and food.

To prevent redundancy and foster greater cooperation, commander and deputy should divide their duties. This can be arranged in an unofficial talk, in an atmosphere of fraternity and good cheer. A commander must not be afraid to devolve powers to his deputy; otherwise he would turn his second-in-command into a useless appendage and frustrate his career progress. Even the most centralized commanders should give their deputies the free rein, full backing, and responsibility with which they can prove themselves as fully able to take over.

At long last, at the beginning of 1973, the battalion was mine. David Yisraeli was appointed deputy commander of Barak Brigade on the Golan Heights, and the 77th — "Oz 77," so-called for its valor — was handed to his second-in-command. I gathered my equipment from my office, crossed the clerk's room, and set up shop in the command office across the way.

Having long felt "at home" in battalion command headquarters, I was able to forego the period of study and adjustment that so many officers need on assuming a new post. At once I embarked on the routine work of a battalion commander. The weight of this responsibility, however, struck me suddenly. I was stunned at how a commander feels the full brunt of his duties within a few minutes after taking over a formation.

Eitan Kaouli, one of my company commanders, was now promoted to the position of deputy. We quickly learned to work together efficiently, almost fraternally. It was Eitan's thankless task to command former equals, literally yesterday's roommates. I was apprehensive about his leadership ability. On more than one occasion I advised him to try to stay on good terms with the company commanders, even though his duties sometimes required head-on collisions with them.

By weird coincidence, Battalion 77 was set up near Egyptian Milestone 77, i.e., 77 kilometers from the Suez Canal. The battalion had more open space at its disposal than any other battalion, so much so that four companies could train new tank crews at once. The expanses of Sinai, well-suited to open field maneuvers, were the most convenient training grounds I had known.

As if to make my work more difficult, some higher authority had decided to house my battalion in tents. Thus many soldiers, faced with the choice between my battalion in Sinai and the 82nd in Beersheba, preferred the latter. Comparison between the two battalions was inevitable, and we frequently found ourselves isolated, neglected, and forgotten. Brigade Commander Yanush took action to sweeten the bitter pill. When he felt that things had come to a boil, he summoned the brigade staff from home and gave them a lesson in working procedures, starring Battalion 77... .

Despite the distance, we were frequented with many visitors. Some of them dropped in so they could claim they had been there — to sign the visitors' book, as it were. We detested them.

Yanush, by contrast, was a regular visitor. He always kept me off guard; one could never predict his reactions or even guess how he would behave. As time passed, the other battalion commanders in the brigade were replaced. Yossi Eldar was appointed commander of the armored infantry battalion, and Haim Barak commander of the 82nd. Thus I became the "old man" of the group, maintaining correct and amiable relations with my commander all the way.

Being stationed far from civilization had its advantages, too. Everybody was preoccupied with drills and preparations for war; this, after all, was what we were there for. Far from the temptations of the big city, I circulated at leisure among the companies as they trained, set standards and made sure they were upheld, modified the ways in which we used our training grounds, computed new firing angles, and set up new targets. In camp I ran paths and access routes wherever I pleased. My style of command was altogether different from that of my predecessor, David Yisraeli. Rather than announcing the change, I just went about things my own way. I was very much the hands-on commander. I had plenty of time and lots of desert to forgive all my sins.

Battalion commander

An IDF battalion is an autonomous formation that does everything required to meet its personnel's every need and see to their lives in routine matters and during maneuvers. The battalion is divided into several companies, each with its own commander, all subordinate to the battalion commander.

The battalion commander — usually a man in his late 20s — is responsible for everything that goes on in the battalion. Because the formation comprises several hundred soldiers aged between the teens and early 50s, assigned to groups of different quality and dealing with diverse tasks, the battalion commander must be an expert on everything. When he visits the mess hall he should be able to address himself to its cleanliness and order as well as the quality of the food. In the armory he should take notice of how the ammo is organized and assess how well standing orders in this regard are being upheld. Throughout he should be able to verify routine compliance with procedures.

In his battalion the commander is king. When he has an itch, everyone else scratches. He determines the training program and tells the company commanders what to emphasize. He serves as liaison between his men and other army authorities, attends the reading of orders for the battalion, and represents the battalion in dealings with brigade headquarters and higher echelons.

In his residential quarters or his office, the battalion commander's nostrils sense the exhaust of the cars, tanks, and personnel carriers in the field. His intuition is deemed capable of fathoming his men's states of mind, to which he should be alert and attentive just like everything else in the battalion. He can never present his commander's instructions verbatim, using them as a shield. Only if adapted to the men and their esprit will they attain the best results, and only a battalion commander who knows his men can present them this way.

The same goes for his own orders. Rarely does a battalion commander face the ranks. Thus his instructions are liable to change direction and spirit as they filter through the company commanders and others. When a company commander is not at peace with his superior's orders, cannot explain their importance and rationale, or perhaps simply does not understand them, how convenient it is for him to rule, "'cause the commander said so!" Yes, the order will be carried out, but surely not in the manner desired. In extreme instances it might even produce results opposite of those intended.

Therefore the battalion commander has got to maintain direct contact with his men as best he can. He should meet with them, talk with them, explain, persuade. He should never state his case, about-face and walk out, as if he feared confrontation or had not planned his schedule properly. He should always let his listeners ask questions and express attitudes, and should permit them to engage him in personal conversation, if only brief exchanges in random meetings.

The battalion commander has got to be a top-grade professional. Never should an ordinance officer be allowed to feel that his commander is somehow unfamiliar with the technical problems pertaining to his equipment. Never should a battalion commander display impatience when the headquarters company commander presents him with administrative problems. He should be able to assure even the lowly artilleryman that he is indeed familiar with this domain, and can draw up an artillery fire plan adeptly. Heaven help the battalion commander whose men doubt his professional competence. Soldiers miss nothing. A commander whose professional competence is not up to snuff can fool them only up to a point. Then the truth comes out. The men will respond not with mutiny but with silence, because they'll feel there's no one to speak to, and will not want to humiliate their commander publicly.

There was a time when, because of the way wars were fought and the broad parameters of the battalion framework, the battalion commander hardly ever showed his face on the training grounds or the battlefield. In Israel's War of Independence, as battles raged for the Jerusalem areas of San Simeon, Radar Hill, and Nebi Samwil, the battalion commanders were several kilometers away. Today no battalion commander can afford to be anywhere but on the front line, leading his men. As the first to storm the enemy target, the commander should demonstrate valor and serve as an example and a model for emulation. His position among them will do much to determine the success or failure of an operation. Being in the right place is more useful than delivering a thousand inspiring speeches. Onstage, around the clock, the commander should lead his men with neither reservation or challenge. They want to see him close by, and as they mount the onslaught they have to know they are acting in his name and with his awareness.

Here the battalion commander faces a dilemma. In wartime, he can stay in touch with his troops only by radio. This limits the number of listeners to his company commanders and a few staff officers. The enlisted men do not hear him as they should; the direct impact on those who fight the war and press the trigger, the kind of impact that knows no parallel, is lost. It is precisely these men, too, who are most in need of their commander's authoritative, supportive influence. These are the men who should follow his instructions in letter and in spirit. Therefore the battalion commander has to go out of his way, even by artifice, to make sure the last buck private in his formation sees and hears him. The conventional way of doing this — at least in the IDF armored corps — is to break into the company-level radio network and talk with the men. Only thus can even the jeep drivers, for example, receive unmediated orders from the battalion commander himself.

In mid-campaign the fighting man keeps the image of his commander in mind. Essentially, he is fighting for his commander, and he should be sure that his commander is aware of his efforts to do as told. When you are charging into hellfire, nothing matters more than the absolute certainty that the man who gave you the orders knows, at that very moment, what you're doing and where you're doing it. There is nothing like uninterrupted and intimate communication between the fighting man and his commander to ensure that the commander's decisions are the right ones.

All this notwithstanding, there is no denying that even a battalion commander, as a man and a soldier in every sense, is afflicted by all the feelings that beset all fighting men under fire. Principal among them is fear.

When fear grips you in the middle of battle, it slackens a bit if you know that everyone around you feels the same way. Fear diminishes when it is not yours alone. It further diminishes when you are willing to be wounded for something, for someone.

Coping with fear is easier for a commander. Because he is an "actor" on stage, his actions followed by many pairs of eyes, he must repress his emotions and behave as his audience expects. Nor is there any doubt about what those expectations are: a constant display of dynamism and initiative, judgment, knowledge, and sagacity before issuing orders, and, above all, a show of leadership, taking the men to their objective with confidence and courage.

Battalion command undoubtedly puts an officer to his true test. I had been given a great privilege when I was assigned to serve in the 82nd under a commander who, I knew, had passed all the tests: the late Kalman Magen. For him I would storm any enemy objective.

11. THE YOM KIPPUR WAR

The 7th Brigade, including Battalion 77, had been designated for the Egyptian front. It was to take part in the defense and subsequent crossing of the Suez Canal.

Late in the summer of 1973, Yanush, the brigade commander, had a premonition that we might be called on to bolster the forces arrayed on the Golan Heights, facing Syria. Therefore, we went to the Heights for reconnaissance, familiarizing ourselves with the area and studying operational plans for war with the most resolute of our enemies. Defending the Heights at the time was Barak Brigade, equipped with only two tank battalions, under the command of Col. Yitzhak Ben Shoham and his deputy David Yisraeli. Barak shared the front, from Mount Hermon in the north to the Yarmuk River in the south, with another line brigade. The positions along the border were manned by platoons and companies belonging to two infantry battalions, one under Golani Brigade (infantry) and the other under Nahal Paratroops. A reserve division was assigned to the Golan Heights. Its commander was Rafael Eitan — "Raful" — a brigadier general at the time, on study leave in anticipation of leaving the service. This division, headquartered in the Galilee panhandle, would take part in the defense, once mobilized.

Barak had one tank battalion, under Yair Nafshi.

Its platoons and companies were scattered in the various front positions and would blunt enemy offensive moves. A second battalion, under Oded Erez, held the rear and was presently engaging in maneuvers. Dispersed behind these formations were several batteries of artillery, ready to fire, and a small engineering force at the service of all forces on the Heights. All of these, for reasons of economy, were subordinate to and coordinated by a single regional command, Northern Command, situated in Nazareth. The line brigade would activate the infantry in its positions and the tanks between them; only after coordination and approval by Northern Command would Barak be allowed to intervene in the fighting.

Rosh Hashana 5734

Rosh Hashana 5734 (1973), the Jewish New Year, fell on a Thursday and Friday. With a two-day holiday, the eve of the holiday, and the Sabbath immediately afterward, Israelis geared up for a four-day weekend. Many headed for the country, and crowds thronged the beaches from Sharm el-Sheikh at the southern tip of Sinai to Lake Kinneret at the foot of the Golan Heights. I went home on furlough, pleased at the thought of a vacation. Finally I could finish renovating the house I had bought about two years earlier. In particular I wanted to lay the roof shingles before the onset of winter rains.

No sooner had I climbed up to the roof when a phone call from brigade commander Yanush brought me down. I was to report to the Golan Heights at once and take part in its defense. My wife Dalia, surprised and disappointed, took the news with a stony, sad silence that expressed more than any vocal complaint or irritation. Again she would spend a festival without me.

Proud of my new mission, I wasted no time. The men who stayed with the battalion for the festival were airlifted to the north; the tanks remained in Sinai, locked up in the battalion area. I summoned the platoon commanders and my deputy, Eitan, by telephone and headed north. I took advantage of the trip for a much-needed nap. The previous evening my brother Emmanuel had wed his girlfriend Ruthie, and the festivities had gone on until dawn.

Reaching the Golan Heights, I reported to Ben Shoham, commander of Barak Brigade. We requisitioned tanks from the brigade's emergency depots. Tersely Ben Shoham summarized the task facing Battalion 77:

"You're gonna be a counter-attack force on all sectors of the front."

The battalion had 22 tanks at that stage. That very night, the first night of Rosh Hashana, we finished equipping and arming them. As the Jews of Israel recited festival blessings and dipped apples in honey, the battalion's soldiers loaded ordinance into the bellies of their tanks and then sat down for their festival feast: sandwiches brought over by the company sergeant-major... .

Even though we were ready to move by dawn, Northern Command ordered us to stay put in our shelters. We used the time to scout the Syrian border. The area looked quiet and pastoral. None of the many sightseers on the Golan Heights felt the tension in the air.

I had to reconnoiter extensively to get to know the units along the line and make sure we spoke the same language. Nor did I know the Golan Heights well enough. I suspected that we would not have time to learn every path, every dirt road, every position, every incline as an army must if it will conduct effective defensive warfare; one has to know how to use every fold in the terrain as a firing position against the enemy. I had never encountered a Syrian fighter, but I, like my men, had been schooled in the conventional wisdom: the Syrians were tough men and tough fighters, firmly resolved to liberate the Golan Heights.

We did not waste a moment. We scouted the area repeatedly and repaired problems we found in the tanks, building confidence for what might await us. Our 105mm Centurions were considered good machines; their firing systems were thought to be efficient and their armor better able to withstand enemy shells than that of the Patton.

Until Friday, October 5, we were the only representatives of the 7th Brigade on the Heights. Now brigade command joined us, and with it another three battalions: the 75th armored infantry under Yoss Eldar; the 82nd, a tank battalion, under Haim Barak; and the 71st, another tank brigade, under Menahem Meshullam Rattas.

On two matters I brooked no compromise: the condition of my tank and thorough familiarity with my crewmen. The tank was gone over from top to bottom. We checked the firing system, the automatic mechanisms, the auxiliary equipment. I had to be sure I was going to war without risk of being killed by a loose screw or an uncalibrated sight. We found the engine and transmission in good working order, capable of coping well with the tank's bulk. Technically at least, we had a good tank.

I knew none of the crewmen. Swiftly I presented

them with my demands and sought to figure each of them out. My remarks gave them the feeling of being under pressure. To ease the tension, I joked around a bit, as was my habit. The young men, excited at their encounter with the new "boss," found it hard to absorb my message in the right spirit.

"No one gave me permission to die at my age," I told them. "So you gotta take care of me and wipe out anyone who goes for my neck!"

An embarrassed half-smile flitted across the men's faces.

Yuval Ben-Ner, the driver, seemed puzzled and confused at having stumbled into such a thicket. Imagine, being a big-shot's driver... . David Kilyon of Kibbutz Beit Hashita, the gunner, took a different attitude, displaying self-satisfaction with his role as the battalion commander's gunner. Kilyon radiated a self-confidence that befitted his physical dimensions. The loader-radioman, Gideon Shemesh of Kibbutz Re'im, blonde as a Scandinavian, tried to treat the occasion as just one of those things. Only Lt. Gidi Peled, the operations officer, greeted me with a real smile. I had appointed Gidi as operations officer after having appreciated his performance as platoon commander in the battalion. I liked the man and worked well with him.

All the assessments before Yom Kippur indicated that something was afoot on the Golan Heights, but two possibilities — a war of attrition or a Syrian attempt to wrest part of the Heights from our control — were believed more likely than outright war. It was reasonable to foresee a Syrian attempt to capture Tel Faras, the town of Kuneitra and the hills around it, or Mount Hermon.

The Golan Heights had few artificial obstacles. Most salients had no anti-tank ditches, and only some areas were protected with minefields. Several tank ramps had been built near whatever anti-tank ditches we had, their locations determined by how well the forces dispersed on the front could resist an enemy breakthrough in their respective areas. These positions, less than two dozen in number, were smack against the border fence. Each was manned with 12-16 infantrymen. The positions were supposed to integrate into the defense, even though none was equipped with firing stations that would protect the men's heads. One had to climb into trenches on the roof of the bomber. The border fence was the ordinary chain-link type. A road ran along it on our side, with a strip of sand between it and the fence to reveal any attempt at infiltration. All the forces were stationed very close to the border. The purpose was to meet force with force, bullets with bullets, and any enemy incursion with the best response possible.

Just before Yom Kippur the Soviet families residing in Damascus and Cairo were evacuated, a clear indication of Syrian and Egyptian intentions. The General Staff was in turmoil: were we really on the threshold of war? If so, what should we do? We fighting men never imagined that our superiors might be misreading the situation, and we were oblivious to their vacillation. Never, until that Yom Kippur, had I harbored any doubts about the decisions of my superiors. I obeyed them with confidence, pledging everything I had to fulfilling my own mission: making my formation the best in the world, the best prepared for the ordeal of war. In his biography of Maj. Gen. Daniel Elazar, *Dado*, Hanoch Bar Tov describes the arguments that raged among members of the General Staff about how to size up the prewar situation. Most of them believed war was not imminent. The dispute reached its peak on the morning of Yom Kippur, when Dado and Defense Minister Moshe Dayan went at loggerheads. Dado demanded large-scale mobilization of the reserves; Dayan wanted to call up only several tens of thousand. The dispute was bumped upstairs to Prime Minister Golda Meir. She would decide.

By this time the Egyptians and the Syrians were ready for zero hour. The Egyptian chief of staff at the time, Gen. Shazli, described the months of circumspect, painstaking preparations in his book, *Crossing the Canal*. They were planned so as to mislead us totally and conceal their true intention.

On Israel's side, the major objective was to maintain calm. This was our undoing. Elections were only a few weeks away, and the government was afraid to do anything that would upset the electorate or undermine its support. Calling up the reserves was one such action. Had this been done, the first days of the war would have been totally different.

The IDF regular forces can defend the country's borders for a limited time only. To discharge anything more demanding than this, it must integrate the country's civilians — the reserves — into its ranks. Once the reserves are called up, it takes time for them to report to the front with gear and weapons, ready for battle. That time lapse is crucial, and our enemies know it well. Their feints were meant above all to trick us into postponing the mobilization, and we should assume that this will be a major goal of theirs in the future, too. Opening the war against our regular forces alone gives them a tremendous advantage that could carry them to victory.

But we, too, learned our lessons. The Yom Kippur War produced a major change in our thinking on the subject of preparing the reserve formations for war. If put to the test again, we shall summon the reserves well in advance, using all the methods we've got — some public, some secret — and requiring only the shortest period of time to turn them into fighters.

Yom Kippur, October 6, 1973

In a bunker in Nafah, where the line brigade had its headquarters, the Command-level orders were read out. At approximately 1000 hours OC Northern Command, Maj. Gen. Yitzhak Hofi, briefed his subordinate commanders. After the briefing I stepped out of the office and waited for 7th Brigade commander Yanush. I was still under Barak command and wanted to return "home" to the 7th Brigade. I asked Yanush to approve this move, which entailed switching my tank's radio frequency; Yanush, consulting with Ben Shoham, gave the OK. Then he brought me up to date: Gen. Hofi had announced that war would almost certainly begin at 1800 hours that very day.

So now I knew for sure. Nothing could postpone or cancel it.

By Yanush's order we were ready by noon. The tank crews were on alert under the netting that covered the vehicles. I locked up the camp synagogue and ordered the worshippers to eat something and return to their tanks. The Yom Kippur fast was liable to impair my fighters' performance. Mine, too.

Five minutes before noon, jeep tires screeching, I hurtled into Camp Nafah for a final briefing with brigade command. Suddenly several bombs fell within the camp confines. Aircraft passing overhead at low altitude issued roars of their own.

I threw myself to the ground, face down, hands protecting my head. Surely they were Israeli aircraft whose pilots had gone off course. As the camp burst into commotion, I searched the sky. They were Syrian MiGs. I felt humiliated. We had been caught with our pants down. Within seconds I was back in my jeep, racing to my battalion a few kilometers away.

"Shoter stations, this is *shoter*," I called into the mike, using the network's code name — "cop." "Start the engines. Get ready to move. Over and out."

I pressed the gas pedal to the floorboard with all my strength, as if this would produce greater speed. As I rushed forward I looked up, scanning the skies for aircraft.

The nets had been taken off the tanks. Thundering engines were heard everywhere. With a screech of brakes I stopped beside my tank and hopped into the command cupola. The crew was ready and waiting. That was a relief. In the turret I noticed some empty shell casings near the cupola machine gun. Someone had fired at the enemy aircraft. I didn't need to guess who. Kilyon, the gunner, nodded as if to confirm his "guilt."

I was number two on the brigade level radio network and number ten within the battalion. Northern Command ordered the 82nd Battalion to move into the southern sector, where Ben Shoham had taken charge; the 82nd stationed itself alongside Barak Brigade's two battalions, under Oded Erez and Haim Barak respectively. The 7th Brigade assumed responsibility for the northern sector. Yanush sent Yoss Eldar's armored infantry battalion, bolstered by tanks reassigned to him from my battalion, into the area between the Bustar hills and the Little Hermon — the easternmost sector of the central Golan, that closest to the enemy. Rattas' battalion was to defend the area north of the Little Hermon along with the vicinity of Bukata, a Druse village between the Little Hermon and the town of Kuneitra. My battalion was sent, at some delay, toward Kuneitra and the Bustar hills overlooking the town from the north. Groups of tanks from Yair Nafshi's battalion were strewn along the line in stationary positions. Yair himself joined one of the formations right on the border, east of Bustar. This deployment of tank battalions among the brigade commanders gave the 7th Brigade an advantage.

"Where's the war?" I asked myself, looking east. Artillery shells were landing all around, especially near the crossroads. Still, I had not seen the enemy with my own eyes. We moved several hundred meters east and deployed the battalion in the field. The tank companies — Company F ("Vespa") under Lt. Yair Sawet, Company G ("Big Boy") under Capt. Menahem Albert, Company H ("Hummous") under Lt. Ami Plant, and Company I ("Tiger") under Capt. Meir Zamir — took up position as if it were a drill. Alongside them was a single platoon-strength formation under Amnon Lavi, a company commander in the battalion. My deputy Eitan sat in his tank, not far from mine. The operations officer, Gidi, brought the map down from the turret and spread it in front of me.

Then, in a tone permitting no argument, Yanush ordered me to transfer one of my tank companies to Yoss. I sent Ami. A few minutes later I had to part with Zamir, too, in the same fashion; he was sent to defend the Tal Hazka salient, a few kilometers south of Kuneitra, under brigade command.

In close formation we advanced through cultivated fields to the area assigned us, the town of Kuneitra and its northern outskirts. Taking up position on the Bustar hills, I sighted indications of enemy forces for the first time: clouds of dust churned up by the Syrian tanks, still far away in Syrian territory.

Artillery shells began landing on our positions. Impressed with the enemy's accuracy, we quickly sought safer ground. Syrian aircraft circled overhead in quest of prey. Occasionally they swooped and emptied their bomb bays. The explosions reverberated into the distance and pillars of black smoke rose to the heavens. I did not need binoculars to make out features of the Syrian landscape; I had learned the area and knew it well. If only I were as well informed about the deployment of our own forces! I had to know for sure who was on my right, on my left, up ahead, and in the positions.

I sent Menahem Albert into Kuneitra to prevent a Syrian incursion into the town. Then I climbed the Bustar hills with Yair and Amnon. My artillery liaison officer, Avraham Snir, requested permission to shoot into Syrian territory. I okayed this, although I did not know exactly what he intended to shoot at.

A shell landed near me, its shrapnel scarring the tank. I ducked into the turret. I have always felt helpless under artillery fire. Not only can't I prevent it; I can't even strike back at the enemy gunners responsible for it.

Late that afternoon we began to notice enemy tank columns approaching the perimeter fence. As night fell, our tanks' disadvantages manifested themselves.

We could not hit enemy tanks in the dark. The Syrian formations, by contrast, were equipped with an infrared system with which they could illuminate our area, identify us, take aim, and fire with deadly effect. All we had were our headlights, which we were afraid to turn on. We fired illumination shells that lit up the area briefly, but these ran out quickly. The men sized up the situation as being intrinsically unfair. Naturally they turned to me, expecting a logical, satisfactory solution. I had nothing to say. The most effective tool we had was our tank commanders' infrared binoculars, with which they could make out the enemy's infrared lights. Thus we knew approximately where the Syrian vehicles were headed and could fire in that direction.

We suffered heavy losses that night. The combat was harsh, complicated, and frustrating. The Syrians stopped to regroup only after several of their tanks had crossed our path. Under cover of darkness they crossed the border fence and the minefields. We had dug an anti-tank trench on our side of the minefield, but they filled it with dirt and reached the very midst of our forces. At last we could see and hit them. Every time we did so, we used the light of the flames to zero in on their comrades. On Saturday night, I moved from Bustar Hills to Yoss' territory, where I discovered that Yoss had been wounded and evacuated to a hospital. Ami Plant returned to Battalion 77 along with his company, and I attached this formation to mine for the purpose of defending the area south of the Little Hermon. Menahem Albert, commander of Company G, was seriously wounded later that night; his second-in-command went down, too. I sent my own deputy, Eitan, to command the forces in Kuneitra.

I knew that if only we could hold on until morning we would beat them. We silenced our engines and listened to the Syrians' movements, no one sleeping all that night. The Syrian tanks were massing on our side of the anti-tank trench, evidently waiting for dawn to resume the offensive. Tensely we waited for the morning's first light.

Sunday, October 7, 1973

With the first glow of daybreak I spotted them, 80 or 90 tanks clustered about a kilometer and a half to the east. They began to move toward our sector, dust billowing in their wake. At first we found it hard to take aim; the sun had not yet come up. The moment it did, however, we turned many of the enemy vehicles into flaming torches. The enemy was astonishingly resolute and courageous. Even when their comrades were hit, they went on in normal fashion.

We worked more effectively by daylight. We identified all the paths in the field and put them to the best possible use. We had one advantage over the Syrians: we were in positions, whereas they were in motion. But they outnumbered us by at least eight to one. We fired at them as if infuriated by their determination and audacity. We delivered accurate hits and took plenty of our own. Several of my tank commanders and a number of officers were wounded. Once a tank commander goes down, his vehicle is taken out of action and evacuated. Thus our numbers dwindled with each passing moment, as did our ammunition.

My tank and its crew performed superbly. We fired like madmen. Throughout, I tried to strike a balance between commanding my tank properly and running the entire battalion. At first it seemed complicated, but eventually I learned where and when to attend to my own vital needs and when to focus on the tanks under my command. The Syrian observation officers were obviously training their sights on us with great precision, using the best observation point imaginable: 9,000-foot Mount Hermon, 30 km. to the north, which we had called "the eyes of Israel" when we used it to look into Syria. Now it was in enemy hands.

By now the Syrian tanks had pulled up alongside our cannon. We were in the very heart of hell. Yair Sawet, commander of Company F, was killed, as were additional commanders in the battalion: Avinoam Shemesh, Amir Bashari, Yisrael Barzilai, Amichai Doron, Boaz Friedman, and Eli Edri. One of the crewmen, Herzl Hai, was also killed. Other commanders were wounded; a tank was set aside to evacuate them. The evacuation teams worked without letup and with supreme valor. I had placed two personnel carriers at their disposal and ordered the technical squads to help them evacuate the wounded. All this imbued the men with confidence that no casualty would be abandoned in the field.

The medical team under Dr. Eshel split into two squads. One, with the doctor and his assistants, received the wounded a few kilometers behind us and administered first aid. The second squad rushed to the disabled tanks and, under fire, evacuated their men. Technical squad personnel who were not engaged in evacuating casualties waited in the rear for the disabled tanks to arrive. Then they extricated the casualties and made every effort to restore the tanks to operational condition with the greatest possible speed. Every tank was crucial. Without those that had been repaired and returned to the positions, we could not have stopped the Syrian onslaught. My deputy, Eitan, spurred and prodded our battalion ordinance officer, Ze'ev, and his men, to return every repaired tank to the front.

In mid-combat I realized that I had not done enough to train the ordinance and medical personnel for the additional functions that the demands of war would impose on them. To be ready to save human life in the middle of a battle, these units, the medical teams in particular, have to undergo extremely difficult and complex drills. Now, without the benefit of practice, they discharged these tasks with supreme devotion. I was proud of them and could not help letting it show.

Syrian MiGs were assisting the ground offensive. I will never forget how they thundered as they flew by, their pilots diving low and turning sideways to get a good look at us. With a slight effort I can recall the color of their eyes.

A round fired from the air struck my tank's gun. The enemy did not score many hits, but we could not repress the sensation of helplessness. Why wasn't our air force protecting us? Why had it abandoned us to the Syrian pilots? Obviously we returned fire, but to no avail. Having selected their prey, the enemy aircraft returned at attack angle, spattering machine-gun fire and dropping bombs directly into our positions. As veterans of the Six Day War and the War of Attrition, we remembered the Israel Air Force in its full potency. We had all seen the film *Three Hours in June*, which displayed the IAF's impressive achievements in June, 1967, with emphasis on the clear skies under which the land forces operated at all times.

Not in our wildest dreams had we imagined Syrian aircraft crossing the border.

I could not communicate with the air force. I did not know how to contact air command and direct our planes to the battlefield. I could only shout at the sky, radio brigade headquarters, and plead for air cover. With anti-aircraft weapons I knew we could down many of the Syrian craft. They were flying so low that no anti-aircraft weapon could miss. But I shouted in vain.

Tanks are helpless against enemy aircraft. Their might comes to the fore in ground combat, armor against armor. Once the enemy's air force goes into action, it becomes our air force's duty to provide an aerial umbrella. Otherwise the fighters begin to approach their breaking point, jeopardizing the entire campaign. Apart from its potency, the air force does much to raise morale and sustain the fighting men's psychological strength.

By dawn on Sunday the Syrians had registered impressive accomplishments on the southern Golan. Barak Brigade under Ben Shoham was mauled. Its men and tanks decimated, it was forced to retreat. The Syrians had captured half of the Golan Heights; by noon they advanced as far as Camp Nafah. Division commander Raful, who had used the camp as his headquarters, had to move to the rear.

During the retreat the brigade's three senior commanders fell in action: Ben Shoham, the brigade commander; operations officer Benny Katzin; and Ben Shoham's second-in-command, David Yisraeli. The brigade was leaderless. Oded Erez's battalion fell apart and retreated to the central Golan. The 82nd Battalion under Haim Barak took heavy losses. His deputy, Danny Pessah, fell in action, and Barak himself was wounded and taken to the hospital. There was no choice but to disperse the companies among other formations.

Dan Lenner took command of the southern sector and kept his reserve division fighting throughout Sunday. That night Raful took responsibility for the northern sector. Golani Brigade (a conscript infantry brigade, normally stationed in the North), reaching the area at reduced strength, was redirected northward and integrated into Raful's division. Only on Sunday did a command structure worthy of the name take shape on the Golan Heights. Until then, Northern Command headquarters was supposed to pull the strings. It couldn't, of course.

Mussa Peled's division, sent north by Central Command, reached the area on Monday. It staged a two-pronged counterattack, one force starting from the vicinity of Ein Gev and Moshav Bnei Yehuda and the other moving on the Gamla axis, farther up the Heights. Four bloodsoaked days later, the two reserve divisions succeeded in driving the Syrians off the southern Golan.

On the northern sector, the enemy had taken Mount Hermon straight away on Saturday afternoon. This was a national catastrophe and a serious blow to our intelligence system, as expensive, delicate, and sensitive equipment fell into Syrian hands. Many of our men were taken prisoner in the process, and the mountain, previously considered impregnable, became an objective for recapture at any cost.

The 7th Brigade engaged in local action on the second day of the fighting. Rattas fought north of the Little Hermon. My battalion, the 77th, saw action to the south, on the outskirts of Kuneitra. Yoss' battalion was integrated with other formations until their wounded commander came back from the hospital. Yair Nafshi's battalion was dispersed along the line in small groups; Yair himself went back to the Bustar hills north and east of Kuneitra.

Monday, October 8, 1973

While I was busy impeding moderate-strength enemy offensives across the front, Yanush ordered me to capture the valley below our positions.

I took the battalion into the valley, the tension indescribable. I weaved among enemy tanks, some abandoned and gutted, some still manned and battleworthy, their cannon trained on us. I could not tell them apart. The Syrians, frightened by the sight of our artillery pointing east, opened fire with everything they had: aircraft, amazingly accurate artillery, and Sagger missiles, a weapon we had not encountered until then. Mercilessly they savaged our tanks and our men.

After scouting the area, I requested and received permission to return to my positions upland. Even though these positions were in the rear, they had their advantages. As we were pulling back, Zelig Haverman, one of my tank commanders, was killed; his men left him in the field in his tank. No good. I attacked the area again in order to extricate Zelig. I could not live with the possibility of having an MIA in my battalion.

That night I was given yet another task: defense of the northern outskirts of Kuneitra. More precisely, I was to keep the Syrians out of the town and prevent their outflanking us from the north. I spent the night with Ami and his company near Kuneitra's northernmost houses.

Despite our tremendous fear and crackling tension, we could hardly keep our eyes open. The war against sleep — never drowse in the turret! — had become the major battle. Sleeplessness is more powerful than any fear. An exhausted body does not function. When it yields to fatigue, it submits to fear, too. Our every fiber and organ cried for rest, even for just a moment.

Tuesday, October 9, 1973

Late Monday night Yoss came back from the hospital and took over the area south of the Little Hermon. He went through a difficult night. I listened to him on the radio — contending, struggling, always persevering. At daybreak on Tuesday, Yanush took me off the Kuneitra sector and sent me with eight tanks, including several from my battalion, to the vicinity of Kibbutz Merom Golan. From there I watched Yoss struggle against an overwhelming Syrian offensive. I wanted desperately to help him. There I was, "unemployed." Nevertheless Yanush withheld permission, vacillating about where to draw our defense line that day.

A little while later eight Syrian command helicopters passed low overhead. We downed one and the others landed behind us. Now there was no doubt: enemy commandos had blocked our route of exit to the rear, from the Little Hermon area to Kibbutz Gonen via Merom Golan! Our forces wiped out the commandos some time later, but no one thought to tell me. I went on fighting with the impression that the only route by which we might evacuate casualties and take on vital ammo and fuel was blocked.

After thinking hard and long, Yanush ordered me to go help Yoss. His force comprised tanks from the 77th Battalion, commanded by my deputy Eitan Kaouli and Amnon Lavi, commander of Platoon 40. Fighting with Yoss were two tank companies under brigade headquarters, commanded by Eli Geva and Meir Zamir. I headed for the valley with all possible speed, far outpacing Ami, who followed me with his company. I had to master the terrain; only then could I bring Ami's company straight to our new area of operation.

The major feature of the terrain was a low hill on which two formations were fighting. On the hill I could see several disabled Israeli tanks, including several on fire, with a number of Syrian tanks in similar condition next to them. Frightened soldiers, wounded and sooty, in Syrian and IDF uniform, raced about in search of a place to hide. At the top of the hill we had no one to look into Syrian territory. The whole scene resembled something taken from a good war movie, made by a talented director.

To the left of the hill was a gully. This was my objective; on Sunday the Syrians had used it to outflank me and attack my tanks from the rear. I moved north, intending to bypass the smoke-filled battlefield.

I could see Israeli tanks moving west, as if retreating. A few of them, their ammo exhausted, were seeking to rearm. Others were evacuating casualties and looking for the medical officer, stationed several kilometers to the rear. Rather than contacting Yoss, the sector commander, I looked for a position from which I could halt the Syrians. Then, skirting a row of boulders, I beheld a terrifying sight.

"Stop!" I shouted at Yuval.

The tank stopped on a dime, jarring all the men inside. A few meters away were three Syrian tanks, two stationary and one in motion, looking for prey.

I ducked into the turret, leaving only my head exposed. I grabbed the cannon swivel-stick and aimed at the nearest enemy tank, the one to the right.

"Fire fast," I roared, pulling my head inside so as not to be struck by my own shrapnel.

"What's the range?" Kilyon asked innocently.

I thought I'd go out of my mind. The tank was so close that Kilyon hardly needed to aim, let alone worry about range. Then I understood: his sight was obstructed by a sea of green. He hadn't imagined that the object blocking his view was a Syrian tank.

"It doesn't matter. Fire already," I shouted, kicking him to emphasize the point.

The shell rocked the tank as it exited. I peeked through the hatch while Gideon reloaded. The Syrian tank was not ablaze as I had hoped, but its commander had leaped out, done for. I trained the gun on the second tank, several degrees to the right.

"See it?" I asked. Kilyon nodded enthusiastically.

"Fire fast." Another shell struck its target, opening a gaping hole in the enemy turret.

Now I aimed at the third tank, a T-62. It had stopped in the meantime, its black, massive muzzle aimed at us. Behind it a fourth tank came into view, moving quickly, its gun aimed at us.

"Fire, fire," I cried.

"It's busted," he shouted back from the turret. Perversely the empty casing of the last shell was stuck in the muzzle. Gideon grabbed it and yanked with all his might. Gidi and I leaped over to help him.

The giant gun of the T-62 continued to menace us. Death stared me in the face. I gripped the handles in the command cupola, ready to spring. I would not be trapped in a burning tank this time!

We heard an explosion and took a sharp jolt. The explosion was ours: Kilyon had unblocked the muzzle, reloaded, and fired. The Syrian tank, hit, burst into flame. I swiveled the gun to the right and Kilyon fired again, without hesitation this time, at the fourth Syrian tank. It took another shell to bring the last enemy vehicle to a stop, totally disabled.

I sighed with relief, allowing myself the briefest of pauses to calm down. My next task was to move toward the gully to the left of the hill. I was sure the Syrians were using it to outflank us.

Yanush radioed me for an update. Optimistically I described the chain of events: with my tank positioned at the opening to the gully, facing several Syrian tanks seeking to break through, Kilyon had knocked them out easily.

Now I could observe the Syrian-held territory and the other side of the hill that had been taken from us. There was the valley, strewn with the tanks my battalion had wiped out on Sunday. Immediately I noticed additional enemy tanks, several dozen, crossing the valley about 1.5 kilometers from the hill. Following them were several dozen more, now located in the vicinity of the border fence.

Yanush turned the sector over to me. Yoss had moved his personnel carrier into a stationary position. He had to pack up and move; he could no longer defend himself. If we did not take the hill, I knew, we'd lose this battle. I ordered Ami to advance to the nearby positions and gave him directions on how to do this; even so, he could not reach them. Amnon returned to the battalion, only a few tanks at his disposal. My second-in-command, Eitan, came back, too. We had additional tanks in the sector, but they were not on my frequency. I urged Shalom, the brigade communications officer, to order them to switch over to my Shoter network and join Battalion Oz 77.

Sizing up the situation, Yanush called Rattas, situated north of the Little Hermon. In short order he dispatched eight of his tanks to help me. Rattas then moved into position behind me, and thus we split up the territory. With the trepidation of a soldier asking his commander for a favor — Rattas had once been my company commander, and I the loader-radio man in his personal tank — I asked Rattas to take over for me and seal up the gully. "Affirmative," he replied and moved forward. A few seconds later, he was struck and killed.

A few of the tanks that arrived with Rattas were hit; the others fell back. I wanted one of the retreating tanks to take over for me in the position blocking the gully. Amir Naor, a young officer, volunteered for this perilous task even though he was totally out of ammo. Now I could join Ami's company and attempt to recapture the hill.

By this time all the tanks in the area had tuned their radios to Shoter; thus I could speak to their commanders and crews personally. Nevertheless, I could not motivate them to storm the hill. I was afraid of what might happen next. When I had been at the entrance to the gully, I was perhaps the only man to spot the dozens of enemy tanks that were moving toward the hill. Now I could no longer see them, but they were no less menacing for that. I tried raising my voice, but most of the tanks stood still. Then I applied persuasion, explaining what awaited us past the hill in logical terms. Finally I moved forward, toward the hill. Only Ami came along. Just then, the first of the Syrians began to line up on the other side of the hill, facing us. They opened fire. We were clearly on the verge of a frantic retreat.

That was unthinkable. I had to find the language and the style that would propel my fighting men toward the hill together with Ami.

"Shoter stations, this is Shoter." Now they knew they were dealing with their battalion commander. "Look at the enemy's guts! He takes his position and looks us in the eye. Now what about us? What the hell's happening to us? Who's stronger, us or these puny Arabs? Start advancing and line up with me. I'm waving the flag. Go!"

I spoke quietly throughout, shouting only the last few words for emphasis. Then, as if an unseen spring had been released inside them, the tanks began to advance.

"Don't stop, don't stop," I roared at several hesitant crews lagging behind. I felt a surge of pride at the sight of the metal monsters to my right and left, now advancing and spitting fire. We climbed the last few meters to the top of the hill carefully, so the enemy would not discover and smash us. Reaching the positions, we could all see the dozens of enemy tanks clattering across the valley floor. There were other tanks here and there, too — motionless ones, which we had hit previously.

The crews began searching for targets. "Shoot only at the moving ones," I ordered, anxious not to expend ammo on anything but living targets. We fired like maniacs, every man fighting for his life. The shells followed each other rhythmically, the gunners performing like musicians in an orchestra under a passionate conductor.

No, the Syrians would not drive us out of here. All

we had to do was shoot continuously, quickly, and accurately. We held the advantage, for the Syrians were down below. At first agitated and nervous, then with gusto, we pelted them with artillery fire. It was our lives they wanted; every pull on the trigger attested to our fierce will to live.

We fired until we ran out of breath. Several tanks to my right were hit, and the casualties either fled to the rear on foot or were evacuated by their comrades. I glanced at them for a split-second and refocused on the advancing enemy. When facing a mortal enemy, you take care of yourself — and your gun — before anything else. So instead of contemplating the tanks that had been downed around me, I looked for another Syrian tank to destroy.

An eleven-tank force under Yossi Ben Hanan — leftover tanks from Barak Brigade — was inching up Bustar Hill to our right. His deputy, Shmuel Askaroff, had been wounded in combat and evacuated, his chances of survival slim. Zamir, who had manned the same positions, had to evacuate for lack of ammo. Hence this move by fresh forces to occupy the positions.

We stopped them. Now we watched many uninjured Syrian crewmen racing among the wrecked tanks and personnel carriers. We looked down, methodically zeroing in on individual tanks that continued to threaten us. Our men contemplated each other in disbelief, half-smiles on our sooty faces, not yet aware of the magnitude of the victory, unable to come to grips with the price it had extracted. Hardly any of the tanks around me had a shell to spare; only a few were undamaged. The victors stood erect in their positions; the vanquished were scattered, bloodied, across the valley.

The vale of tears, we called it. The Psalmist's vale of tears, quoted in the Sabbath greeting hymn *Lekha Dodi*, which we knew so well: "Too long have you dwelt in the vale of tears."

The vale of tears.

The radio network crackled as the brass lined up to congratulate us. Raful lauded us right and left, and Yanush gushed with praise.

"You stopped the Syrians!" With this simple assertion Yanush defined the hellfire we had just come through. "You're a hero of Israel!" he added with emotion, bringing a deep flush to my cheeks. "Stay on the hill; don't endanger yourself!" Yanush's warmth was embarrassing, his personal concern for my safety profoundly touching.

We allowed ourselves a brief respite to let the experience soak in. I sat there in the tank, listening to the brigade radio network. The brigade recon company, under Uri Karshani, had gone out to attack enemy commandos near the Druse village of Bukata. As I listened in, I could clearly make out the contours of the battle taking shape. The Syrian commandos, hiding among the boulders, ambushed the company's personnel carriers. I heard the fighters' cries of agony and pleas for assistance. I shuddered. Uri, the company commander, was killed, as were many of his men; others were wounded. The company was scrapped from the brigade's order of forces.

With my superiors' permission I sent some of my battalion's tanks to the rear to restock with ammunition, food, and fuel. I joined them. Stopping at provisional brigade headquarters, I looked for a quiet corner and a stone to lay my head on. Instead of rest, however, I quickly found myself in the middle of an emotional family reunion.

"Avi!"

"Arnon!"

My brother Arnon, an ordinance man, had been assigned to my brigade as a tank mechanic. We embraced in the heat, speechless, peering into each others' eyes and restraining tears of excitement. Arnon's colleagues in the battalion's technical squads crowded around to congratulate me, their faces wreathed in stubble and their eyes red with lack of sleep. It was not hard for me to guess how I must have looked to them.

In that state of inner turmoil, I was summoned to the brigade operations officer for an update briefing.

"Tomorrow, Wednesday, October 10, you're going into Syria!"

I was stunned. "Let 'em do it by themselves," I blurted.

I had no idea about my battalion's condition. I had not yet been given a report on the number of casualties and the equipment that was no longer usable. It was clear to me that we could not go on without pausing, regrouping, rebuilding the force. Still, I regretted my slip of the tongue. I was a soldier; my job was to do as I was told, not to give flippant free rein to my feelings.

My disquiet aside, I knew that thrusting into Syria and terminating the war there was the right thing to do. The war undoubtedly had to end at a point that would facilitate the onset of political negotiations. A government with a strong army and unchallengeable achievements in the field would come away at an advantage. The decision on how to end the war, I believed, was not the fighting man's. The war had to end under the terms most conducive to a political dialogue.

The objectives and goals of the war were set by the political echelon; the armed forces would act astutely to attain them. To do so, it had to understand the objectives and goals correctly. Otherwise it would find it hard to select its ways and means. The military planner must apply all his experience and wisdom in pursuit of the objective, and can do so only if he is not afraid the objective will change in mid-combat. Only thus can he draw up and consolidate his plan wisely, infusing it with all the cunning and sophistication he can muster. A plan meant to be halted in mid-stream is of necessity simple, unsurprising, and, at times, dangerous.

The idea now was to reach the vicinity of Damascus, hardly 50 kilometers away on the inland downslope of the Golan Heights. This seemed logical. No one doubted the wisdom of those who were setting the objectives. They were right. I imagined "they" in the form of a stern-faced man, flecks of white in his beard and hair, radiating broad, profound understanding of historical processes. He sat in the bowels of the earth, safe from all danger, sketching colored arrows on a large map. All he lacked — and I wished with all my heart that he would overcome the deficiency — was some experience at pulling the trigger, so he could understand those who obeyed his orders. Us.

When you pause between two battles, having acquired bitter experience in the first, you need much more psychological strength and valor for the imminent second round.

Courage and fear

From earliest childhood I felt I was not brave enough. It always troubled me. My younger siblings were always considered "gutsier" than me. Showing off in front of their big brother, Ilana and Emmanuel lost no opportunity to display their victory over fear. I always sought to be the sort of guy who has more courage than blood in his veins. My childhood champions were fearless movie stars. Another model for admiration and emulation was Meir Har-Zion, the intrepid commando in legendary Unit 101 of the 1950s, who kept all of Israel secure by mounting instant, devastating retaliatory strikes whenever Arab "fellahin" raided our border settlements.

A "real" man doesn't know the meaning of fear, I used to say, drilling the message into my head. I soon learned that the "real" man is one who knows how to conquer fear.

In my youth I tested my ability to stare fear in the face. First came all-night hikes; later I would ready my bicycle for a "mission." I abused the bike terribly, doing stunts and acrobatics at mortal peril. I even put together a circus act on the bike.

Then came my father's motorcycle, a massive and heavy machine with a 5.5-horsepower engine. I controlled it, too. At the age of 14, my legs not yet able to reach the ground as I rode, I would take the bike for secret spins around the yard and nocturnal sorties. The heavy, wild beast obeyed me, even in dangerous, impassable territory, giving me a feeling of satisfaction and pride.

Over time I learned something else: you can thwart fear by superior know-how. As my date of induction approached, I vowed to be the kind of soldier I had read about in my youth. The IDF, I sensed, was the setting where one could pass all the tests.

Fear will dominate you unless you repress it first. No one is truly fearless, but some know how to put their fear "on hold." Anyone, and I mean anyone, can muster the strength to overcome fear. By deliberate simulation and practice we can train ourselves for our encounters with the real thing.

When fear grips us, our bodies do not bend to our will. We break out in cold sweat and our pulse races uncontrollably. "Knock-kneed" becomes more than a cliche: our knees really shake. Our voices change, as does their tone.

To function properly in the midst of all this, one must drill and redrill one's responses until they become second nature. Only thus, working automatically after thoroughgoing drill, do we deny fear its opportunity to paralyze us.

Then we can take matters further by putting ourselves "on stage." Anyone in such a situation will try to meet the audience's expectations, even if they're scared. Those expectant, demanding eyes, trained on you, prod you to go out and do it, irrespective of fear. Commanders, I have found, display their valor more easily than enlisted men do. Leaders, with eyes boring into their hearts, cannot be cowards. Rather, they can attain pinnacles that would surprise even themselves.

Togetherness magnifies the courage that resides in each of us.

Thus, motivated to overcome fear and demonstrate bravery, and aware that courage is the only key to survival and victory, we learn to acquire the trait of valor.

Counterattack

The commander's hardest moment of all is that which
comes after the battle, when he is informed of his
unit's casualties. Such news is easier to take when
you're under fire. The tumult of combat leaves no
time for contemplation; your attention returns immediately to the war. In those quiet afternoon hours after
the Vale of Tears, however, I totally lost my peace of
mind when Amnon informed me of the death of his
loader-radioman, Eliav Sandlar, and when I learned
how Barak Brigade had been mauled and its commanders, Ben Shoham and Yisraeli, killed. I was also
given a list of the battalion's disabled tanks and, with
it, a partial list of casualties evacuated to hospital.

We spent the rest of Tuesday and all of Wednesday regrouping. The plan to occupy a Syrian enclave,
formulated at brigade headquarters, provoked the
opposite inclination: a preference for defensive warfare. Now that we knew the territory and understood
that our achievements were no longer in doubt, that
we were the victors, I didn't care if the Syrians did
attack us again. They couldn't beat us, and everyone
knew it!

The incursion into Syria was a journey into the
unknown. We did not know exactly where and how
powerful the enemy was, but a couple of things were
clear: the terrain was difficult, and the enemy would
need only a small force to stop us. It was indeed one
great obstacle course, and we'd have to master it as a
first prerequisite for success. When we go on the
offensive, the initiative is ours alone. We determine
the location, the intensity, and the timing of every
action.

Preparation is the key to victory on the battlefield. While readying the force, I did not know in which sector I would be operating. So I did everything I could to prepare for all contingencies.

"Round up as many tanks as possible," I instructed my deputy, Eitan, and the company commanders. "I don't care how. Get good tanks and crews. Give special emphasis to the commanders. Go out to the field and apply all your powers of leadership. I want a big battalion."

That's just what my men did. The technical squad brought some downed tanks back to fitness, and thus, when the time came to push through, I had 28 tanks.

Reading the orders on the morning of Thursday, October 11, Yanush groped for a code word to use in activating the force. Everyone looked at me.

"Give us something, Panther," called Hagai, our operations officer.

As I tried to evade this duty, all voices burst out in unison: "Black Panther, Black Panther!"

Yanush approved the code without hesitation.

A few days later, as my battalion slowed its advance under heavy Syrian pressure, I was warned over the radio about Syrian tanks that sought to circumvent us. Make every effort to hold them back until reinforcements arrived, I was ordered.

"They won't get past **me**. They know they're dealing with a panther," I replied.

"And what a panther," Hagai shouted. "Black panther!"

I smiled. Never had we had such an apt code word... .

A quick glance at the brigade's battle sheet told me that my battalion would be the first to push into Syria. That calmed me; I had feared that the difficult task of crossing the border first would go to some other battalion. The offensive was structured in two columns. Oz 77 would lead the left column; behind us was Lt. Col. Amos Katz with a newly-constituted battalion made up of men who had returned from overseas. The right column would be headed by Ben Hanan, followed by Yoss with a new battalion he had assembled. Geva and Zamir were company commanders in the latter formation.

All the commanders bent over their maps, swiftly updating them with some new information and rushing back to their formations. It was almost nine o'clock, two hours before we were to move, and I had not yet spoken with my men. I began to worry, hiding with difficulty the tension I felt.

"Kahalani, come here a minute," Yanush ordered abruptly, tearing me from my work. He took me aside, out of earshot. As we walked, he laid a hand on my shoulder, a sign of the deep friendship that had developed between us.

"Listen," he said. "I met with the Chief of Staff.... I wanted you to know.... I spoke with him about you, told him how you stopped the Syrians...." Yanush's voice broke with emotion. I, too, was agitated.

"I told him you're a hero of Israel."

Tears choked his throat; he fought to restrain them.

"I wanted you to know that," he added tersely. Now sensing that things were getting too emotional, he summed up quickly: "It'll be OK. See you."

He shook my hand. Flushing deeply, I spun on my heel to return to my tank. Yanush held his ground for another moment, his eyes following me. Then he, too, went on his way.

I was embarrassed, strangely guilty about his having chosen just this moment to share this information with me. Still I was tense and concerned about the imminent incursion. Might this be the reason for Yanush's timing? One thing was beyond doubt: I had to conceal my emotions! We parted as men do when unsure whether they will meet again.

Eitan, my deputy, gathered the battalion. I stood up before them all, officers and enlisted men, to brief them on the battle we were about to face. Many of the faces were new; now we got to get to know each other. Now, too, I decided once and for all on the three company commanders who would lead the breakthrough: Ami Plant, Amnon Lavi, and Ephraim Laor. Until the previous night, the latter had been second-in-command to Eli Geva in Yoss' battalion. It had taken a thorough persuasion campaign on my part to have him transferred to my command.

"Black Panther, Black Panther," the order crackled on the brigade network. Battalion 77, too, got its order to move. I led the convoy south via Kibbutz El-Ron toward Bukata. Then we turned north, toward Mt. Hermon. After passing through the Druse village of Massada, several kilometers south of Hermon, we headed east, toward Tel al-Ahmar, our first objective in Syrian territory. Ami followed me, the rest of the battalion in his wake. At the border fence he passed me and led the offensive toward Tel al-Ahmar personally. The aim was to reach Mazra'at Bet -Jann, about 20 miles from Damascus, that very day.

This time our air force had strafed the entire area before the tanks reached it. The festering grudge I had harbored against the air force since our defensive battle vanished immediately and totally. Our artillery, too, advanced a short distance in front of our tanks, leading us on like the Biblical pillar of fire, striking the Syrian positions and the paths leading to them.

Everything went exactly as planned — until we reached the minefield. The minesweeper tank we called "Stranger" did not arrive. The bulldozer tank got stuck on the way. Five tanks set off mines while searching for a way through the field. Time was not on our side. Already I feared we were starting the attack on the wrong foot.

After tremendous efforts we heard Ami call excitedly: "I found a way through!"

Indeed he had. It was a path used by Syrian "fellahin" to cross the cultivated land near the border. Ami went ahead as a vanguard and got through safe and sound, the rest of us trailing behind. Thus we crossed into Syria without setting off additional mines and incurring no casualties.

Ami captured Tel Al-Ahmar. Many Syrian fighters surrendered to us and were taken PoW. Once Ami had carried out his mission, I ordered Laor to lead the battalion column. Laor pushed through to the road and raced eastward. Following the 77th battalion was Amos Katz's new battalion, in the manner we had coordinated. On the axis to the right moved Yanush and his two battalions, under Ben-Hanan and Yoss. This array resembled that in which I fought the Six Day War. Then, however, I led the column with its two companies by myself, with the battalion commander and deputy commander in the second column.

Laor had just returned from prison, where he had

been serving time for overturning a jeep that he had been driving without a license. He came back to the battalion on Yom Kippur by his own initiative and took part in the defense stage. Now he galloped down the road, shooting every which way.

The men in Laor's company, newcomers to the battalion, were beset by enemy forces from right and left. I feared that he himself would be hit. We came upon a Moroccan brigade in charge of the area's defense; it fled at the sight of us. Mount Hermon loomed to the north. Since we had recaptured it, we knew that at least from that direction, contrary to the Biblical prophecy, no harm would come. I was happy to be in the field; thus far I had known the area only through the binoculars, from maps, and from aerial photos. Laor continued to charge as the rest of us, behind him, fired relentlessly in all directions. By evening, still leading the column, he reached the hills overlooking the Syrian village of Mazra'at Bet Jann. It was too late in the afternoon to move on the village then and there; we would occupy it the next day, I decided. We regrouped to the west of the village and restocked with ammo and fuel — which, to our good fortune, reached us just before dawn.

Mazra'at Bet Jann sprawled at the foot of its surrounding crown of hills. Our positions controlled the entire village. During the night, however, Syrian forces had begun to move in. This was a danger signal for us: it meant the village would not fall easily.

Amos and I reached agreement on how we would mount the attack. My battalion would provide cover, and his would storm and occupy the village via the east-west highway, in fact the only way into the village.

At earliest dawn on Friday, October 12, the tanks of Battalion Oz 77 settled into their positions and began hitting enemy tanks and personnel carriers moving about the village. While gratified at the sight of pillars of flame emanating from the stricken machines, we knew that many others were hiding among the trees and that only the incursion force could wipe them out. Amos was well aware of this. He had acquired a wealth of combat experience in the Six-Day War and the War of Attrition in Sinai. Visiting the United States when the present war broke out, he had rushed home and evidently found his place in the fighting quickly and efficiently.

Syrian aircraft closed in on us, trying to deny us the village. We tried to hit them without success. A plane diving from our rear dropped its bombs right on us. Gidi, our operations officer, saw them coming.

"Aircraft! Into the tanks!" he shouted.

Frantically I plunged into my tank. Gidi saved my life.

The bombs hit the ground a few meters behind my tank. They rocked the vehicle and filled it with black, thick dust and smoke. My crewmen began to retch and suffocate. Yuval, the driver, brought us to the rear, where we climbed out for recuperation.

Two men — Ofer Ben-Neria and artillery auxiliary officer Avraham Snir — had not managed to take shelter in their tank. Both were killed. Later, when we came under artillery fire, Second Lieutenant Amos Nahum was wounded. He died *en route* to hospital.

At an agreed-upon signal, Amos' battalion burst forward. My battalion, in the hills, beheld an incomparably impressive scene: a tank battalion galloping down the road, enemy aircraft and artillery peppering it with bombs and shells in an attempt to stop it. Syrian tanks tried to stop Amos' machines, but my battalion wiped them out from its positions. By now Amos was fighting in the middle of the village, his men downing the Syrians at close range. In the course of this he lost several tanks and their crews. The difficult terrain, further complicated by dense vegetation in many areas, made it hard to control our forces in the village. At this juncture I drove into the village in my tank, to meet with Amos and observe the results of the fighting.

Amos had sustained a head wound and was bandaged. At his side I met comrades from previous wars. Capt. Menahem Dror, a company commander seriously wounded in the Six-Day War and classified as a disabled veteran, had volunteered to climb into a tank and command a company. Lt. Amos Luria, Amos' operations officer, had lost a hand in the War of Attrition. He, too, had been defined as a disabled veteran, and he, too, had volunteered to serve as a tank battalion operations officer. All had served, as I had, in the first Patton battalion.

The right-hand column of the brigade, under Yanush, took Jabta al-Hashab and the village of Taronje. Yoss continued toward the village of Harpa and took it, and Ben-Hanan turned right in an attempt to capture Tel a-Shams. This offensive failed, and Ben-Hanan was wounded. A special paratroop recon force under Yoni Netanyahu extricated Ben-Hanan and his crewmen after great toil. A reserve paratroop battalion took the tel that night.

Dan Lenner's division moved south of the 7th Brigade toward Khan Aribna, with intent to continue to Tel Ashas on the Kuneitra-Damascus axis. The divi-

sion finally broke through in a difficult and complicated battle that ended in victory but claimed an
intolerably high price in blood. The division continued south and broadened the area under its control,
stabilizing its boundaries the next day by capturing
Kafr Nassaj and Tel Mar'i. Swiftly this area acquired
the sobriquet of "Enclave." Within two days, in fact,
the IDF had occupied a vast swath of territory, bor-
dered by Mount Hermon and Mazra'at Bet Jann on
the north, Tel a-Shams, Tel Mar'i, and Kafr Shams to
the east, and the southern outskirts of Kuneitra to the
south.

On Friday night, Oz 77 was transferred from the
Mazra'at Bet Jann sector to another part of the enclave, where it sat until the end of the war.

The war winds down: Oct. 13-24, 1973

Life in the enclave was a mixture of moments of
tension and hours of peace and quiet — even these
disrupted by Syrian artillery. Tensely we followed
the news, as American Secretary of State Henry
Kissinger pulled strings in an attempt to bring about
a ceasefire. The tank men took advantage of the calm
to regroup, rest up, and successfully carry out missions meant to expand the enclave. We managed this,
to our delight, without losing any men.

I convened my battalion's companies for the first real
talk we were able to have since the war broke out.
The crews had gone slack with the dispelling of tension, attempting to shed the entire burden of the last
few days. I contemplated the men. They were men,
boys who had grown up before my very eyes. Their
faces had 18-day beards; their tank overalls were

sooty and dusty, clamoring to be laundered. A single hidden thread, a kind of invisible glue, bound the men together, as if they could not consider the thought of distancing themselves from one another. They leaned on each other's shoulders, articulating their thoughts with slight gestures or a single word that conveyed everything. They exuded a special interdependence, born in the crucible of this war. Then I understood: what I saw before me was comradeship-in-arms.

Friendship and comradeship-in-arms

The fraternity of fighting men originates in friendship. A military career is such that friendships start up and end with great frequency. It begins with induction. The green soldier in boot camp gropes about in his new surroundings, looking for help and explanation, and finds a friend with whom to share his doubts and ordeals, acquire missing information, and get a helping hand. But army life is fast-paced, its turnover high. The chances of two men remaining tent mates for long are slim. They are assigned to different training courses, different corps, companies, and platoons. All this works against the forging of true, long-term friendships. Quite often I had hardly established real friendship with someone when our ways parted with no advance warning. Then I was back to square one, looking for another friend. Sometimes this back-and-forth routine sapped my emotional strength and left me indifferent to the whole matter. Then I would merely wait for friendship to develop by itself.

Most of us have very few friends; we can count them on the fingers of one hand. We are surrounded by acquaintances, but intimate friends are few. A friendship that survives the years originates from more than two people's quest for togetherness. It depends above all on their adjustment and acquiescence to each other's traits. Accepting friends is something like a "package deal." Some of their attributes are just what you want to see in someone, those very traits that make you want to be close to someone. Others you find downright unpleasant. With these, too, you must make your peace. You can't set out to change them. This is the only way to develop genuine companionship — a relationship put to the test in a moment of pain, of need for help, of yearning for an attentive ear or a shoulder to lean on.

Again, the fraternity of fighting men originates in genuine friendship. True, a powerful, shared ordeal on the battlefield strengthens the ties between friends, but even this isn't enough. Comradeship-in-arms is but another layer of an existing relationship, which gains intensity and strength under fire.

I have always perceived the comradeship of fighting men in terms of personal sacrifice. One accepts high personal risk for a friend. Fighting men in all IDF formations — tank crew, platoon, company — are in close contact. This uninterrupted group existence spawns a high degree of interdependence, manifested in extreme form on the battlefield, sometimes so much that the men entrust their lives to their comrades.

Experiences engraved in blood never disappear, never fade from memory. Deeply embedded in us, they eventually rise to the surface. Comradeship-in-arms signifies the integration of these experiences with genuine friendship and personal sacrifice.

The IDF uses this term regularly. Anyone offended by his comrade's attitudes is likely to assert that "That guy doesn't know the meaning of comradeship-in-arms!" True, companionship amplified under fire does nothing to guarantee long-lasting friendship or relationships. But that warm spot in the heart lasts forever; memories that surface at some unpredictable moment rekindle the mutual commitment. I have often seen high-ranking officers and commanders who got their jobs by virtue of unforgotten comradeship-in-arms, by which "service buddies" are committed to each other all the way.

On a few occasions, however, I have seen the highest command echelons of the IDF abuse that comradeship-in-arms. The ambition to succeed and protect oneself occasionally lead to wanton, ill-conceived actions. During Operation Peace for Galilee, the War in Lebanon, I was accused of having ordered the capture of Beaufort Castle contrary to instructions. Comradeship-in-arms lost its meaning before my very eyes: men who had once fought at my side now argued that my headquarters had acted contrary to orders!

As a commander who advanced side-by-side with his men under enemy fire, I used judgment in the decisions I took, considering the conditions of the place and the time. No one asked me about my motives and rationale. I was made to pay for the actions of others who, occupying well-lit, air-conditioned bunkers, failed to do their work properly. Everyone makes mistakes, of course, but comradeship-in-arms demands that every fighting man be willing to protect his comrade with his body. Unfortunately, our highest echelons do not always keep this in mind. When this became clear to me in that episode of June, 1982, something shattered inside me.

As I have said, comradeship-in-arms finds its full expression within the tank crew, the platoon, and the company. To keep it from flickering out at higher echelons, we would do well to foster it there, too. Every soldier should know that he will never be abandoned on the battlefield, that his comrades will defend him with their lives, and that he is duty-bound to reciprocate. The first of the fighting man's unwritten ten commandments should be that dealing with interdependence, comradeship-in-arms.

The Syrians tried to drive us out of the enclave but had to settle for long-range gunfire. Slowly we gained "international" experience, identifying the Saudi, Moroccan, Iraqi, and Jordanian forces fighting us alongside the Syrians. Similarly we became familiar with the fighting men's habits: some did not change their clothes, did not write letters, made sure to wear a certain piece of dress while in battle, carried a book of Psalms, and kept their stubbles of beard — superstitions meant to ensure their well-being. Now we let our thoughts stray to home. We began to miss things back there.

Only on the last day of the war was my battalion supposed to disengage from the Syrians and retreat a little for regrouping purposes. On the night of October 24, I heard on the news that the Syrians had agreed to a cease-fire. We were surprised, too cautious to believe it. Even the next morning, by which time it had become a *fait accompli*, we were still itchy, staying on alert until the last moment. Then Oded Erez's newly rebuilt battalion replaced me on the sector.

We left the enclave after nightfall. I was impatient;

Yanush had asked me to get out quickly and report to him at once for a personal talk. What could it be? I asked myself. As if to compound my troubles, Laor's company got itself stuck amidst the boulders; to help get them out I had to inch into a gully with my tank, annoyed about the precious hours we had lost.

At long last I reached Yanush. We drove in his jeep toward Nafah, the battalion's tanks following. Throughout he maintained a strange silence, keeping his eyes on the road. Finally he said:

"Kahalani, I really called you over to tell you that there's been a tragedy in your family. Your brother's dead."

I was stunned. A violent shudder wracked me from head to toe. My thoughts went vague, formless.

"Which brother?" I asked, groping in shock. Since we had met before the breakthrough into Syria, I had heard nothing about Arnon. Emmanuel was fighting in Sinai. I had received no word about him, either.

"Emmanuel," said Yanush, now looking at me.

I could not hold back my tears. Emmanuel's face danced past my eyes — laughing, clowning features enveloping his sad eyes. Only a few days ago, beaming at his wedding, he had captivated us all.

"When did this happen?"

"A few days ago. I had to keep it from you; I couldn't get you out of the enclave. Your parents have been waiting for you some time now. Go home at once!"

Now I understood why I got no mail for the past few days, and why the mobile phone had gone "out of order" just when it was my turn to call home.

But Yanush had more bad news to relate. Ilan, my wife Dalia's kid brother, had also fallen while crossing the Suez Canal as communications officer in a tank brigade. He, too, was a newlywed, his wife five months pregnant.

The pain was unbearable. Of course I had to go home. But how would I restore the battalion to fitness? Furthermore, since my deputy Eitan had been wounded several days ago, who would command it?

"Don't worry," Yanush said soothingly. "Your buddies will get over it. I trust them."

I handed the battalion over to Ami, who undoubtedly had the experience and ability for the job. Ami took the battalion to Camp Nafah. From there, late that night, I headed for Nes Ziona. Home.

Citations

Regrouping after the war, the commanders were asked to evaluate their men — officers and rank-and-file soldiers — in writing. Then, on forms sent to us from brigade headquarters, we were to recommend those we believed worthy of citation. I was surprised that this was being done so soon after the war. In fact, the whole business was strange to me.

After the Six-Day War, as I lay wounded in the hospital, I was impressed by the large number of men given postwar promotions — and even more impressed by those awarded citations. I knew nothing about the method and criteria under which these men were chosen. I believed at the time that only casualties, or those who had extricated casualties with particular derring-do, merited this prize.

My first thought now was to hand the forms to my company commanders and let them decide. Quickly I changed my mind; that way the matter might fall between the stools, provoking controversy and heartache, contrary to its intent. So I shut myself in my room and tried to concentrate, mentally reconstructing exceptional feats worthy of commendation. I got nowhere. All the men had been heroes, all of them. Now what?

I summoned the company commanders and staff officers for some joint deliberations. Laor, Amnon, and Ami, with whom I had wound up the war, participated actively in the talk.

"I don't understand what they want from us," Ami began heatedly. "I don't think I can fill out a form like that! For me they were all heroes. No on retreated from their positions. I can't think of anyone I could recommend more than anyone else."

Amnon was calmer. One commander, he thought, did deserve special commendation, but he wanted to consult with me about it.

Laor apologized. "I wasn't a company commander when the Syrians were stopped. I can't recommend anyone until I consult with my own commanders."

I balked at this. "Listen," I pressed, "We've got top-notch fighters in our battalion. I understand your problem, but try to think hard. We can't let this drop without presenting someone as our representative!"

This upset Ami. "If I give it to one of them, how will I look the others in the eye? I know our battalion. There's no doubt: we stopped the Syrians. But each of us did his job! Show me one man who didn't!"

Half-asking, half-answering his question, Ami looked me straight in the eye. I could not help but answer.

"Everyone knows this job is hard, complicated, and sensitive. All through the IDF commanders are going to recommend their men. Then they'll set up a committee to approve the recommendations, and just us, because we can't make up our minds, aren't going to recommend anyone. Then we'll have to face our men — and there's no doubt they're the best Israel's got — and tell 'em what happened.

"A commander who recommends one of his men for a citation puts himself on the firing line. He's embarrassed, the guy who gets it is embarrassed, and the men feel you've discriminated against some of them. They'll ask 'Why him and not me?' It's inevitable. But more than the men's reactions, I'm concerned about ourselves, our leadership. How are we going to take soldiers whom we didn't recommend, who feel what they've done is worthless, and lead them into war?

"Therefore, so we can finish this job and be at peace with ourselves, let's keep something in mind: citations like this are not supposed to be gold stars for outstanding pupils. They're supposed to call attention to courageous fighting men and exceptional actions. They commemorate feats of heroism and add them to the battle heritage that we pass on to the next generation.

"A few years from now, a new generation will have to defend the country. They won't be any worse than we are. These stories about our fighters are trivial and important at the same time. They'll determine the patterns of military conduct that will serve the next generation as a basis. Today we don't have to decide on the level of award that we're recommending. The committee will make that decision; they have an overview of the whole army. But we *will* have to tell our men what kind of rationale we used to make our decision, explain what the decision means. It's for posterity, for our children."

A few months later, the citations committee summoned my company commanders to describe the sto-

ries behind the citations, the truth behind their recommendations. They invested their comments with a
fervor that went to my heart. I was proud of them.

Twelve fighters in the 77th Battalion were given
citations. The committee didn't give us a chance to
describe the rest of the men.

First Sergeant Amir Bashari, a superb commander
about to leave the service, was stationed in his tank in
a position overlooking the Vale of Tears. From the
stony hill he succeeded in wiping out many Syrian
tanks. Even when alone on the hill, even when his
comrades around him had been struck, even when he
had become a target for Syrian cannon, he did not
retreat. He continued to fight, continued to inflict
losses — until he was hit and killed.

First Sergeant Yoav Blumen, Amir's good friend
and a member of his induction group, had been taken
to the rear in a damaged tank. He left the tank with
the technical squad and leaped into another tank.
This machine was hit, too, but Yoav did not give up.
He went to Camp Kurdani near Haifa, far from the
battlefield, and drove a new tank back to the Golan
Heights. Two officers in his company wanted to join
him and climbed into the tank. Because Yoav insisted
that he occupy the commander's cupola, the two officers became his gunner and loader-radioman. As
we counterattacked, the tank was hit. Yoav was killed;
his crewmen were uninjured.

Posthumously, Amir and Yoav were awarded the
Medal of Gallantry.

208 • Avigdor Kahalani

Medals and Citations

In 1970, the Knesset enacted the IDF Medals Law,
instituting medals for acts of valor, gallantry, and
distinguished service by soldiers and units.

The Medal of Valor is given by the Minister of
Defense per recommendation of the Chief of General
Staff for supreme heroism in combat at the risk of
one's life. The Medal of Gallantry is given by the Chief
of General Staff for bravery in the course of discharging combat duties, again at the risk of one's life.

The Distinguished Service Medal is given by the
Chief of General Staff for exemplary courage. The
medal, worn on one's uniform shirt next to the special pin denoting participation in war, is a two-piece
adornment: a medallion bearing various symbols of
Israel's battle heritage, and a colored plate. The Medal
of Valor plate is yellow, reminiscent of the yellow
badge, an emblem of Jewish resistance during the
Holocaust. The Medal of Gallantry plate is red, and
that of the Distinguished Service Medal purple.

In addition to the medals are four levels of citations, each composed of an olive leaf superimposed
with a diagonal sword. Citations are attached to war
participation pins. The four levels are named for the
officers who recommend their recipients: Chief of
General Staff, Major General, Division Commander,
and Brigade Commander.

These officers forward their recommendations to a
special committee that convenes as warranted, dis-
cusses each case on its merits, issues its opinion, and
recommends the type of decoration to award each
candidate. Medals and citations can be given to entire formations, but these are not publicized, for obvious reasons.

From the War of Independence to the present writing the following have been given:

41 Medals of Valor

218 Medals of Gallantry

601 Distinguished Service Medals

176 COGS Citations

191 Major General Citation

63 Division Commander Citation 71 Brigade Commander Citation

It takes only one glance to notice that Armor garnered the highest number of citations: 284 out of a total of 426 citations and medals. In second place is Infantry, with 195 medals out of 262 citations and medals.

Of 41 recipients of the Medal of Valor, 13 were from Armor and 10 from infantry. Armor has garnered 70 medals of Gallantry, compared with 60 for infantry.

Air Force personnel earned 57 medals and a total of 123 decorations of all kinds; corresponding figures for the Navy are 43 and 58, respectively.

The first citation was given in March, 1948, two months before Israel was established but well into the country's War of Independence. Twelve medals, all for valor, were awarded during the War of Independence proper. Another five Medals of Valor were awarded to veterans of the Sinai Campaign, eleven of the Six-Day War, and eight of the Yom Kippur War. The other Medals of Valor were given between the wars. Twenty-one of the 41 Medals of Valor were posthumous.

Conspicuous among these data is the fact that most recipients of special citations were commanders. No wonder. We have a tradition in the IDF, spawned by the legendary Gideon Ben-Yoash, who ordered his fighters, "Watch me and do what I do." Ever since, is the commander who spurs his storming unit with the cry of "Follow me!" Citations are awarded for exceptional behavior, in which, by nature, few enlisted men in non-command functions have an opportunity to engage. Most rank-and-file soldiers operate within a given structure or crew with defined tasks. Even the lowliest of commanders, by contrast, is expected to take mid-combat decisions in volatile battlefield situations. To attain his objectives he applies leadership skills, initiates action, and modifies the tactics used. All these factors are conducive to behavior that departs from the accepted standard.

Moreover, as noted above, all eyes are on the commander. Thus he must display greater courage than his men, lead the attack force, display initiative, and set a personal example. Anyone who studies our rosters of war casualties will notice that the commander corps also pays the highest price by far.

The table below illustrates this well:

CORPS	TOTAL CITATIONS AND MEDALS	THEREOF: OFFICERS	THEREOF NCOs	THEREOF: POSTHUMOUS
Air Force	123	105	16	10
Navy	58	34	17	7
Infantry	262	149	77	79
Armor	436	294	121	166

Following the Yom Kippur War, one commander in Battalion Oz 77 was awarded the Major General Citation. Seven received the Distinguished Service Medal, three the Medal of Gallantry, and one the Medal of Valor. Five of the awards were posthumous.

Another factor should be borne in mind. Those who wear a citation or medal on their chest owe more than they are due. As great as their honor and acclaim is, the commitment pinned to their epaulets is greater. The account of their valor is now and forever part of Israel's military heritage, and the young eyes following these men around view these people as models for emulation. They have to keep it up, raising the standard ever higher.

12. REHABILITATING THE ARMORED CORPS

After parting with the 77th Battalion and the Golan Heights, I went straight to the Armored Corps School as its deputy commander. My superior, the school's first commander after the war, was Lt. Col. Shlomo Arbeli; he was later replaced by Col. Yaakov Pfeffer. For me it was an abrupt transition after having been responsible for a battalion in the midst of rehabilitation after a bloody war. My new home was a rear formation in central Israel, where the missions were totally different. Armor had taken much heavier losses in the war than the other corps; its command echelon, in particular, had been decimated. The Armored Corps School, based in Camp Julis near Ashkelon, was supposed to replenish the tank formations with new personnel as quickly as possible.

For this, the corps needed new sources of manpower. Attention focused on infantry officers, and indeed, many of them were sent to my school for retraining.

Retraining for armor, however, entails more than a few months' "occupational" studies and a ceremony at the end. It also means a profound change in mentality, especially for men coming from infantry. The pressures of the time merely magnified the effort necessary. Thus I presented Maj. Gen. Aden with some crash courses for new men and further training for tank crews: I knew the subject matter in my sleep and could differentiate between what mattered most and what mattered less. Together we cut the time spent in maneuvers by about half.

"You're training cannon-fodder," the critics said. But my experience on the Golan Heights had taught me the significance of a tank disabled for lack of a gunner, a commander, or some other crewman. When it comes to that, you don't draw distinctions. It's everyone's responsibility.

The men of the Haruv ("Carob") reconnaissance unit, stationed in the Jordan Valley, were among the candidates for retraining. So vehemently did they resist this reassignment, however, that we — Brig. Gen. Dubik Tamari (Chief Armored Corps Officer) and I — went out to apply some persuasion.

The result was a harsh exchange that left me stunned. The "red berets" in the recon unit balked, it turned out, because Armor had suffered so many casualties. They were not ashamed to say this in so many words. To my surprise I felt that the fighting men of Armor, ordered to defend the country, were doing it alone as the others kept at a safe distance. These recon men, the cream of our youth, had done much less in the war than my tank crews had. Whatever happened to justice? How could the best Israeli youth, volunteers in their present assignment, have pressed the trigger less than my fighting men? Among the tank crews, to be sure, there were men who grumbled about the duties assigned to them. All, however, swallowed the bitter pill. All the more, I thought, should these recon men. After all, no one had ever questioned the quality of the fighters in this volunteer formation!

The "Carob" men plunged my school into a tumult of commotion and nuisance. Forsaking any pretense of self-control, they threw smoke grenades into their tent compound and tramped into the mess hall as might an outlaw gang in a Wild West movie.

Having no choice in the matter, I had to whip them into line. It was quite a crackdown, with lots of reprimands, fines, and even a few jailings. When the men realized that they could not misbehave their way out of Armor, they lined up at the base clinic, seeking to lower their medical profiles so as to exempt them from any combat duty. A large contingent took matters one step further, presenting themselves to the Chief of General Staff — by chance an Armor man — to tell him that the army was wrong. Dado replied without hesitation:

"If a terrorist slips in through the Jordan Valley, the population at large is not in danger. If we're short one tank company, the whole country's in trouble!"

The episode came to a sad and embarrassing end: only three of the recon men became rank-and-file "tankists."

Another group of men assigned to the Armored Corps School had been POWs in Egypt during the war. Some had been tank commanders, others tank crewmen. Liberated several months later, they reported to me after brief recuperation. In view of the sensitivity of this matter, I interviewed each of them personally before assigning them duties commensurate with their training and ability.

The festivities that greeted them upon their return made me sick. That it was an exciting reunion I understood; this was only natural, especially considering the accounts of valor that accompanied their having fallen PoW. But the message transmitted by this outpouring — that being a PoW was a great honor — was totally contrary to my way of thinking. I was concerned.

About half the men in the group were assigned as instructors in various parts of the school. The others tried to dodge this duty; the school wasn't cushy enough.

"I did my share. No way I'm gonna serve here," one of them said in so many words.

"All we want you to do is be an instructor in the artillery section," I answered patiently.

"I'm not gonna do anything around here. I'll serve in administration headquarters in Tel Aviv, in Unit 805: start at eight, do zero, and go home at five."

I boiled with anger, wanting only to smack the kid and show him which way was up. Even a mere slap in the face would have jarred him back to reality. Instead, I tried some tough verbal skirmishing. When that got me nowhere, I locked him up in my unit's jail. The whole world flooded me with phone calls: "Reconsider, Kahalani." I could just see the screaming headlines: "Kahalani Busts PoW from Egyptian Prison to Israeli Prison." But I did not yield.

I had always given the PoW problem a lot of thought. I had never personally gone through that experience, and was not totally at peace with myself when I dared form an opinion or judge the young men who had come home. Talking with many of them, however, I was able to peek into the world of these men, the happiest men on earth when they set foot on Israeli soil.

The former PoW surely spends the rest of his life believing it could have been different. He finds it hard to refrain from blaming himself for his capture.

He may even think at times that it might have been better to die in action. After talking with Dr. Reuven Gal, former IDF Chief Psychologist, I understood that these feelings — especially guilt — probably never vanish. Only therapy can liberate the returning PoW from these chains of the mind and get him back on his feet quickly. Nor did Dr. Gal rule out the idea of court-martialling PoW's upon their return — if only for their own good.

Be this as it may, there's no doubt about what matters most: to make the PoW confident that he has returned to a warm, loving society. He won't resume normal life until he's sure of this. Thus, when encountering those who have undergone one of life's worst traumas, if not the very worst, this should be our goal.

Very slowly the Armored Corps School came back to itself, re-establishing its study routine and accepted standards. The staff were still reeling from the impact of the war, in which they had fought as tank crewmen, and they found it quite a challenge to resume their previous calling as experienced instructors. Furthermore, the school had been given a new duty: receiving new tanks. We equipped them, armed them, and took them down to Sinai or up to the Golan Heights. There they were distant partners of the machines stationed in their positions. At all times we felt the ambiance of the front line.

In the aftermath of the Yom Kippur War, the IDF became more aware of the need to care for casualties' surviving brothers, the wounded, and former PoWs. Whenever I decided on the placement of men whose brothers had perished, the images of others in that agonizing situation crossed my mind: Amnon Giladi, who fell in the Six-Day War, and his brother Gideon, who died in the Yom Kippur War; Adam, my close friend, who perished in the 1969-1971 War of Attrition, and his brother Gideon, who died in the Yom Kippur War; Shimon, my wife's older brother, killed in the War of Independence, and Ilan, his younger brother, who fell in the Yom Kippur War. When reassigning the wounded, I considered my friend Benzi Carmeli, first injured in the 1956 Sinai Campaign, reinjured in the Six-Day War, and killed in the Yom Kippur War as commander of an armored reconnaissance battalion.

A family once bereaved should never be forced to re-experience this most terrible pain of all. No surviving son of such a family should be put on the front line unless the family itself approves it. Many such families withhold their permission, and nothing could be more understandable. However, I greatly admire those who volunteer for combat units out of desire to follow in their deceased brothers' footsteps — with their families' backing.

One morning a woman stumbled into my office, hysterical, clutching a letter from her husband, a soldier in my school.

"Forgive me," the husband wrote. "I intend to commit suicide. I can no longer stand being a soldier. But before I go, I would like to fire a bullet straight into the head of Avigdor Kahalani. I intend to sit down and shoot him between the eyes with his wife and children looking on."

I was floored. I knew the man. A chronic AWOL, he would spend one day in the camp and the next 18 days in parts unknown, show up for a little while and disappear again. His commanders had sent him to me for court-martial, after which I put him in the camp lockup with the intention of sending him to military prison. He broke out; even his wife had no idea of his whereabouts. She did tell me, plainly worried, that at the age of 17 he had stabbed his father in the heat of a family quarrel.

Considering the experiences of officers who had been assaulted by their soldiers, I sent my family away and had them replaced with security men, waiting in ambush for the wound-be assassin. I went about on the alert, a handgun on my hip. A few days later the soldier was caught, drugged silly, wholly out of touch with the world... .

During my tenure at the Armored Corps School I continued building my home. For lack of spare time and cash, the work developed into many weeks of toil. We hopped from one floor tile to the next, side-stepped piles of sand between the rooms, and fought off stray cats who invaded the house through the paneless windows. One night I woke up noticing a strange weight on my chest. I opened my eyes to discover a slightly frightening sight: a feral cat sleeping comfortably on my chest — just the place to wind up a long day of scavenging... .

Once the construction was finished, we could only pray that the house would not collapse on the heads of its engineer-architect-builder-carpenter-metal worker-owner and his patient kinfolk.

All that time the entire country was in turmoil about the war, its origins, and its outcome. Screaming newspaper headlines repeatedly invoked the buzzword "mehdal", (blunder), as representative of the political-military decisions preceding the war. "Failure," the public ruled. Their efforts to fathom the motives and analyze the political moves only strengthened their verdict. The war itself was almost forgotten. So were the warriors.

Personally, I knew and fully believed that we had registered a tremendous victory. Now I was seized with a powerful urge: Write!

Write? To whom? Who would read it? How would my comrades and men react? What would my commanders say? In what style? Who would publish it? And how would it be written at all? After all, I had barely passed my high-school finals in composition!

I resolved to try nevertheless. The moment I began, my hand raced across the pages uncontrollably. Within a few months my first book came out: Oz 77, translated into English as The Height of Courage (Greenwood Press, 1981), named for Battalion Oz 77, which fought heroically under my command. That's what oz means in Hebrew, after all — valor.

Reconstructing a Reserve Training Base

Late in 1974, Maj. Gen. Mussa Peled, commander of the armored corps, asked me to take over and revitalize an abandoned training facility in the remote, desolate Negev — Tze'elim. This facility, where most of the armored formations were trained, had fallen into disuse when the war broke out, its men reporting to Sinai for tank crew service. I had other ideas: I wanted to return to the Golan Heights and told Mussa so. I acceded to Mussa's request only when he promised that it would not frustrate my explicit ambition. Thus, in my Israeli-made Carmel automobile, with my veteran driver and a new clerk, I headed for Tze'elim.

What I found was something like a ghost town struck by a cyclone. I toured the camp, inspecting the warehouses and classrooms, and held my head in despair. Were our war maps wrong? Had the Egyptians overrun and looted the place? We knew very well that its only occupiers were our own forces, who used it for emergency maneuvers *en route* from Sinai to the emergency depots. The classrooms were wrecked. Study material that took years to compile fluttered across the dunes. Teaching aids had vanished, office equipment was but a fond memory, and telephones and light sockets had been ripped out of the walls. Spare parts of tanks and other vehicles lay about the camp like junk. Tanks in search of shade had parked on the grass, crushing the sparse greenery that had sprouted only after years of effort. The fences were ruptured, and only one warehouse was found intact. Trite as it sounds, the idea of starting all over seemed like "mission impossible."

Searching about for a working telephone, functioning electricity, and an office worthy of the name, we took up quarters in one of the camp's most remote corners. I called the Armored Corps School and secured — on loan — a typewriter; the moment it arrived, my clerk began to bang out a wish-list that I would send on to headquarters. With an improvised key we could even lock the door on our way out. There it was: the base had a commander with an office, a clerk, and a driver. A new unit was born in the Israel Defense Forces: the reserve formation training facility. Slowly officers were posted to Tze'elim, trailed by a few enlisted men. All were given the privilege of a personal interview with the base commander; all were assigned to duties commensurate with their ability.

The firing grounds around the base had been a treasured Armor Corps asset for years. They permitted large-scale maneuvers, in which many tanks and armored infantry units could fire freely in every direction. When news of the re-establishment of this facility became known, the first brigades sought to reserve maneuver time without delay. So we, the "founding fathers," hurriedly organized the classrooms and reconstructed the drills, once performed with kits whose traces were now lost in the dunes.

At the time, I was working directly under armored corps commander Mussa Peled. Here I discovered a Mussa I had not known. Treating my base like a devoted personal nanny, he displayed a sensitivity and fairness of which I had been unaware. The grudge I had borne Mussa since graduating Command and Staff College now gave way to affection and appreciation.

I loved the wide open spaces of the Negev, that great, untamable kingdom. I was still a lieutenant colonel, even though my position warranted a higher rank. The rule up to that time was that any officer assigned a brigade command was promoted to full colonel. Just as I took up my position, the law was amended; to gain this promotion now, one had to be a lieutenant colonel or brigade commander for at least three years. I found it no easy task to stand up to brigade and division commanders who treated lieutenant colonels as servants — "hewers of wood and drawers of water," in our familiar Biblical jargon. In lengthy arguments with them I insisted that my facility would govern the formations' comprehensive training, maximizing the use of resources and time.

In due course I also demanded a broader range of

operations for Tze'elim, informing the Chief of General Staff, Motta Gur, of the need to send infantry, engineering, and artillery formations to my facility along with armor units.

"There's not enough room for everyone," he answered.

I led him to a map on the wall and drew an imaginary line around the camp perimeter.

"There's no problem of room. What there is, is a problem of will and vision," I pressed.

Motta began to see things my way and ordered his Instruction section to handle the matter. Now I met with the vigorous opposition of the chief paratroop and infantry officer, Brig. Gen. Dan Shomron.

"No way. Never!" he ruled. "I'll lie down in the road!"

Tze'elim was soon renamed: Not many days went by and the facility was renamed the Field Formation Maneuvers Base. Infantry moved in with all its formations and luster. Engineering was pleased with the privilege of training there, and Artillery, situated not far from Tze'elim in any case, completed the circle. I could not disguise my pride at the sight of the bustling camp. Classrooms hummed with reservists mastering their duties, and the tanks came and went, breathing new life into the desolate training grounds.

Allocating the training areas required intellectual effort and weighty responsibility. Growing numbers of units that had trained in Tze'elim before the Yom Kippur War wanted to return. Augmenting them was a unit I myself established at the time: a new tank formation staffed with men who acquired vast tank experience in the war. Frustrated at my inability to devote full attention to my own unit, I handed routine administration of the camp to my deputy, Yitzhak Ben Shoshan. My tank unit was of incalculable personal importance: I refused to be caught without a unit to command if war broke out.

Now we invested all efforts in the routine of maneuvers, a routine that had often proved to be tumultuous and memorable.

Around the clock we commanders and instructors pursued the rushing tanks, and, in my case, stormed alongside them in my jeep. One night, advancing without lights with the "attack force," I found myself trapped between two tanks. In mid-rush the tanks converged, not noticing the jeep between them. I looked death in the eye. I gunned the jeep forward, miraculously avoiding a fatal encounter with the two metal monsters — only to meet with murderous machine-gun fire from their comrades. I came out unscathed. God protects even stupid fools... .

One Friday afternoon, I raced into the field alone for some pre-maneuver reconnaissance and toppled my jeep into a gully. Those were the early days of Tze'elim, and my jeep still lacked basic equipment. Thus I found myself with no radio, no weapon, no map, no steel helmet. What I had was an upside-down jeep in the middle of the desert, about ten kilometers from the base, on Friday afternoon — just when everyone had gone home to prepare for the Sabbath. No one knew where I was. For lack of choice I began hiking back to the camp.

You have it coming, I told myself. My adventurer streak was as strong as my driving curiosity; I have never overcome either trait. But to commit all possible sins in one trip?

One day, without warning, I was ordered to report to the Orthopedic Department of Sheba Hospital near Tel Aviv, a major medical facility along side one of the largest IDF bases. The reason: Chief of Staff Motta Gur, hospitalized for back trouble, wanted to interview me. So he did, bedridden, half-prostrate and half-seated, covered with a sheet from the shoulders down.

"You're gonna be commander of the 7th Brigade," he greeted me, as if summarizing a protracted discussion.

Surely he was kidding. Amram Mitzna and I had been vying for command of the conscript brigades on the Golan Heights, Barak and the 7th. Mitzna himself had told me that they had already decided to give him the 7th, and I had made peace with this defeat, if sadly. Now, of all things, my dream had come true. No one had dropped hints, no one spread rumors. What a pleasant surprise!

Some time later my successor, Lt. Col. Nattke Nir, reached Tze'elim, was promoted to Brigadier General, and assumed command. He gave my "baby" tremendous momentum, making it a central training facility for all field formations.

Officer placement

The IDF establishment is always concerned about how its officers are placed. Field officers stay in one position for one to two years; those in rear units hang on a little longer. In view of the dizzying turnover of officers and the gentler movement of career NCOs, reassignment is by necessity the topic of frequent deliberations. When a given position becomes available, the would-be appointee inevitably goes through several days of tension. New duties sometimes entail uprooting one's family. The very assumption of new duties within an unfamiliar system provokes uncertainties and doubts. When the change involves a promotion in rank and level of duty, these, too, compound the candidate's curiosity and stress.

The "outsider" may imagine that commanders reshuffle their subordinates all by themselves. Not so. Every change of position within a formation requires the approval of headquarters. A battalion commander cannot replace a platoon commander without consulting the brigade commander. Neither can a brigade commander appoint a new battalion commander without his division commander's approval; division commanders, too, act on the basis of consent from higher up. A major general cannot replace a colonel unless the Chief of General Staff approves — and the Minister of Defense signs the order.

All that is theory. In practice, powerful officers often succeed in giving their cronies the jobs they want, emulating a *modus operandi* that has gained legitimacy in other governmental institutions. The way decisions are made, too, provokes questions. An officer is supposed to climb the military ladder in accordance with documents attesting to his/her past achievements and present performance. Sometimes, however, an assignment is based on old friendships, comradeship-in-arms, or the shared background of appointee and appointer. Quite often, perhaps too often, the appointers do not use written opinions about the officer wisely and correctly. Sometimes an oral opinion is considered more important than a written one.

Commanders review their subordinate officers every six months. The review is forwarded, for record-keeping purposes only, to Army Administration under the General Staff Manpower Branch. Because both the author and the object of the opinion are afraid of the written word, these evaluations do not always reflect reality. If a commander is weak and knows it, he tries to avoid confrontation with his subordinates, thus often "rounding" his opinions upwards. It used to be worse. Once an attempt was made to set a minimum grade, beneath which perks such as loans would be withheld and officers forced to undergo reassessment if they wished to continue their career service. By the nature of things, very few officers were "flunked."

IDF formations are subject to constant review and audit. Their adjutants, ordinance personnel, medical team, routine operation of facilities, and many other aspects of their performance are frequently checked, monitored, and evaluated. When an officer's future comes up for discussion, achievements and military past should be the criteria. And since written opinions do not reflect reality, the army system should use additional tools at its disposal. Examples are the achievements of the officer's formation, i.e, the results of formation-level audits; its performance in drills; the motivation of its personnel; the percentage of those who sign for career service or request transfer; and the number of training and traffic accidents.

Those who decide on officer placement do not always take these last points into account. An officer can bust his gut for his unit, devote hours on end to operational issues or manpower problems, and come up with fantastic results. Still, when the moment of reassignment comes, personal relations between him-

self and the decision-makers can outweigh everything.

Reassignment of colonels and higher-ranking officers is carried out after special Monday afternoon deliberations in the bureau of the Chief of General Staff,
with most of the General Staff in attendance. The list
of candidates is presented to this forum in advance,
and in most cases all the information in this document is leaked so that every last officer on the list
knows everything. Several candidates compete for
each vacant position, and the tension mounts high.

I attended many such discussions. I could not help
but notice the generals' reluctance to discuss the candidates freely and frankly. So apprehensive were they
that one could rarely tell what their position was.
Their discussions are supposed to transcend the mere
formulation and presentation of opinions. Their fear
originates in one factor only: the leaks they can expect in the aftermath of their "confidential" meeting.
Candidates usually find out what was said about
them with no effort at all; some go so far as to complain about remarks made about them by one general
or another. In this embarrassing climate, the task of
officer placement has acquired an evident ambience
of "politics," in which decision-makers ensure their
ability to retract or change their positions as warranted.

With all this in mind, many officers feel it necessary to "market" themselves before the discussion.
Before being interviewed by the generals, they line
up at their office doors in order to marshal the broad-
est possible personal support.

It's not a bad idea. These generals play a very
significant role in determining assignments, and their

clout with the Chief of General Staff is great. None of
the generals will let unwanted persons intrude on his
turf. Sometimes he prefers a less worthy candidate
who is one of "his" men over better candidates who
are "outsiders." The worst fate of all awaits a candidate who had never been under the command of any
of his judges. All one can do when facing such a
forum is pray... .

As soon as the COGS (Chief of General Staff) decides
who goes where, even before the Minister of Defense
confirms these decisions with his signature, the officer is notified. The candidates wait for the phone
call tensely. The COGS's office clerks become officials of the highest order. They are the ones who
break the news!

Consider that. How can it be that such sensitive
information is conveyed by lowly office clerks? And
what about the "losers"? Why aren't they informed,
too? Why aren't they updated officially and honor-
ably, with words of encouragement as they ponder
their alternatives? Only in the best cases are the lucky
winners summoned to their commanders, who inform them officially of their new duties. Usually they
are summoned to the COGS's bureau, where, along
with other officers changing functions, they are given
letters of appointment, new ranks or both, in a quick
mass ceremony.

IDF generals are chosen and appointed by the Chief
of General Staff, with the approval of the Minister of
Defense. Since the latter usually relies on the General
Staff's decision, the Staff wields unparalleled clout.

In civilian government, the Prime Minister, the
country's highest official, does not know who his/

her ministers will be even after the election returns are in. Various kinds of pressures are brought to bear, and the decisions usually reflect a compromise between the Prime Minister's desires and the system's demands. The Chief of General Staff, by contrast, has unlimited decision-making prerogatives and can easily persuade the Minister of Defense to approve his selections. The turnover of generals in the past few years has been high, too high. The Minister of Defense's approval signifies acceptance of the COGS's wishes. All this attests not to any criticism of the considerations but rather to the COGS's power.

All of us have to submit to judgment, explaining and elucidating our steps to our superiors. Ministerial responsibility for officer placement should be more than a rubber stamp devoid of governmental judgment. Without a supervisory system, those who carry out the decisions will find it hard to withstand undue pressure. Officers not handpicked by the COGS need a strong, objective agency that can overrule the COGS and act in accordance. Another possibility should be explored: requiring government approval of generals' appointments, as is the case with ministry directors-general and other senior civilian officials.

Those who determine people's future surely need to be sensitive and alert. Even as our decision-makers make their appointments as they see fit, they should also be forthcoming with the candidates, disclosing their considerations frankly. As for officers' "lobbying" with the generals, I find it tasteless. It does nothing for the men's own dignity, and it takes place in a climate of trepidation that only does harm. Above all, once an opinion or an evaluation is written, we've got to look the candidate in the eye, stand behind what we've written, and stand behind what we've written, and resist outside pressure concerning its substance.

Duties involving the safeguarding of soldiers' lives are entrusted to our very best commanders, the individuals best suited to command responsibility. It is important to appoint as field commanders only persons who have undergone their baptism of fire. Such men are like steel — the tempering they've gone through makes them better. Even for the purpose of persuading subordinates to sign on for career service, these men have the "right stuff"; everyone knows that nothing affects this particular decision as much as a commander's influence. A top-notch command corps attracts others of its kind — to everyone's benefit.

In mid-1975 the IDF awarded citations and medals to its most outstanding fighting men in a festive ceremony at Jerusalem's major convention center. Several of the recipients had fought with Battalion 77. Some were young fighters who had proven themselves under fire; others were seasoned veterans, now given appreciation for their role in but one of their many battles.

One of the men awarded the Distinguished Service Medal was my late brother Emmanuel. When his name was called, my parents mounted the stage, visibly moved, choking on their tears. I was proud but tormented about my brother, who had not lived to receive the medal himself. Emmanuel, I now knew, was the true hero of the family. All I could do was emulate him.

After this event we went on to the President's residence. There, in the courtyard, the President of Israel, Prof. Ephraim Katzir, awarded me the Medal of

Valor. There were eleven such awards, three of them posthumous. The latter were given to the parents.

The courtyard was packed with dignitaries seated amidst wreaths of flowers. The IDF General Staff, government ministers, public figures, and media personalities waited for the ceremony to begin as we, its objects, were led to the front row after refreshments.

One of those present, I noticed, was Dado — David Elazar, Chief of General Staff during the Yom Kippur War. He had come upon hard times. A commission of inquiry under Supreme Court Justice Shimon Agranat had found him responsible for the outcome of the war's first few days, and he had resigned from the service. I had not met with him since, but I shared his agony. I wished to approach him and shake his hand, but I refrained; he was mobbed with people. All I felt for him was esteem and admiration; he had played a major role in determining the course of my army career. In fact, it was his audacious decision to admit me to OCS against everyone else's judgment that had brought me to the President's residence.

Seated on the platform in the courtyard was the country's senior leadership: President Ephraim Katzir, Prime Minister Yitzhak Rabin, Defense Minister Shimon Peres, and incumbent COGS Motta Gur.

Once the award ceremony got underway, I found it highly impressive. From my position on the platform I knew beyond doubt that I was representing all the fighting men of Oz 77, from whom I derived my strength. Decorations such as these are not meant to assert that their bearers are genuine heroes. They indicate the presence of people and fighters who functioned successfully under fire, overcoming fear and dread. One of many such men, I was chosen by fate to represent them.

Yes, it's exciting to go about with the decoration on my chest. It's also a "heavy" experience. The yellow medallion stands out from afar, and its wearer is put the test wherever he goes, ever troubled by the possibility of disappointing those around him.

There on the platform, an emotional audience at my feet, I contemplated my brother Emmanuel, my wife's brother Ilan, and my close friends who had fallen in battle.

Israel has many heroes. Some were thrust into the limelight, others less so. Many of my country's genuine heroes will never be decorated, for they took the stories of their valor to their graves.

To the Golan Heights via Israel TV

On my way to the Golan, I stopped off at home. With tension riding high on the Heights, the transfer of command of the 7th Brigade from Ori Orr to myself was postponed. I tried to refrain from attaching further significance to this decision. Rumors of the kind that only an army can generate sniggered that I wouldn't get the brigade after all. Like many of my colleagues, I never considered a new appointment as "sewn up" until the baton was in my hand. Last-minute turnabouts were everyday occurrences.

But a two-month postponement? Tensely I waited for the redeeming phone call that would confirm the command position I had long desired. I was sure it wouldn't fall through this time. I'd get the brigade. I took advantage of the unplanned furlough to tour America with Dalia — a long-delayed honeymoon and our first such experience. It was unforgettable, instructive, and exciting.

As I stayed "on hold," some schemers back home

concocted a plot. Amos Ettinger of Israel Television, producer of the local version of "This is Your Life," dug into my past and set me up. Apart from several phone calls in which the other end disconnected before I could answer, I noticed nothing. Behind my back, however, Amos interrogated relatives and friends, culling particularly piquant bits of information from Dalia. Everyone but me was in on the secret.

At this stage, I was invited to appear on a TV program for teenagers called "Lad and Lass," the idea being to improve the motivation of youngsters on the verge of induction. I was hesitant about being interviewed, fearful of too much media. My book was about to come out; I'd have to face the spotlights in any event. I did not want to hog the stage, crowding out my comrades. Their role in the Yom Kippur War was no less valorous than mine; I had merely been luckier and had stayed alive.

My indecision did not help. By order of armored corps commander Mussa Peled, I was brought to the TV studio. There the surprise awaited me: members of my class, teachers all the way back to kindergarten, army buddies, and, of course, my family — all were seated in exemplary order and wearing smiles that said "We put it over on him!" When they turned the microphones and the spotlights in my direction, my embarrassment faded. All I needed to do was to act like a tank commander in a firing position... .

The show was televised a few days after I reported to the 7th Brigade. For one evening I was a guest in many Israelis' homes. The "ratings" were upbeat and the reactions enthusiastic, but they left me with a clear-cut task for the short term: to lower my profile.

Otherwise people around me would let their resentment get the better of them.

I then went through a hard period, contending with a difficulty I had not previously known. Suddenly I had to make sure my friends stayed friends. They looked at me in ways that did not always suggest affection or comradeship. I felt I was being pricked with little knives, and soon I learned what they were. Scurrilous, vicious gossip sprouted all around me. Kahalani had become a target, the man everyone loved to hate.

It's inevitable, logic and common sense told me. At the age of 31, still young and thin-skinned, I stood alone, sopping it up, swallowing hard, marshaling all my patience so as not to react. To my displeasure, people always "volunteered" to update me on information I did not care to hear. "He's already over his head." "Even battalion command was too much for him." "He's OK for operating a few tanks in the field, but no more." "No command and leadership ability." "He's destroying the 7th Brigade," "All the attention went to his head." "In the 7th Brigade they salute Oz 77, not him." Those were the remarks of people in uniform. I could only contrast them with the sympathy I received in civilian circles.

I had believed that my commanders, if no one else, would stand in the breach. But drops of venom trickled to them, too, and fissures appeared even in their stone wall. I knew I could respond in one language only: achievements in the field. No one could attack top results with fabricated tales. I resolved to force those who ridiculed me to agree on one thing: that the brigade under my command could and would discharge any duty and pass any test. I swallowed my bile, counted to ten — and went to work.

13. THE SEVENTH
BRIGADE

In early December, 1975, I reported to the Golan Heights to take over the 7th Brigade. Excitement and festivity were in the air at brigade headquarters as it came time to exchange commanders. I was thrilled, too. Understanding why, Yanush led me outside.

"Kahalani, there's a lot of work to do with the brigade. The way I know you, you'll get under everyone's skin and make them perform. I just wanted to tell you ... that I really hope for your sake that nothing's happened to you — that all the publicity and media around you lately haven't done something to you." I wanted to interrupt him, tell him what was on my mind. I restrained myself.

"I want one thing from you," Yanush continued. "Try to stay the same Kahalani, the one everyone knows."

He meant it, and I was embarrassed. I stared at the ground, bent over, picked up a small basalt stone and rolled it in my fingers.

"You see this stone? No matter how much I roll it, it doesn't change its shape. Believe me, I haven't changed and I won't change."

I appreciated Yanush for his remark. It's best to hear such things directly, not in the form of rumors behind your back.

Ori Orr, my predecessor, handed me the brigade banner in a brief ceremony. With a few sentences I set forth several principles I would apply toward the brigade. Then I replied to the well-wishers, stressing, of course, my awareness of the weight of responsibility I would assume from that moment on. Ori Orr had been very highly regarded by his men. I had no fears about stepping into his shoes when it came to human relations, but I knew that the other aspects of my arrival would prove to be an obstacle course.

By that afternoon, having received my letter of appointment from Chief of General Staff Motta Gur, the brigade was mine. Yanush left his position as division commander the same day, handing command to his deputy, Amir Drori.

At the time the 7th Brigade was responsible for one sector of the Golan Heights, extending to the border fence. The customary "overlap" with Ori was unusually short this time, about two days, leaving me to toil day and night to master every detail. I was used to that.

My command methodology was different from that of my predecessor. Ori believed in decentralization, making routine battalion life easier. I took more of a hands-on approach. Therefore I set myself two aims: maximizing my own knowledge and immediately alerting the men to the nature of the change, even if my demands would put them under pressure.

I set one inviolable rule: never to besmirch my predecessor, even by way of hint. I acted as I believed best, my attention focused on the future. Many commanders brag about their unit's achievements, emphasizing the "shambles" they had found upon assuming command. "The battalion just got back on the track." "Finally we dug ourselves out of the mud." "For the first time in years you see soldiers smiling in our unit." "Since I came aboard, not a single tank has missed its targets." "It took me a long time to bring the unit up to the level you see today." This manner of speaking, so familiar, is not to my liking. Yes, any commander wants to make himself look good. This kind of talk, however, leaves the opposite impression: such a commander devalues himself... and my opinion of him.

I plowed into the brigade full-force. I sat with each commander, discussing his plans and the kinds of maneuvers he was to perform. We still bore the scars of the Yom Kippur War. The next war, we imagined, would be like the previous one; therefore we arrayed our forces for the sector's defense, the specific aim being to stop the Syrians at some distance or in the Golan minefields.

Then I took up the matter of discipline. Instinct told me that my orders, the results of profound thought and many hours of work, were not always being obeyed in the field. The men were receiving them in muddled, meaningless form. I understood the problem: a brigade commander is liable to lose direct contact with the men and may pay for that with the obfuscation of his orders. To ensure success, I would have to face the men and convince them to trust me and my approach. Unmediated contact is always the best, most reliable kind. To achieve it I would have to work hard, sometimes sacrificing precious time designated for the administration of my vast formation. However, I would not ever accept the possibility that my orders would be either disobeyed or obeyed as their recipients deemed convenient.

In 1976-77, defense of the Golan Heights was entrusted to infantry and armored brigades under the command of a single headquarters. Their orders were to hold the Syrians back along the border. Tank battalions were set up several kilometers from the border. At an agreed-upon signal they were to move toward the border and deploy among our positions along the border fence, deployed for what we call "current defense." Thus the sector would be covered. Given the nature of this deployment, the defense of a given salient or position was sometimes entrusted to a few tanks only — a grave responsibility for their crews.

The forces that controlled the sector in "peacetime" included regular infantry, armored, engineering, and artillery units. In case of attack, these forces would hold on until the reserves mobilized and reached the Golan Heights. These fresh, strong reinforcements would take up position in the next of a series of obstacle positions, thus presenting greater resistance to any attempted Syrian incursion. The reservists were virtually part of the Golan landscape in their behavior and their familiarity with the field, the enemy, and the regular forces. To this day, this defense array has never been put to the test. Still, we engaged in maneuvers and drills without letup, until we became a well-oiled machine.

The Heights bustled with intensive civilian settlement activity at that time. New settlements had been founded since the Yom Kippur war, as if the war had intensified Israel's determination to cling to the territory. We came under pressure to hand over firing grounds between the roads for cultivation and pastures. Other areas were earmarked for building. The cornerstone for a new Israeli city, Katzrin, was laid. It seemed as if the planners were deliberately out to consume our firing areas.

The nature of service on the Golan was and remains totally different from that in Sinai. Everyone felt the burden of responsibility and was required to be on high alert. Tension hovered overhead, cloud-like, without letup. All we needed was one quick glance to the west; the sight of Lake Kinneret, hardly 15 miles away, to remind everyone who and what we were defending. Watching children on their way to school every morning intensified this feeling.

The civilian settlers considered their role in defending the Golan as no less important than the army's. Something like a partnership of fate developed between us. Commanders on the Heights were given broad authority, and we were often torn between the residents' demands for farmland, pasture, roads, and our own training needs. When we let one of our training areas fall into disuse for several months, we suddenly found that it had become a wheat field. Moreover, it was easier to resolve that by pushing paths through the basalt boulders than by thrashing through the wheat... .

My brigade's three battalions were stationed at several kilometers' distance from one another. One of the battalions, the 82nd, was commanded by Meir Zamir, who had spent part of the Yom Kippur War under my command. Zamir guarded his battalion jealously, letting no outsider enter. At all costs he tried to prevent brigade-level interference in the battalion's affairs, as my protesting staff officers often told me. However, I was less concerned about

Zamir's methods than about his results, and these spoke for themselves.

The commander of Battalion Oz 77, Ori, had been my classmate in Command and Staff College. We had known each other since then but had never been more than casual friends. New to the brigade, Ori found it hard to integrate. He toiled energetically to care for bereaved families and develop battalion pride. This, to me, was a sign of maturity and experience.

The third battalion, known as "Romah" (Hebrew for "spear"), was entrusted to Avner. Avner was a devoted and honest man who used straight talk and knew how to take it. That is how brigade headquarters addressed itself both to him and to his battalion. Avner was a "technocrat." He could always pinpoint any malfunction in my jeep and explain why the number of the brigade's tanks that got stuck in the mud was X and not X plus one. Before or during drills he could be seen plying the fields of the Golan on horseback. I ordered him to equip himself with a two-way radio and an antenna before going out on these journeys, so he could respond when we searched for him.

Amir Drori, my superior as division commander, was available around the clock. Rarely have I encountered anyone with a stronger work ethic. I never saw him twiddling his thumbs. He worked ceaselessly, always serious, nails always neatly trimmed. Our relations were amicable although never intimate; Amir kept himself at a distance even at times when, I sensed, he yearned for an attentive ear.

Throughout Amir's tenure, Barak Brigade and mine competed regularly in drills with such ferocity that an unhealthy state of tension developed between them. Competition itself is meant only to help. Unfortunately, however, we had to judge each other's performance in the drills, and we found ourselves dragged into arguments every time. The rules and the judges' impartiality were continual bones of contention, which always left a bad taste in our mouths.

The drills were innumerable. I volunteered for every possible drill, accompanying every formation that reached the area. My crewmen and their commanders gained more from the drills than training experience only; they had the opportunity to fire more ammo and to run the tanks longer than their allotments permitted.

As brigade commander, I had the privilege of being surrounded with superb officers with especially strong work ethics. My operations officer was Chen Y., who later took over Avner's battalion. Jackson, my quartermaster, had come with me from Tze'elim. Amir, followed by Asher, were my intelligence officers. Ya'akov was my adjutant officer until he was replaced by Carmi Ness. Yosha was responsible for ordinance. My second-in-command turned out to be Ami Morag, my late brother Emmanuel's battalion commander in Sinai. Ami was subsequently replaced by my good friend Yossi Melamed, who in turn gave way to Avner.

Dalia and I decided without hesitation to move to the north. We applied to Kibbutz Degania Bet, a renowned, long-established collective settlement at the southern tip of Lake Kinneret, and after some time were admitted. Dalia's sister Yona and her husband Arye Yoram, members of the kibbutz, were delighted at our arrival. We were given our own house — something of a luxury in the kibbutz mindset — which accommodated the whole family with room to spare.

Dror was in fourth grade, Vardit in kindergarten. Dalia taught guitar on the kibbutz and divided her remaining time between the kindergarten and the kitchen. Only I had the privilege of being exempt from the duty rotation.

The warm welcome quickly made us part of the local landscape. Relocating my home to the base of the Golan Heights, however, did not enable me to spend more time at home, nor did it increase the number of furloughs. It took me only about an hour to drive home, but endless work and innumerable alerts determined my schedule. Dalia soon understood that her proximity to the Golan Heights was an optical illusion. Although I, too, could almost see our house from the camp, we both knew my responsibilities made home much farther away than it looked.

The Four Officers Affair

One night, as I was about to turn in, I got a call from Zamir, commander of the 82nd Battalion.

"Sorry I'm calling so late," he began.

"It's never too late for a brigade commander," I said reassuringly, indicating that he should continue.

"Four of the officers we're supposed to promote to lieutenant tomorrow don't want to be given the rank by you," said Zamir, matter-of-factly.

An unusual request indeed, undoubtedly concocted by someone with malicious intentions. Zamir was referring to his battalion's operations officer, a deputy company commander, and two platoon commanders. I knew them all. I also knew that at least two of them had fathers with glittering military histories and key positions in the national leadership. Their kids were "sons of so-and-so." That didn't frighten me, but I was concerned about the public repercussions liable to result from the episode.

Zamir then explained the motives of the strange quartet. I had interfered too much in the battalion's routine. Now I understood everything. This was their reaction to an action I had taken against Zamir's operations officer. On several occasions my own operations officer had complained that the man had failed to appear at brigade-level meetings and had hidden behind Zamir's excuses. After repeated warnings, I had put the officer on disciplinary trial.

I had considered the episode a battalion-level problem that Zamir could have solved by himself. Now that they'd thrown the ball into my court, however, I would handle it my way.

"Have 'em report to me tomorrow morning," I concluded.

"To get promoted?" Zamir asked.

"Negative. For a talk. Then we'll see."

I was looking forward to that talk. It was clear, however, that the others were looking forward to its results with greater anticipation. I did not know how far the story had spread or who knew about it, but one thing was sure: after the talk it would spread like an epidemic and give my "admirers" further evidence of my inability to control the brigade. In short, it was another attempt to test my patience and endurance.

Thoughts raced through my head. Finally I decided that they would either accept their new ranks from me or get kicked out of the brigade, with all that this implied.

The four rebels, along with Zamir, stepped into my office the next morning and seated themselves at either side of the table. They exuded self-confidence, enjoying the game, proud as roosters for having proven their manhood. Contrary to my custom, I did not smile. Instead I examined them gravely from the moment they entered.

I got straight to the point, sparing the prefaces. "Zamir, your battalion commander says you object to getting your lieutenants' bars from me. I understand you have some complaints about how I run the brigade."

The four shifted nervously in their chairs. Thus far none of them dared to look me in the eye.

"I thought I should talk with you and clarify a few things that you may not understand. In the 7th Brigade, I'm the one who gives out the ranks, so I'm not going to discuss that with you. But if you've got complaints that you'd like to tell me about, my door's open, just as it always was and always will be for any soldier in the brigade who wants to contact me."

It was my opponents' turn to speak. By now they were looking at me, but their response was brief and confused. Somewhere in their stuttering I heard something about excessive interference in battalion affairs. Then Zamir spoke, stressing that he had tried to elucidate the brigade commander's attitude and had made every effort to talk them out of their protest.

Before answering, I looked each of the recalcitrants in the eye.

"I won't address myself to each of you separately, because you're all giving me the same message. What you're accusing me of, even if not in so many words, is that I tried your operations officer just because I felt like it. Do you imagine that I would just ignore an infraction of discipline that's been committed who knows how many times? An operations officer who hides behind his battalion commander so he won't have to report to the brigade operations officer! I won't let things like that go on. I don't interfere with how the battalion is run, but if I ever have to, it'll be between me and your battalion commander. I assume that even you platoon commanders don't let Tank 3A dictate your agenda to you. I'd also like to believe that if Tank 3A doesn't perform as it should, you'll know how to climb in and tell 'em how to make it perform better."

No one said a word. Zamir shifted his gaze from me to the unhappy four and back again. I could almost feel my words sinking in.

"The way you decided to protest is unique and original," I went on. "I won't try to talk you into accepting your lieutenants' bars in my office. I just want to make it clear that not accepting them in this office means not getting them anywhere else in the brigade, and I presume the candidates for the rank will not stay with the brigade."

"Sir, could we have some time to think it over?" one of them broke in.

"I've got no time for negotiations. At 1000 hours we'll hold the ceremony here, in this office. Whoever shows up will get the rank, and whoever doesn't — I'll understand that he doesn't want it, and he'll understand that within a few hours he will no longer be part of the 7th Brigade. Dismissed."

I gestured to indicate that I was unwilling to discuss the matter further. Zamir signaled to the four to wait for him outside, and stayed in his seat.

"Sir, are you really going to kick them out of the brigade?"

"Yes. Within an hour after the end of the ceremony."

Zamir looked surprised. "Let me talk with them," he said in an attempt to calm me.

"Zamir, I ask you in no uncertain terms to say nothing to them. Nothing. Let 'em mull it over. They'll decide their future for themselves."

At exactly 1000 hours the four men reported to my office, joining several other officers who were up for promotion. After the brief ceremony, they asked for permission to remain in my office for a moment.

One of them began hesitantly: "Sir, we want to stay here and explain.... We feel uncomfortable about the whole matter and want to apologize."

One of his colleagues, more confident, went on: "I think, sir, that we thought you didn't understand us.... In any case, I think we didn't know you personally until now. We're sorry for what happened, and we hope you'll understand." The four fixed their eyes on me, waiting for my answer.

"I understand," I answered. I gave each of the men a parting handshake.

Subsequently, I got to know these men well, and all of us forgot the bitter aftertaste of the episode. One of them, Doron Levy, asked for career service in brigade headquarters, and I appointed him as the brigade's operations officer. He became one of those closest to me.

Never, however, did I forget the lessons of the affair. I learned then that my orders were not being construed and obeyed as given. Now, too, it was clear to me that my brigade's personnel did not know the real Kahalani. By being involved in all brigade affairs, I had earned myself the image of a martinet. Still, I had always made sure never to lose sensitivity toward those around me, and to make myself available and attentive to them at all times. Even though I refused to sweep painful subjects under the carpet, I tried hard to avoid personally offending officers and enlisted men. This particular affair took place shortly after I had joined the brigade. I had not yet reached every corner, had not yet talked with all the men.

I'm facing a different kind of leadership problem, I told myself: that of the commander of a vast system who can neither establish a relationship with nor apply his influence to each and every one of its personnel. I had to bypass the battalion commanders and try to devolve something of my authority to the company and platoon commanders. I had messages to convey to them, lessons to contribute to them, and the distance from my office to the lowest-ranking field commanders was great, in a sense other than that of kilometers.

Unlike a battalion commander, a brigade commander simply cannot meet with his soldiers on a day-to-day basis. Battalions are by nature their commanders' little fiefdoms, as mine had been when I occupied that position. A brigade commander's orders, by contrast, pass through a lengthy hierarchy from the brigade's staff officers to the battalion commanders and battalion staffs. The effect is reminiscent of the children's game "telephone." Thus far I had always known how to face my men and look them in the eye, and had always felt that if only they understood the spirit of my instructions they would follow me. I still met with the soldiers, to be sure, but from their standpoint I was someone who had descended from the Pantheon. I'd finish my remarks and walk away, leaving only the platoon and company commanders at their side. Leadership and command on my present level were different from anything I had known. The brigade commander has to downscale his expectations of his ability to motivate his fighting men by mere personal example. He has to acquire and apply additional techniques.

Command and leadership

The issue of command and leadership takes on a different hue on each rung of the army ladder.

The traditional IDF cry of "Follow me!" prevails on the platoon and company levels. Platoon and company commanders march at the head of their formations, pulling everyone else in their wake. Battalion and brigade commanders exercise leadership and control from a position in the middle. On the division level, a general is entrusted with large forces deployed over a much larger area. Here the commander's physical location is not important, as long as he can motivate and control the forces from wherever he is.

There is no doubt that the true test of a commander and leader is on the battlefield. It is to pass this test that he runs the formation when it is not in action, and on this basis he applies his leadership. Montgomery defined leadership as the will to exercise control combined with a nature that evokes trust. Each of us may posit his own definition, but it is the "final exam" that counts.

Leadership is the ability to make people and groups do what you want. The method varies from one commander to another, and the formula that motivates one person may not budge someone else. Two commanders may lead their respective formations in their own ways, each obtaining equally good results.

The test of leadership is whether soldiers are willing to go to war under your command. Soldiers follow the leaders in whom they believe, who know how to command and get the most out of them, and who can get them home safe and sound by the time the guns fall silent.

Those who aspire to leadership should consider several facts at the heart of the issue:

—Soldiers look for commanders and leaders.

—Soldiers are willing to give everything they've got for their commanders.

—Fighting men want to trust and believe in their commanders.

—There can be no leadership in the absence of personal, direct contact.

—One cannot lead without a desire to control events.

—One cannot lead without a goal for which to strive.

—One cannot lead without the ability to inspire enthusiasm in an entire formation and in individual soldiers.

—One cannot lead without the ability to bring about victory or achievements.

—No leader is indifferent.

—No leader is insensitive to human life.

—Leaders do not necessarily have to be similar in their traits or methods.

It is also important for the would-be commander to be aware of several attributes and skills, without which he or she will find it virtually impossible to motivate people. The commander must:

—have self-confidence and faith in his or her ability to attain the goal.

—inspire trust.

—understand the soldier's psyche.

—be conscious of what others are thinking about him.

—display thorough professionalism.

—be courageous and steadfast.

—prioritize.

—be informed and up-to-date.

—know his or her subordinates personally.

—take the initiative.

—know how to make decisions.

—have and use common sense.

—be consistent.

—display humor and tact.

The more leaders follow the path expected of them, the greater their chances of success will be. Even the lowest ranking of subordinates have to know who they are fighting for, the figure behind the orders. A formation's attitude towards its commander depends on the position he chooses to adopt within it. Commanders have to be themselves, developing and emphasizing their natural attributes rather than adopting those of others. They have to know how to elucidate and persuade — and, when these tactics prove inadequate, how to twist arms.

Commanders who meet with difficult situations and find themselves unable to continue motivating their units should never sink into indifference. Once indifference sets in, loss of control is not far behind. Inconsistency on a commander's part sows doubt, confusion, and loss of faith in his subordinates' minds.

Any commander who thinks this is too much to demand should request reassignment. And the faster he do so, the better it will for his country's security.

Routine in a wasteland of basalt

Within a few months the brigade had become part of my body and soul, and I became part of the Golan landscape. I got to know the place and, while scouting for new training areas and firing directions, enjoyed the scenery.

One of my activities involved the creation of new tank roads. One day I loaded the brigade staff into a personnel carrier and set out to examine the route the Syrians had used to fool us. Just then the personnel carrier tumbled over a cliff, ourselves inside. Its front end was smashed to pieces, and the passengers almost met their Maker, but miraculously, no-one was injured.

Too impatient to wait for the tractors to level the road, the first tanks began to use the route, disregarding the hard going. Since then this path has become one of area's busiest, with heavy two-way traffic of tanks and personnel carriers during maneuvers.

I have always considered symbols very important, not least among them being the national flag. When I first joined the brigade as a junior officer, I tried to memorize the brigade's anthem but quickly forgot it; it was poorly suited to the spirit and the place. Now I rewrote the lyrics for the Golan Heights and our times, adding a stanza on the Yom Kippur War and mentioning the names of the battalions. I required all enlisted men and commanders to memorize the anthem; until they did so they were to carry copies of the lyrics around in their shirt pockets. I remember their triumphant smiles when I ordered to them to produce that scrap of paper.

Field days, contests between battalions, and study of the brigade's combat history added to the men's feeling of uniqueness and inspired them to demand more and more of themselves. Another fact magnified our pride: every tank newly placed in service in the IDF was sent to the 7th Brigade to be broken in. The head of the General Staff quartermaster's branch, Maj. Gen. Arye Levy, gave us a present: a spacious new building which we quickly designated as our "battle heritage" room. It rapidly filled up with documents on the brigade's battles and casualties. All the men visited it, entering with curiosity and exiting with a combination of respect and awe.

Eventually, Chief of General Staff Motta Gur tried to appoint Lt. Col. Menahem Einan as my replacement. Menahem, who had been waiting for the assignment, pressured Motta, while I made it clear that I had no intention of leaving the brigade until I'd presided over it for two years. This was good enough for OC Command Rafael Eitan ("Raful"), but Motta, while understanding my feelings, made no promises. Plenty of young officers were pressing him for command of regular brigades. In the end, I won: the brigade remained mine for two years.

Commanders and staff officers in the brigade were replaced several times during my tenure. Ephraim Laor, who fought in my battalion in the Yom Kippur War, took over the 82nd from Zamir. Ilan M. was given the 77th, followed by Moshe P. Chen Y., the brigade operation officer, took over Romah. A brigade's greatness lies in its ability to develop its own commanders; almost all commanders in the 7th Brigade were home-grown.

In early 1977 I began to limp; my right knee could no longer take the strain. Surgery was the only solution. After Dr. Horoshovsky had cut, repaired, and stitched, I woke up in a cast.

During recuperation, one of my visitors was Yanush. Since I had been out of touch for some time, he described a little of what was happening behind my back.

A few months after I had been appointed brigade commander, Yanush asked Raful, then OC Command, to crack down on me. According to reports he had received, I was treating the brigade in cavalier, roughshod fashion.

"I don't know what you all want from Kahalani," Raful replied. "I can tell you the 7th Brigade is top-notch. Everything it does, from maneuvers to operational activity, it does very well. That means its commander is a real commander. Leave him alone."

I was pleased to hear Raful's opinion. I considered it more important, however, to know that he could examine the facts and see through malicious gossip.

A senior commander is a man alone. He makes most of his decisions after serious contemplation, consulting no-one. His circle of friends and close acquaintances contract; his physical distance from them grows. He has no way to share his experiences and no one to share them with. If he tries to use his subordinates for this purpose, he may quickly destroy a system built with great toil.

During most of my two years as commander of the 7th Brigade, I had the privilege of having Yossi Melamed as my second-in-command. Our friendship, already close, took on special meaning at that time. Both of us, however, had the sense to draw the line between friendship and the business-only relationship between a commander and his deputy.

A commander's attitude toward his staff officers varies in keeping with his nature. Staff officers are a commander's executive arm, and, as such, the commander has to give them the executive power and maneuvering room they need to make decisions. Every commander often meets with a dilemma: when staff and field unit decisions clash, whose side do you take? You can back your staff against the formations, or allow the field commanders to carry out only some of the staff officers' instructions. If you take the latter course, currying favor with the formation commanders at the staff's expense, you'll quickly find yourself swamped with papers. From that moment on, every document and operational order will cross your desk.

Obviously a staff officer is prone to error. Most such mistakes can be corrected. But if they know the commander's philosophy, act in its spirit, and keep sight of the goal he sets, their work will be easier.

It is the staff officers' duty to see to the entire formation's needs rather than serving as their commander's personal aides. If they succeed in keeping their personalities distinct, the units subordinate to them will appreciate them more — as of course will their commander.

The kind of staff officer I always sought was the autonomous type who minimized the number of loose ends brought to me for resolution. I always felt that a staff officer who found it hard to reflect his commander's intent and chafed under the burden of maintaining loyalty should find other duties.

Throughout my service on the Golan Heights, the 7th Brigade's primary concern was maneuvers. We engaged relentlessly in planning them and devising schemes to augment them. Commanders were judged by the size of the allocations they gathered for their formations, and spared no effort to obtain quantities of ammo and tank motor hours beyond allocation. Leaving our fighting men inadequately trained, we knew, was unforgivable.

Occasionally we were informed of budget cuts. These forced us to switch to centralized resource control and a relentless quest for efficiency measures. For the first time we began integrating others corps in our maneuvers. To Amir's credit as division commander, I note for the record that his decision to turn infantry, engineering, and artillery formations into armor units was a wise one, and well-implemented.

By this time our scavenging for additional ammo broke all records. Things reached such a state that men dragged ammunition meant for periods of alert from positions and ammo bunkers. On one of my visits to the training grounds, I was told that the shortage of ammo and tank hours was the most pressing problem of all. In contrast to all these, our old Centurions, now revitalized, were highly satisfying. They served us faithfully, never letting us down.

The brigade was given new radio protocols during my first week of command. I, too, acquired a new code name, Dror. That means two things in Hebrew: a swallow and a free spirit. I liked it so much that I kept it, even though the other protocols were changed every few weeks for security reasons.

Another practice I kept up was the "race to the ramps." Without warning I would activate a battalion's siren or fire a few rounds into the air. The battalion would leap to its feet, and within a few minutes all its tanks would race to the tank ramps abutting the border. To display my personal commitment to this "nuttiness," I timed them with a stopwatch. Sometimes I let the men see me advancing to one of my special observation positions; they would track me, pinpoint my position, and warn their comrades to be ready to "jump"...

All our actions had one ultimate aim: to make the residents of the Golan Heights confident that our soldiers were looking out for them at all times. All the fighting men knew that if the Syrians attacked, the victor would be the side that acted with greater speed and sophistication. A small force could stop a large one if it made correct use of terrain, minefields, and tank ramps. Our weapons were no better than the Syrians', and as for quantity, there was obviously no room for comparison. We were sure the Syrians would face us on equal terms one day, even though that day might be far off. The men hardly had to open their eyes to carry out their tasks. To prevent confusion in moments of agitation and tension, we knew we had to drill and redrill, practicing our operations and defense as often as possible.

Then my two years were up; it was time to yield my position and move on. I hoped to return to the Golan for a third stint, but I knew I was parting with the 7th Brigade itself for good. It was not a pleasant thought.

Friday morning, October 28, 1977, came too quickly for me. In a festive ceremony I handed the brigade banner to my friend Yossi Ben-Hanan, who had won the "traditional" competition for the brigade commander's job, and pinned the brigade tag to his shirt. Ori Orr, fresh on the job as division commander, congratulated both of us, the departing and the incoming. Gabi, my veteran driver, had already loaded my car with all my personal possessions, including souvenirs that had accumulated in my office. Together we headed for the coastal plain.

Dalia and I had already bid farewell to Degania Bet and returned to Nes Ziona. The children could hardly tear themselves away from the kibbutz, and Dalia, too, found herself wishing to stay. Life on the kibbutz had been an memorable experience for all of us. Dalia was also on the verge of giving birth, and our schedule was such that the newborn would first see the world in Nes Ziona. So it was that our third child, a son, Dotan, was born three days after I left the brigade.

The birth was an ordeal for Dalia. Dalia was in agony and labor had to be induced. After she and Dotan were discharged from hospital, the pain returned. All the doctors but one agreed that the cause was an infection that would "go away." Only one woman physician was suspicious. After paying Dalia several house calls, she decided to take no more chances, and sent her back to the hospital for tests. A few hours later she was on the operating table; her uterus had ruptured in birth. Her life was in danger.

I sat outside the operating room, watching people run to and fro, without knowing what was going on inside. After great efforts and 12 transfusions they succeeded in stanching the hemorrhage. The family was engulfed in days of round-the-clock stress and anxiety. We sat at Dalia's bedside, hoping and praying, tensely monitoring every sign of recuperation.

I brought baby Dotan back to the hospital. I had no idea what to do with him; having spent my fatherhood years in the tanks, I had no experience in the care of infants. Surely the hospital had somebody who knew how to diaper and feed him! I met with point-blank refusal. They would not readmit an infant who had already been discharged. Delicately but stubbornly I explained the whole story until I made my breakthrough. The stone wall of dedicated nurses crumbled, and Dotan returned to the infants' ward. A few weeks later Dalia came home, and the demands of the expanded family slowly put the episode behind us.

14. TO THE UNITED STATES FOR STUDY

I had long dreamed about doing some advanced military studies in the United States. I knew I would have to wait a few years for my next promotion, and tried to persuade my commander that this trip was of special importance to me. While the decision was pending, I was assigned the position of deputy commander of a reserve division.

This was my first encounter with forces of a kind I had not known. It was also good training for a brigade commander who aspired to command a division. I had always regarded the division as a complex, massive organization, whose commander needed especially massive shoulders to stand up to its burdens. As I plunged into my temporary assignment, Armored Corps commander Mussa Peled gave me the good news: in May, 1978 I would go to the United States as a cadet in the American land forces' Command and Staff College in Kansas. About two months before departure, thrilled and well into the bustle of preparations, I got another call from Mussa: the Chief of General Staff had canceled my trip. Another officer had been chosen, a younger man who been given preference because of family problems.

I hung up and turned to Dalia. "Just what I was afraid of," I fumed. "We're staying put. Again they favor the ones who know how to apply pressure. Whoever said, 'Don't believe you're going until the plane's in the air,' was right!"

I asked for an appointment with the Chief of General Staff, if only to tell him what I thought of his decision. A few days later I was summoned to Motta. I tried to be polite, but in vain. Motta's bureau chief, my friend Haggai, had let him know what was coming before the meeting; all I could do was express my feelings in so many words. I'd been rooked, I said. I did not agree with his considerations and did not accept the motives. I left his bureau disgruntled and informed Dalia and the kids, "Unpack the suitcases and put the dreams on hold!"

But the surprises were not over. A few days later came another phone call. The Americans had approved a second IDF cadet. We were going after all!

There was still one more obstacle to cross: an English test at the American embassy. All the candidates had to pass it. I postponed this as long as I could, cracking the books day and night. After all, one of the purposes of the trip was to overcome my English language barrier once and for all. To this day I don't know how I managed to pass the test. Even had I failed, of course, the flight was two days away. It was too late to stop me.

Shortly before take-off I parted with Yanush, now OC Northern Command.

"Put one over all of them: take a junket all over the U.S.!" he said. "It'll be good to let your hair down for awhile. And don't worry about what'll happen later; when you get back you'll be a division commander!"

Yanush sounded like he meant it. Moreover, he was a man of his word.

Innocent abroad

This journey into the unknown — foreign, strange America — enchanted us all. More enchanting still was the idea of embarking on a full year together as a truly nuclear family. I would come home every day. Imagine!

We touched down in New York. Little Dotan was indifferent, dozing placidly in a little basket. Today he has to open the photo albums to realize that he was really there. Dror and Vardit were tense and excited — everything was so big, and nothing but English all around. So they'd have to learn English, too!

As we were going through passport control, I heard the strains of familiar, pleasant Israeli-Yemenite music. Proceeding to the arrival terminal, we were surprised to find a group of several dozen Israelis — a reception committee — showering us with enthusiastic singing and wreaths of flowers. Had we landed in Rosh Ha'ayin, Israel's Yemenite capital? No, these were Israelis of Yemenite origin living in New York. Ovadia Ben-Shalom, president of the Society for the Promotion of Israeli Society and Culture, had let them know we were coming.

Hardly giving us time to recover from the surprise, they loaded us and our baggage into their cars and drove us to a sumptuous Yemenite feast. The traditional, familiar delicacies suddenly seemed tastier and more plentiful in New York than in Israel. As a disciplined soldier I did as my hosts instructed, following the program they had drawn up for me. My flightmates — Col. Amos Katz, a comrade from the 79th Battalion, Lt. Col. Amiram Levin, and their families — did not believe their eyes. Only in our dreams could we have asked for the warmth and love that were lavished on us.

We moved on to Washington for another two weeks of English study. From there we drove to Fort Leavenworth, near Kansas City, taking a long, interesting route. At Leavenworth we were greeted warmly by an American officer who had been appointed our "foster parent"; a local Jewish family, too, tended to our every need. It was indeed a soft landing.

The dimensions and scale of the American command and staff college defied any attempt at comparison with the Israeli version. It had 1,000 cadets, including 100 from fifty foreign countries. As a veteran soldier I took little interest in the purely military studies. The subject matter on diverse security, on the other hand, enriched me greatly, and this first close-up encounter with the United States Army was fascinating. I discovered that my American colleagues were dedicated, highly motivated officers who loved their homeland and were proud of it, saluting the flag with whole-hearted respect and singing the national anthem with fervor. Many had completed master's degrees, a feat of which few Israeli officers could boast. Among the three Israeli officers in attendance, none even held a B.A.

I made friends with the cadets from the allied countries. In our many hours together they taught me much about their countries — things one does not find in geography books — and forged highly satisfying relationships that have lasted to this day. The only people who steered clear of us were our "cousins," and there were not a few of them. That was the year Israel and Egypt had signed their peace treaty; even so, neither side initiated contact, each ignoring the other.

The nature of studies in the American Command and Staff College, too, was different from that offered at the Israeli facility. The cadets, coming from every part of the world where American forces were stationed, displayed strong values and cultured, firmly-rooted behavior patterns. But in the military sphere, to my surprise, they proved to be outrageously inexperienced and, consequently, unforgivably naive. Real war, of course, was nothing like its depiction in the books that served as the basis for their military training. One could not help but notice an imbalance in the study program: heavy emphasis on senior-echelon and national issues, in contrast to the little time allotted to practical discussion of the daily routine of a major or lieutenant general commanding a formation of fighting men.

Each class had about 60 participants, and almost all instruction was in the form of frontal lectures. Each cadet was given a number by which his test scores were listed on a bulletin board. Group work was rare. Joint discussions, too, were infrequent. Even on those few occasions the groups were too large, making it hard to follow the discussion and impossible to express oneself individually.

My own personal war was with the English language. At first I listened to the lectures without understanding much; when the lecturer had a heavy Southern accent, my ordeal was twice as harsh. Every day I spent hours in the language lab, drilling nouns and verbs into my head. The effort paid off: by the end of the year I felt I had won. In mid-year a friend of mine, Lt. Col. Shlomo Cohen, reached the U.S. Desperately he phoned me for some advice: he was losing his war with English! Having survived this baptism of fire, I put him at ease: "If all the kids in the street speak English, so can we!"

Dror and Vardit, too, found it hard at first. In time, however, they picked up the language, adjusted to their peers, and took to the country as a fish to water. Only Dotan got by with no difficulties at all. He spent most of his time with his mother, who spent her time taking advantage of sales and, together with the rest of us, helping our youngest progeny develop. We were not house-bound, of course. We exploited my year of studies for innumerable outings, spending every day sightseeing near and far, crisscrossing the U.S. east to west, north to south.

Near the end of the year my parents, too, came to Kansas. What a thrill it was to greet them at the airport. Imagine: from little Nes Ziona straight to the heartland of America! To be sure, airport inspectors confiscated the avocados, lemons, and Yemenite delicacies they had carried with them, but the taste of home they had brought was not impaired. My mother was disoriented for a few days, stunned by the magnitude and the affluence of the new surroundings. And my father? The very next day he set out alone to explore the town's streets. He hardly knew a word of English, so he dusted off his Yiddish, set it to an American accent as best he could perceive it, and plunged in without embarrassment. They spent several months with us — a joyous period that ended with a three-week tour, winding up the entire year.

As I have mentioned, our classmates included several "cousins," from every Arab country except for Syria, Iraq, and South Yemen. The familiar sound of Arabic was heard in every corner; briefly I wondered if I had not stumbled into an Israeli university rather than a military facility in the middle of the U.S. When Amos, Amiram, and I tried to greet them as they passed, they either looked down or turned away. Still I could see the hatred in their eyes. Eventually I discovered that the Arabs had checked me out and knew that I was of Yemenite extraction. Whenever I was within earshot they became furtive and taciturn; after all, the swarthy Israeli officer might understand everything they said.

One of the college's traditions was to ask the foreign cadets to present their countries in a lecture to the entire student body and staff. To our surprise, there was no locally-available informational material that might "sell" Israel's beauty and uniqueness to this Gentile audience. Thus we phoned and wrote home for photographs, slides, and films. The lectures were successful in the end, but as we were preparing them we learned, to our chagrin, of the ineptitude of Israel's public relations efforts — the root of its failure throughout the world.

As the project got underway, the Saudis demonstratively insisted on being the last to present. Even though Israel was customarily last on the list, the Saudis got their way. All our appeals were of no use; quietly and obliquely the Americans indicated to us that we should give in.

The Saudis accompanied preparations for their lecture with a broad publicity campaign. Gold-framed photos were mounted in the halls, Saudi flags flapped in the breeze outside the lecture hall, and in a printed background sheet the organizers promised a gold Saudi coin to anyone who attended. All this had its effect, and the hall was filled to capacity. What the audience received was a comprehensive discussion of the enemies of Saudi Arabia: imperialism, Communism, and Zionism. Graphically the lecturers demonstrated Saudi Arabia's greatest problem: too much money. The lecture ended and we kept our mouths shut.

A few weeks later, a local newspaper ran a lengthy article inviting the public to a Saudi lecture on that country's viewpoint of the Israel-Egypt peace treaty, signed several months before. Masterminding these activities was a Saudi prince, son of the country's defense minister, who was attending the College. This young fellow strutted around the school like a peacock. Marines guarded his house 24 hours a day, and he would hop into his private plane now and then to spend a weekend in Paris.

All this made me boil. Unwilling to let it pass quietly, I prodded Amos and Amiram to help me mount a counter-offensive. I contacted Israel's military attache and told him what I had in mind; he gave me the go-ahead and best wishes. I also informed the college commander, who gave up his Saturday leisure and invited Amos, Amiram, and myself for an urgent talk.

We Israelis studied the college's rules pertaining to such projects. They explicitly prohibited outside advertising, allowing only ordinary signs posted on the bulletin boards. Additional media such as newspapers, flags, or photographs were forbidden. Having clarified this, I showed the American general the local paper containing the interview with the Saudi prince. He could hardly conceal his fury. Clearly the college had tried to downplay the importance of the article; perhaps it had deliberately ignored it.

"If the Saudis explain the way they perceive the peace treaty, and if they present Zionism as an enemy — I intend to pack up and leave," I said vehemently, looking the astonished college commander straight in the eye.

"Sir, I do not understand your behavior as commander of this school," Amiram added.

The general's patience gave out.

"Shut up," he shouted at Amiram.

We stood up to leave. Our message was unequivocal: the ball was in the general's court. He had a problem on his hands!

Two days later the Saudis delivered their lecture. The slides presenting Zionism as their country's nemesis had vanished, and not a word was said about the Israel-Egypt peace treaty. Planned to last a full hour, the lecture limped to its end in 20 minutes, and the surprised audience filed out quietly. It was a local victory in a battle whose likes we had not previously experienced — and the victory was ours.

Only when we returned to Israel after our year abroad did we realize how homesick we had been. It was a fine experience to have had, and have finished. For me, an officer who always served far from home, under difficult field conditions, it was a year-long gift. No package tour could have given me this kind of acquaintance with the greatest of superpowers.

My personal experience was also enriched tenfold. In the narrow domain of commanding military formations, of course, I had no need to broaden my resources of information and experience. But I learned one invaluable lesson: Israel must rely only on itself. We dare not hope, even for a moment, that an American expeditionary force will rescue us at our moment of need. It would arrive too late and find itself in unfamiliar terrain. Deep down, too, the American soldier would be an unmotivated fighter, for he would be defending someone else's homeland, not his own.

My intimate encounter with American Jews turned me into an expert on the subject of "aliya" — Jewish immigration to Israel — and shattered all my illusions. Only the handful of "fanatics" would come to live in Israel. What a pity.

"The finest year of my life" — was how Dalia summed up her experience. I wondered how it could be that the finest year in our lives would be the one spent abroad, instead of in Israel!

15. DIVISION COMMANDER — A MAILED FIST

I was swamped with work the moment I got off the plane. I returned to the north as deputy commander of a reserve division, and Raful, now Chief of General Staff, promised me a divisional command within a few years. The incumbent commander of my reserve division, Avraham Baram, was about to leave the service, and he shared with me apprehensions of a kind I had not known: the mixed emotions of a senior officer on the verge of retirement. The United States was quickly forgotten. My batteries were properly recharged; the motor was running full blast.

I took over the division in January, 1980. It was charged with defending the Golan Heights front, and I had to be on constant alert, ready for anything. Although young for a brigadier general — I was 35 — I felt mature enough for my duties. IDF division commanders hold much of the army's land might, much more than the three or four brigades listed in the order of battle. Division command is the springboard to senior positions. It was a new ball game.

The division is the army's fundamental building block. The Israeli division is composed of several thousand soldiers, the precise number depending on each division's internal structure. At its disposal are all the resources needed to wage autonomous warfare of all kinds on all fronts. Division headquarters is fully responsible for the tasks its formations are ordered to discharge.

An armored division has several tank brigades and infantry units. A supply group under division headquarters provides the field formations' needs. It supplies ammo, fuel, water, and food. It manages the medical groups and the ordinance units that repair and restore out-of-order and otherwise damaged equipment. Thus its embrace reaches every unit in the division.

Yet another group subordinate to headquarters is artillery, which deploys as needed to assist the brigades and battalions.

Inevitably, division headquarters has evolved into a coordinating body. It is this coordinating function that makes the division commander's responsibilities so weighty, so relentless.

Given my broad experience, I often tended to compound my duties by delving into battalion and brigade issues, suggesting or ordering my brigade commanders to act this way or that. I tried, however, to restrain myself. I knew my subordinate commanders had to gain their own experience and learn their own lessons. I was not always entitled to butt in. Even when I noticed points that warranted personal comment and emphasis, I contented myself with "ministerial" advice.

The tasks entrusted to a reserve division are difficult and complicated. The country's security depends on the quality of its reserve formations; the regular forces can contain the enemy for a short time but can never

overcome him unassisted. Ordinarily, however, a reserve division commander meets with his men only
once a year, at maneuvers time. A second annual
meeting takes place only when the division is called
up to secure the borders. The question perpetually
facing our senior officer corps is how to train a reservist properly when all we have is a few days once
a year. A second question is how much of our resources, such as ammo and fuel, to allot to the reservist to keep him fighting-fit. In our annual struggle
over the defense budget, the level of reservists' training is always at issue.

The division under my command was going through
a tumultuous training period. I went from one battalion to the next, one brigade to the next, taking full
advantage of my right to participate in the training of
each. I had my sights set on another position down
the line: command of the regular division on the Golan
Heights, the army's best, the one known as "Basalt."
It seemed only natural to succeed my present duties
with another stint on the Heights.

The struggle for division command, however, had
been resolved even before I joined the list of candidates. Command had been promised to Brig. Gen.
Matan Vilna'i, who had just completed his tenure as
chief infantry and paratroop officer. Why Matan, of
all people, a man with no armor background and no
association with this sector? I consulted with Yanush
at length. This didn't help; Yanush promised me nothing. Still I did not give up. I knew Raful himself had
promised Amram Mitzna's divisional command to
Matan. To be sure, Matan's credentials were better
than mine; he was a member of the General Staff and
knew all the generals personally. Mitzna, too, told

me the game was rigged. Everyone gave me encouragement, but even I believed it was a lost cause. My secretary, a woman from Kibbutz Beit Alfa, informed me that the "kibbutzniks" had discussed the competition at length, comparing each candidate's chances. Even Beit Alfa saw no chance of my taking over the Basalt Division.

Despite this gloomy picture, I met with Raful to speak my mind. He listened, smiled, and said:

"It'll be OK."

I stepped out of his office confused. What did that mean?

The day after Rosh Hashana 1981 I sat in my office late at night and went through the mail. I did not go home; it was my practice to spend two nights each week with the division. Suddenly the phone rang.

"The chief of Manpower Branch is looking for you," Ruthie informed me.

I was surprised and puzzled. Who else was working so late? Was something wrong with the division? With the men?

It was none other than Maj. Gen. Moshe Nativ on the line.

"Why the late hour? Should I put on a flack suit?" I asked.

"No. What're you talking about? How are you and how's the division?" Nativ sounded exuberant.

"I'm OK. So's the division."

"Avigdor, I talked with Raful today. We decided you're getting a regular division. Basalt."

"Run that past me again?"

"Just what you heard. It's all sewn up. We'll hand over command a few days from now."

It took me a moment or two to bring my excitement under control. "What about Mitzna?"

"He's going to Command and Staff. I want you to tell no one in the meantime, especially not Amir Drori."

Amir Drori was OC Northern Command, having replaced Yanush several months earlier.

"Amir still doesn't know about our decision. I haven't caught him, and I want to be the one to tell him." I was puzzled. How could Amir not know?

"Who'll take over for me?" I asked Nativ, pushing aside the other questions.

"David Katz." This was a surprise. Katz was not at the head of the list, and I wondered how he had passed the others. He did have two important advantages: Raful's sympathies and a previous tenure as Motta Gur's bureau chief.

"For you," Nativ went on, "there's no problem with Amir. He'll have a little problem with the appointment of David Katz, but that doesn't have to bother you." Nativ sounded sure of himself. There was no doubt: their decision was serious and was about to be implemented.

First I called home, of course. Late as it was, Dalia was wide awake and excited, sharing my delight at the good news. Only at the end did she mention the matter of greatest concern to her:

"And how often will you come home?"

I had commanded the reserve division for about two years. Again, as in the past, I had gained intimacy with the personnel. Again it was hard to part. Less than two days later Amir informed me officially of my new appointment; that very Friday afternoon I reported to the Chief of General Staff to receive it. My second-in-command, Yodke Peled, wanted to stay on as my deputy, and I agreed to this. Berko, Mitzna's deputy, was sent for a period of studies. Yodke and I bid our men farewell and hit the road.

A division in a field of basalt

Officially appointed on Friday, I was asked to hang on another two days before taking up my duties. Mitzna was about to wind up some operation that he had planned and was in charge of carrying out. It was the High Holiday season, the mid-September week between Rosh Hashana and Yom Kippur. Just then the world was taken by storm: Egyptian President Anwar Sadat had been assassinated. The IDF went on special alert, and I stayed home with nothing but a scrap of paper to my name. I was a division commander without a division. Katz had already taken over the reserve formation, and Mitzna was still winding things up with the one earmarked for me.

I blamed myself for my unwanted idleness. I should not have left the reserve division until Mitzna had cleared out for good! We were on alert and I was missing out. Perhaps war would break out, and here was Kahalani at home with a piece of paper! To compound the tension, Amir decided to postpone the transfer of command until things became clear. I spent, all together, three days waiting at home. Finally word came: report for transfer of command. It was the day before Yom Kippur.

A few minutes before the ceremony, an order came through from the Chief of General Staff's bureau: stop everything. Orders are orders; Mitzna and I could only sit around and continue overlapping. It was late morning and the last of the soldiers had gone home on holiday furlough. In another few hours the whole country would shut down for Yom Kippur. When the go-ahead finally came, there was no one around to share the festivities. We rounded up a few officers, had a couple of drinks, and passed the baton. Immediately afterwards I met with OC Command Amir and then went home for the holiday. The heavy responsibility was mine, but I had not yet met my men.

Matan Vilna'i took his defeat like a man. Encountering me by chance, he wished me the best of success. They'd promised Matan that he would get the division after me, once he'd completed his studies and retrained for armor. The latter would be especially demanding; as a paratrooper, Matan had about a year's worth of retraining ahead of him. The transition from infantry to armor entails relearning at every stage, from crewman to battalion commander.

My entry into the division met with no obstacles. After all, I knew the men — army people and civilians alike, knew the enemy well, and was as familiar with the Golan Heights as with the palm of my hand.

My new division, the conscript Basalt Division — formerly a reserve division commanded by Raful in the Yom Kippur War — was responsible for a sector of the Golan including Israeli settlements and Druse villages. The civilian residents of the Heights are considered an integral part of the area's defense forces. The division commander and his staff are in close contact with them, and it is the army that allocates land for maneuvers or for pasture and farming. The latter is a sensitive matter and the source of constant complaints and confrontations.

The casual observer may consider the Golan a vast domain, but that appearance is deceiving. Its width is

20 kilometers at most, and its length — from Mount Hermon to the Yarmuk River — is barely 100 kilometers. Much of the area is carved up by gullies and streams and does not lend itself to civilian settlement or army maneuvers. The territory near the border, too, is useless. So anyone in charge of dividing up the area has to be very judicious, making every effort to find the delicate balance between military and civilian needs. Much of the Golan terrain is good for agriculture and pasture, and the civilians know it well.

To carry out its maneuvers, the army often has to block roads so as not to endanger civilian travelers. A tank about to fire a shell needs about 20 kilometers of clear firing range, which is unavailable on the Golan Heights unless major roads are closed. There's no other way, but we know it's a real nuisance. Children do not get to school. Delivery of bread, milk, and other foodstuffs is delayed, sometimes for many hours. Everyday life is totally disrupted.

During my term as division commander on the Heights, I liaised with one Kobi, the civilian settlements' "operations officer" who communicated the residents' grievances to me. Kobi was an enormous man who traveled the Golan highways in a powerful American car with front-wheel drive, virtually sagging with communications gear. He never seemed to sleep. Thus the confrontations between military and civilians were harsh and frequent.

We also had trouble with the national water company, Mekorot. In the past few years Mekorot has been trying to keep the Golan's ample rainfall on the heights, thus pockmarking our firing grounds with little catchment basins. The momentum of civilian settlement also benefited from our involuntary contribution; one of our firing areas, its boundary several hundred meters east of the town of Katzrin, was suddenly rezoned for urban development, and the tanks had to further constrict their deployment in an area that was cramped to begin with. We even had to contend with cattle, which crossed the fences and grazed among the targets we had set up in the field.

I had to learn to walk a tightrope. I could not discharge my duties, I knew, unless I tried and tried again to strike the needed balance.

The division had had many commanders before me. Shmuel Gorodish had established it and was succeeded by Raful, Yanush, Amir Drori, Ori Orr, Uri Saguy, and Amram Mitzna. In IDF circles they called the commanders in the north the "Northern Mafia." If so, then the "godfather" was Raful, Raphael Eitan. Several of the aforementioned officers had even fought under his direct command. All of them, too, seemed to be one another's "cronies." Men from elsewhere in the country sought command of Golan brigades and divisions — and failed.

Some of the division's officers were old friends and acquaintances of mine. In charge of the 7th Brigade, now refitted with state-of-the-art Merkava tanks, was Eitan Kaouli, my deputy in the Yom Kippur War. Barak Brigade, a Centurion formation, was commanded by Yossi Melamed, my friend and former deputy in the 7th Brigade. Ehud Gross, subsequently the IDF's Chief Education Officer, commanded a reserve tank brigade. Other brigades were under Eli Shalem and Haggai L. The artillery group was under Itzik Gazit, with whom I had worked in the past. The maintenance group, a reserve formation, was under Sal'i. Zion Ziv commanded still another brigade, and

Yomi was in charge of the brigade stationed closest to the border. My deputy, Yodke K., accompanied me to the division, and Ron Bagg spent a brief period of time as chief of division staff.

Several days after I took up my position, the government, at Prime Minister Menachem Begin's initiative, resolved in favor of applying Israeli law and jurisdiction to the Golan Heights. The Knesset ratified this move, initiated by Prime Minister Menachem Begin, with record speed. Henceforth the Golan, Jews and Druse alike, would be treated like any other part of Israel in the eyes of the law.

The Jewish settlements were jubilant; from that moment their future was more secure. The sight of government ministries and courts hastily setting up Golan branch offices attested that no one intended to retreat from this territory. I visited the reveling locals to congratulate them. While acknowledging the crucial importance of the new law, as an army man I refrained from expressing my opinion in public.

For the Druse, by contrast, the de facto annexation of the Golan Heights was a blow. True, the military government was dismantled; no longer were the Druse under occupation, with all that this implied. However, their new status as Israeli citizens was a profound transition for people who lived under Syrian dictator Hafez Assad's watchful eye and did everything they could to display allegiance to "Mother Syria." For some time the Druse seemed to be groping, waiting for the moment they could stage their protest.

My headquarters was no longer involved in Druse village affairs; rather we were engrossed in preparations and alerts for Operation Peace for Galilee. Just then, when our minds were on Lebanon and our eyes on the main objective — defending the Golan Heights — the Druse went into action. The situation soon became intolerable, and the army had to reenter the scene. I became the area commander and part of the Druse village landscape.

Confrontation with the Druse

When the IDF took the Golan Heights in 1967, most of its residents fled; the area's largest town, Kuneitra, was abandoned en masse. Only four Druse communities remained, and their total population exceeds 10,000 today. The town of Majdal Shams, the northernmost and largest of the four, is of major importance in the battle for local leadership. Nebi Yafuri, the major Druse religious shrine and a focus of pilgrimage among the locals, is near the town. The other three Druse villages are Masade, about eight kilometers southeast of Majdal Shams; Bukata, a sprawling village north of the Little Hermon; and Ein Kinya, the smallest and most remote of the villages, west of Majdal Shams on the way to the Hula Valley and pre-1967 Israel.

A few weeks after Israeli law went into effect on the Golan, the Druse woke up. Their first act was a partial strike; some of the Druse who worked in the Hula Valley and the Golan area stayed home. As long as the strike was voluntary, we did not interfere. Later, however, the strikers began to assail anyone who sought to continue earning their living. That included many of the Druse, who carried Israeli ID cards and were considered quiet, devoted workers. The sanction of choice was religious ostracism, so thorough a banishment from the Druse sect that those subject to it would even be denied a gravesite. At this point of internecine struggles these Druse petitioned us, as the government's representatives, to intervene and thwart the violence.

In fact, the Druse were still jittery about the area's future. These fears were augmented by the fact that Israel was about to return the entire Sinai Peninsula to Egypt; the Druse were afraid that under pressure of a certain sort we would hand them, too, back to Syria. Their dread of the Syrians was much stronger than their allegiance to Israel. They didn't take a single step without considering Syria, without proving that "mother Syria" was truly their matriarch. I kept a different fact in mind: during the Syrians' tenure on the Golan Heights, the Druse had needed permits to travel among their villages and had been treated in general as second-class citizens.

One night in early March, 1982, I was summoned urgently to Northern Command Headquarters. Command staff had already convened in Amir's office, and with it, representatives of the police and other government agencies.

Amir pinned a map of the Golan Heights to the wall and turned to his audience.

"By government order, we are imposing a curfew on the Golan Heights starting tomorrow morning," he explained. "More precisely — on the Druse villages. The purpose of the curfew is to isolate the villages from one another and create pressure that will bring the strike to an end. We'll also step up Israeli presence in the villages, to reduce or restrain those who are inciting the people and disrupting normal life."

Amir drew an imaginary line around the Druse villages on the map. He turned to me and went on:

"Of course the division responsible for the sector is in charge of this operation."

Immediately those present — police, judicial system officials, Interior Ministry clerks — broke into stormy discussion. Everyone had one major objective: to keep the matter from reaching the High Court of Justice. Everyone contributed his experience and knowledge, offering advice and recommendations on how to act.

I could not figure them out. Until now I had not realized how sensitive the matter was, and could not comprehend their fear of imposing our presence in the area. As a military man, I set out at once to discharge the duty assigned to me. As soon as I had received that phone call from the Northern Command, I had issued guidelines to my division's operations officer and planned the blocking of roads and the deployment of my formations.

Early the next morning, troops deployed on all roads in the northern Golan Heights. Additional squads positioned themselves at approaches to the village, preventing entry and exit. Tent encampments were erected around them. We at headquarters occupied ourselves with coordination and problem-solving. I set up a front headquarters in the town of Masade, from which I supervised everything personally.

Amir, OC Northern Command, summoned the Druse religious dignitaries and several local leaders to his office. The clerics arrived in ceremonial garb — long black robes and gleaming white, cloth-covered hats. Quietly they gathered on one side of the office, impressive in their noble bearing, and contemplated us obliquely without initiating discussion. When Amir and I stepped into the room, they rose to their feet respectfully.

Most of Amir's remarks had to do with the new arrangements in the area. He spoke in Hebrew; a government official who spoke a little Arabic translated. Nonetheless, the lack of communication between Amir and his audience was obvious. He may as well have addressed them in Yiddish. They understood only Arabic, and the translation was so poor as to be useless.

You could slice the tension with a knife. I waited for Amir to dispel it, but that moment did not come. When Amir invited his listeners to ask questions, he met with absolute silence. The dignitaries wore compliant, submissive expressions. Looking deep into their eyes, however, I saw that they had no intention of modifying the existing situation. For a moment I sought to sweep away the officious atmosphere and start up a lively conversation by which the two sides could build a bridge — but I had no way of doing so.

The dignitaries dispersed, each to his own village, and we decided to wait and see. Deep down we hoped we could reach a compromise with them by which life might return to normal. Behind the dignitaries' behavior, however, lurked a truth we did not know. They were prisoners of the masses. Other, younger leaders were dictating the community's behavior.

The military squads, now on police duty, were ordered to allow only those civilians with Israeli ID cards to travel among the villages or to leave the area of the Heights. In the meantime, reporters and correspondents were trying to slip into the sealed enclave, putting those of my soldiers blocking the roads to the Golan Heights under tremendous pressure. The soldiers, of course, rebuffed their entreaties, turning us into the objects of venomous coverage. Various weird rumors that found their way to the media spoke of starvation, absence of medical help, and abuse of Druse on the Heights. We were put on the defensive. All Amir and I could do was consult with an ever-present lawyer in an attempt to steer clear of trouble.

Amir hated the media and demonstrably avoided them at all times. He considered them nothing but image-builders and idolizers. This did not prevent their reveling in our distress. Finally Amir acceded to my proposal and held a press conference. At that late stage he delivered a convincing and highly important explanation of the truth behind the roadblocks, but by then the damage had already been done.

Members of Knesset, too, sought to confirm first-hand the rumors whose veracity they never doubted. The most infuriating of all were members of Meir Wilner's Communist Party. They incited the local Druse and described in detail the actions they should take against the government. I was frustrated: how could an Israeli Jew be so base as to help the country's enemies crumble it from within? How had we fallen so?

Amir spent most of his time in my headquarters, as if nothing but this operation was on his mind. Occasionally we went out into the street to assess the atmosphere and talk freely with local youth. They behaved politely but did not flinch from verbal confrontation. They asked us intelligent questions and proved to have a well-formed, solid world view.

In one of those encounters an affable young man approached me:

"I know you. I teach in the school here," he said to me respectfully.

"Where did we meet?" I asked, intrigued.

"We never met," he smiled. "But I always wanted to meet you. I read your book twice."

"In Hebrew!?" I was surprised.

"Of course. It hasn't been translated into Arabic yet!"

The Red Cross came into the villages, checked the situation, and found everything sound. This took some of the pressure off us. In Ein Kinya, after a frontal clash between soldiers and residents, I found myself standing in the main square, explaining why the incident had occurred and discussing its results. I joked around with the Druse, and they with me. Before my very eyes the ice thawed and the tension vanished. I was invited to the home of the *mukhtar* — the village "mayor" — and was received with honor worthy of a king. The village dignitaries filed in behind me and sat down all around. At the blink of an eye the table filled with delicacies, everyone seeking to offer me food and drink. So we had found a common language after all. Even though I did not amend my orders, the atmosphere was unconstrained and pleasant. From then on both sides knew that every future incident would be brought up for joint discussion before any action was taken.

Shortly thereafter, a violent incident between civilians and soldiers, in which several people were injured, took place in Majdal Shams, and we had to put the town under curfew. I knew that only a curfew would put the riots to an end and prevent the bloodshed they would ultimately have caused. I did not know the law; perhaps I had no right to take that step. I decided alone, on the spot. It was the kind of decision that puts you in front of a commission of inquiry if it fails. In this case, it didn't fail.

One morning near Bukata, on the way to my headquarters in Masade, I came across a crowd of 3,000

Druse, including women and children, on the main highway, headed north. Three frightened soldiers had spread a barbed-wire fence across the road, blocking their progress. The crowd was howling hysterically. It was positively heart-rending. I approached the roadblock, where community representatives were entreating the soldiers to tear down the improvised fence. Now I realized what the commotion was about: the sect's leader, Sultan al-Atrash of Jebel Duruz in Syria — the Druse homeland and shrine — had died that morning. When word of his demise reached the Golan Heights, the local Druse went into a tremendous frenzy and attempted to set out en masse for Majdal Shams or join up with their brethren in the Yafouri Valley.

The community elders, accompanied by the group of youths that had evidently organized the procession, wished to speak with me. Beseechingly they asked me to let them move northward. This was not my decision to make, nor even that of OC Northern Command. The order prohibiting movement from one village to the next had been given by the government. I had to decide quickly. Any decision, I knew, would trigger a direct confrontation — either with the Druse or with my superiors. I believed it unwise to let the residents of Bukata continue north; on their way to Majdal Shams they would pass Masade, where others would join them. Together they would become uncontrollable. They had been locked up in their villages for quite some time, and the encounter would undoubtedly lead to a confrontation. On the other hand, their wailing and hysteria split the skies. Even a company of tanks would not stop them.

I summoned the leaders of the group.

"I'm going to let you head for Masade," I said

sternly. "Be aware that I am taking this decision by myself, contrary to orders I've been given."

"But we want to go to Majdal," the leaders tried to pressure me.

I refused. "Even Masade is too much," I answered. They couldn't argue. "I won't open the fence until you promise me that after you get there you'll turn around and go back." They promised.

Then I climbed onto an empty barrel. Very slowly the crowd fell silent. With the help of a megaphone I spoke: "I'm opening the roadblock because I believe a Druse's word is his honor. I also believe that just as I respect you, you will respect yourselves, and after you get to Masade you'll turn around and come back."

A glint appeared in their eyes. With the joy of victory they went back and lined up in little groups as before. I had the fence pulled away and drove on to intercept them in Masade.

There, on the main road, another several thousand Druse were waiting for their brethren to arrive. I'll never get another citation after a decision like this, I said to myself at the sight of this crowd. I have more chance of being busted to lance corporal... . Still, the encounter between the two village populations was moving. I climbed to a rooftop to observe events.

Suddenly a group of soldiers burst into the crowd, trying to separate residents of the two villages. This, I could see, was a local initiative by a junior commander. From my rooftop position I roared to the soldiers to retreat before they would be crushed by the tumultuous mob. Hastily they obeyed. Journalists were everywhere and TV cameras were rolling. I could already see the headlines. My two-way radio signaled me to contact Amir at once at General Staff headquarters. That would have to wait; I had an immediate problem to solve.

Now the mob began to chant "Majdal! Majdal!" Again the crowd was gripped with hysteria. I waited a little longer and came back down for a talk.

"I expect every last one of you to go back to your villages. I understand you, but I have no intention of giving you what you want. I remind you that only an hour ago I heard Druse dignitaries give their Druse word of honor that you would return to Bukata quietly. Don't make my men and me understand that a Druse's word is hot air!"

The crowd fell silent. A few seconds later people were already pushing one another on the road back to the village. I was not busted to lance corporal.

A few days later Ein Kinya became the center of interest again. Two soldiers, one a deputy company commander in the Golani Brigade, were wounded in a violent clash, after which their enraged comrades stormed the crowd and dispersed it. I put the village under curfew. What had made the soldiers so tough? I had always argued that they were too "Milktoastish"; now, before my very eyes, they had become "meaty" — insisting on their prerogatives and imposing their will. When facing mortal peril or the possibility of failing to carry out their mission, even a good little boy from a warm, protective home, who had never lifted a hand against anyone, knew how to stand up for his rights.

To conduct affairs among a population that had just been handed from one authority to another, a consistent, clear-cut, and well-defined government policy was called for. Perversely, however, the Israeli ministries that had set up shop on the Golan Heights had displayed an outrageous lack of coordination. Social Security kept on paying, banks handed out money to all comers, post offices provided service as always, the electric company did not cut off the juice, and the Transportation Ministry continued to issue drivers' licenses. All this went on indiscriminately, irrespective of the customer's identity. Israel's sympathizers and collaborators, stunned at our ineptitude, became indifferent. At first they suggested their own ways of resolving the situation, but quickly they realized that we Israelis had no common language even among ourselves. So they gave up.

I could not tolerate the absence of a single agency that would coordinate all the ministries' affairs. I took the initiative, summoned representatives of all these institutions, and sought to introduce coordination. It was an embarrassing scene. Everyone agreed that my way was the right one, but each little clerk feared for his skin, flinching from any innovation and initiative.

Still, we sought a way to instill confidence in the new administration and to consolidate a sound, uniform policy. The first step, we decided, was to issue the Druse with Israeli identity cards.

Operation "Hotem" ("Official Seal")

With a special effort, entailing collaboration with the Ministry of the Interior, we obtained the names of all residents, had ID cards printed up, and set out to distribute them. Yossi R., the division's intelligence officer, and I mapped out the details of the plan in absolute secrecy. It would be implemented on March 31; on April 1, a new era would begin.

Scores of police and Interior Ministry agents, along

with hundreds of soldiers, were to take part in the operation. A brigade commander was assigned to each village, and dozens of squads would go from home to home, handing out the cards. The basis of this method was our impression that the Druse wanted the ID cards but were afraid to claim them at my headquarters.

Personally briefing the men in the field at 1500 hours, I disclosed the details. From that position, equipped with sorted packages of cards and aerial photographs of the village homes, the forces set out. Our job was to hand out the cards; the residents would decide for themselves how to react.

To make the operation easier, we decided to put the villages under curfew. Shortly after this decision went into effect, the commander of Majdal Shams reported that some of the residents were refusing to enter their homes. We rushed to the town's central square, only to find soldiers and residents standing off in the building-lined plaza, tense to the point of ignition. Bolstering my voice by using my radio microphone as a P.A. system, I entreated the people to go home. The reply: a categorical refusal. Amir hovered overhead in a helicopter, trying to instruct me on how to proceed. Because he spoke on the formation's radio frequency, every last soldier heard him. So did the Druse residents, because I had turned my microphone around. I became aware of this too late.

To my surprise, Amir was irritable and impatient. I had known him as an introverted fellow with nerves of steel. He had always been excessively restrained around me, and, to my displeasure, responded phlegmatically even in difficult situations. But this time he was tough. Stuff the people into their homes, he ordered. From his overhead observation post, developments in the square must have looked no less frightening and threatening to him than they did to me. I tried to promise him that I would succeed in restoring order; all I needed was time. Force, I knew, would achieve nothing but bloodshed. I gave no order to use force. My restraint eventually proved itself.

At this stage about 300 youth burst out from a side street, waving five-foot poles, emitting terrifying cries of "itbah al-yahud!" — "Slaughter the Jews" — and storming the square. Obviously this was a preplanned action, its target the man in the middle of the square: me.

A fighting squad of Golani reconnaissance men under recon commander Goni protected me with their bodies from the onrushing mob. I clutched my loaded gun and cocked it, ready to fight back. Never, however, did I cease talking with the massive crowd, my amplified voice reverberating in the plaza. I made sure they knew that I was the man behind the voice and that I had no intention of retracting my orders to honor the curfew to the letter.

Those who listened could hear the patience in my voice and realized that I would indeed refrain from opening fire. Only a few minutes later — an eternity to me — the people began to disperse to their homes one by one. I was pleased that no one was injured, no blood had been spilled. We had been so close to firing at point-blank range, our weapons set on automatic! Yes, we had to impose our sovereignty on the Golan Heights, but it could be done differently!

We began distributing ID cards that afternoon; by next morning they had been delivered to every house. Some residents accepted them and went back inside quietly. Some made a point of throwing them into the street, and others simply refused to open the door. The soldiers considered it their moral duty to pick up the cards that had been tossed out; this angered me and I told them so. I quickly found that most such behavior was for show; once the sun set, the residents retrieved the cards. A few kept them and threw the envelopes out as a sign of protest and as a way of letting the neighbors know they were not collaborating with us.

But that was not the end of the affair. The next day a serious clash erupted in Majdal Shams. After several soldiers were injured while seeking cover, their comrades opened fire in self-defense, wounding several residents in the legs. I went out to talk with the civilian casualties and calm them. However, I could not stop the media; the story made the headlines at once.

Tension surged. At mid-day, the ID cards distributed, I met with Amir for consultation. We decided to remove all the roadblocks and let the residents move freely.

"Talk with the residents and tell them what our motives are," Amir ordered. He had sensed the locals' acceptance of me, noticed my sensitivity to what was happening, and thought that this was perhaps the best way.

My first stop was Ein Kinya. There, meeting the Druse in the square, I encountered a new state of mind. The sympathy they had displayed a few days ago had given way to hatred. As I spoke I could feel disquiet and ferment. Then a shout split the air "How many did you people kill in Majdal Shams?"

Now I understood what the anger was all about. I repeated my opening remarks but explained our motives in greater detail. My persuasion worked. Tempers cooled a little.

In Bukata I found Amir waiting for me on the main street. The residents were summoned to the central square; after my bitter experience in Majdal, I was apprehensive. The situation was volatile, and it was ill-advised to allow people to congregate in one location. I had appointed a brigade commander, Benny Tern, as commander of the village, but he could do nothing. I was the one they were waiting for, and it was best that I act quickly.

Amir greeted me with a smile. "You're the *mukhtar*. They love you. I believe you'll know how to explain this to them."

"I'm not so sure anymore," I answered quietly, looking at the noisy crowd in the square. I stepped into the plaza. Thousands of people had gathered, filling the square and packing all the rooftops around it. Tense and ready for anything, I made my way through the inflamed, hatred-infused crowd, afraid every moment that someone would knife me in the back or brain me with a club. Literally rubbing shoulders with the people of Bukata, I ascended to a balcony overlooking the square. My mouth went dry with agitation, as it did in the first moments of war. I put on a display of tremendous self-confidence; inside, my tension mounted and my heart pounded.

The community elders, waiting for me inside the house, rose to their feet and shook my hand. A few of them even embraced me, recalling my decision several days earlier on the barrel at the roadblock. The mob in the square, on the other hand, howled with rage at the sight of me. I had to summon all my strength and every technique I knew to quiet them. Only after interminable moments did the cries ebb, the tempers cool, and the crowd begin to listen.

I gave the crowd a greeting, explained Operation Hotem, and spoke about our cooperation.

"I'm gonna stay on the Golan Heights a long time," I shouted: "And I'm sure we'll go on working together!"

Stepping out of the house, I was greeted with stormy applause. The crowd parted to let me through and followed me with calls of "Be well!" and "God keep you!"

Amir met me with a smile. "Now that they've got the right to vote, the Druse will elect you to the Knesset."

On routine, on alert

Operation Peace for Galilee was on the horizon, and Basalt Brigade was one of the formations participating in the preparations and alerts preceding it. In the meantime, Dagan had replaced Yossi Melamed as commander of Barak Brigade. The 7th Brigade readied itself for war in the eastern sector, where it would advance into the Beka'a Valley, the broad north-south fault that splits Lebanon. Finally, reserve brigades were forewarned: if war broke out, they would take up position on the Golan Heights.

A regular infantry brigade, Golani, was attached to the division. It underwent some training on the Golan Heights, culminating with a large brigade-level maneuver under my command. The brigade was given information on the missions it would assume in Lebanon. One of them involved training a special force that would capture the Arnon highlands, including the terrorist stronghold at Beaufort Castle.

I joined one of Golani's nocturnal forays and fell

in love. The soldiers carried heavy packs with all kinds of gear. Quietly and intensely they marched for kilometers on end, amidst the basalt boulders. They were cohesive, willing to make any effort, ready for any task. Most impressive of all was their pride. I had never witnessed anything like the pride of Golani.

At that time, too, I was able to observe my staff's teamwork and appreciate its importance. Under bureau chief Danny Aharon and my dedicated secretary Ruthie Goldman, my office functioned well even in difficult situations. My driver, Gabi Shalom, was part of the crew. All of them combined to make my life easier. Family-like, their mutual concern and interest were self-evident. Any commander who has the privilege of working with an efficient, loyal team that understands its "boss" will do better work and more of it.

As division commander, however, I knew I had to communicate my demands, in spirit and in letter, not only to my immediate subordinates but also to the lowest of commanders on the Golan. The driver patrolling the perimeter fence at night had to discharge his duty properly. The observation man in his post had to know his job inside and out, never letting his vigilance flag. I believed it correct to inform the mechanics and technical men, laboring to repair tanks at night, of the value of their work. I made sure everyone training on the Golan Heights upheld security orders and refrained from disrupting routine civilian life.

Every battalion commander rules his roost, but he has to know that his superiors are watching. The night guard detachment on the summit of Mount Hermon and the reconnaissance squad on the Yarmuk River have important tasks, and must behave exactly as they are told and as written in orders. The division's emergency depots have to be on a higher state of alert than any other depot, and those in charge of them have to carry out their duties to the letter. The training plan has to incorporate more than the plan itself; it needs allocations of ammo, vehicle motor-hours, and firing ranges.

Responsibility for action in all these matters, especially in a frontier region like the Golan Heights, is entrusted to the division staff, the commander's executive arm. Thus a division commander's ability to influence the last of his fighting men depends on routine staff work. I made sure this work proceeded smoothly. I also instituted a "tradition" of weekly visits with the battalions, one each week. Each visit began with a meeting of the division and battalion staffs. Afterwards we sat down to a festive dinner, during which we gave the soldiers the opportunity to describe their problems to me and to the division staff. For the staffs, this was no fun; quite often they were taken by surprise, presented with problems of which they had not known. We visited each formation in turn: artillery, tanks, regular and reserve. Sometimes we attended maneuvers; at other times we observed operational engagements. I made use of my "circuit" to present my world-view to the men and, in return, size up the situation and mood in the field, by my own direct observation, without intermediaries.

To work by the book in so large a system, one has to insist on discipline and compliance with orders. This may be the supreme precondition for discharge of duties by all the men, without exception. I never swept discipline problems under the rug if they impaired operational activity or were likely to do so.

Discipline

When the Israelites received the Law at Sinai, they responded, "We shall do and we shall listen." They obeyed their leader with perfect faith, only later considering "the whys and wherefores."

Obedience and action have been interrelated in all societies and at all times. Indeed, any normal society — including the IDF — has first to heed and then to act; without discipline, one is unlikely to attain any goal.

The Israel Defense Forces, like large-scale civilian entities of its kind, is built in the form of a set of systems whose activation and timing are determined by people who, at times, are not in daily contact, if in contact at all. These systems and those who staff them are tremendously interdependent. Discipline is the systems' lubricant; it induces each person to discharge his or her function properly. Indeed, every army seeks to imbue soldiers with a sense of obedience to instructions and orders from the moment they put on uniform.

The IDF came into being in the middle of Israel's War of Independence, and was naturally structured along British Army lines. Its image, however, is more heavily influenced by the spirit of the Palmah — the pre-Independence, semi-underground strike forces — than by the rigidities of the British system. Shorts, sandals, and a camaraderie that knows no distinctions of rank and status, are all too evident in the habits of the Israeli soldier. This informal atmosphere is sometimes detrimental to the imperative of carrying out orders and sticking to the rules.

I have always been troubled by the possibility of

suffering many casualties because of one soldier's negligence. If the glue of our interdependence melts, if even one of us treats the rules with contempt and charts his own course, we shall have many innocent victims to bury. I, myself, bear the scars of those who breached discipline. I have seen soldiers in effect kill their comrades just by violating security rules. Tank commanders fighting along with me could not find their binoculars in the heat of battle, just because the quartermaster clerk was too lazy to complete his job. On the battlefield I saw tanks and other combat vehicles disabled for hours or even days because the mechanic and technician had left their tool kits and spare parts in the rear. I have seen one negligent driver delay an important operational move. On any number of occasions I took part in actions that were delayed because one participant failed to stick to schedule.

I am not advocating blind discipline. I do believe, however, that even the highest ranking commander has to treat even the most trivial violation of orders with seriousness. Sometimes senior commanders should deal with discipline problems themselves, not leaving them to others. Commanders must ensure two things about their every order: that it is do-able, and that it is done. Commanders should have positive reinforcement on hand for disciplined soldiers and firm negative reinforcement for those who belittle the written rule. Otherwise, disruption and contempt for orders become the norm.

"Make 'em shave and they won't go AWOL." "Make 'em look like soldiers and they'll run through walls for you." Insisting on the fighting man's appearance is one technique among many for maintaining a dis-

298 • Avigdor Kahalani

ciplined army. An undisciplined army may not reach the battlefield and, if it gets there, will probably not do well there.

In Israel, where citizens climb in and out of uniform regularly, discipline is of especial importance. As a people's army, the IDF frequently finds itself playing a major role in coping with national problems in ways that arouse public controversy. A soldier, a commander, or a formation that poo-poohs discipline may find it hard to carry out an unpopular mission — just the kind of mission on which the country's fate may depend.

16. PEACE FOR GALILEE — THE WAR IN LEBANON

The terrorists who fled Jordan in King Hussein's action of September, 1970 — "Black September" — sought an alternative base from which they could dig in and attack Israeli targets, in Israel and elsewhere. They found that base in Lebanon, a country with a fragmented population chronically embroiled in bloody civil strife. Here, in their old-new base, the terrorists departed from the "Fatahland" pattern of the late 1960s, when they had seized an enclave near the Israeli border and treated it as theirs. Now they developed their forces and strength throughout Southern Lebanon and farther north, establishing a military infrastructure that amounted to a state within a state.

In the late 1970s, after several years of Lebanese civil war, the Syrians, who have always regarded Lebanon as an inseparable part of a Greater Syria, invaded the Land of the Cedars "to uphold law and order." The insurgency was too big for Israel to ignore. Batteries of surface-to-air missiles, meant for the Syrians' own defense, provided the terrorists with air cover, too. Thus they created a *fait accompli*: any Israeli move into Lebanon would now entail a clash with Syria.

The terrorists stopped at nothing to hurt Israel:

artillery barrages, ambushes, mines, incursions to seize hostages. In February-March, 1978, Israel mounted its first large-scale response, temporarily occupying Southern Lebanon as far north as the Litani River. Following Operation Litani, the UN stationed a force in Southern Lebanon — UNIFIL (United Nations Interim Force in Lebanon) to prevent anti-Israeli activity. In practice, this force not only failed to carry out its brief; its very presence actually sheltered the terrorists.

In July, 1981, after more than two weeks of engagements with the terrorists, during which their organizational infrastructure was seriously damaged by Israel's Air Force, a cease-fire was arranged through the mediation of Philip Habib, special American envoy to the Middle East. Israel honored the agreement, but the terrorists continued to operate against Israeli and Jewish targets overseas. By this time, apprehensive of an Israeli attack, the terrorists increased their alertness, and the Soviet Union made greater quantities of arms available to them.

On March 30, 1982, during a Land Day assembly in Beirut (Land Day commemorates Israel's expropriation of land in Galilee cultivated by Arabs and the resulting protests), Yasser Arafat challenged Ariel Sharon to an armed engagement at Beaufort Castle, a venerable fortress overlooking the Litani in Southern Lebanon.

"We're waiting for you, " Arafat boasted. "*Ahalan wa-sahlan*! See you!"

On April 3, an Israeli diplomat, Yaakov Bar-Simantov, was assassinated in Paris. The IDF went on alert for an offensive into Lebanon, but postponed zero hour in the aftermath of American intervention.

On the evening of Thursday, June 3, Israel's Ambassador to Great Britain, Shlomo Argov, was shot in the head and permanently incapacitated. That was the last straw. The next day, the Government of Israel ordered the Air Force to attack two targets in Beirut and several PLO installations in Southern Lebanon. The terrorists responded by shelling Jewish civilian communities in Galilee. An American attempt to restore the cease-fire failed.

On the night of Saturday, June 5, the Government ordered the IDF to "remove the terrorists, concentrated with their headquarters and bases in Lebanon, out of firing range of [Israel's] northern settlements." The operation was given the name "Peace for Galilee."

When I took over the division from Amram Mitzna, I received the contingency plan to occupy Southern Lebanon, code-named "Oranim." All missions subsequently added to it were called "Big Oranim", "Rolling Oranim", etc. Since taking up my new position, any number of approvals for plans had crossed my desk, as well as innumerable alerts for near-incursions to Lebanon. From our standpoint, all preparations had been made.

On several occasions forces from central and southern Israel were dispatched to the Golan Heights as a basis for entering Lebanon. These moves, like every attempt to react to the terrorists' operations, disturbed us. They seemed to reflect decisions taken in the heat of emotion. In a talk with Amir, and afterwards with Chief of General Staff Rafael Eitan and Defense Minister Ariel Sharon, I and other division commanders demanded a longer lead time for invasion once the decision was made. We were apprehensive about entering Lebanon just as other forces were moving from elsewhere in Israel to the Golan. That was a sure recipe for chaos; it might also reduce the prospects of a successful operation. The number of alerts in the north, and the pace at which divisions were rushed up from the south, became the subjects of jokes.

My own division of regulars was less put upon than others by all this. Mine was one of the divisions routinely responsible for the Golan Heights when there was no war and in the event that the Syrians should start one. Because the Syrians were unlikely to meet our action in Lebanon with a response on the Golan, the Heights could be defended by calling up the reserves.

My colleagues, commanders of the regular divisions, frequently asked why I had to be taken from the Golan into Lebanon, when my whole *raison d'etre* was to defend the Heights. "It's a waste of power," they claimed. "There's no force like your division to defend the Golan Heights!"

I would not hear of it.

"My division will be the first to cross into Lebanon. It is a northern division, it is the most available, and it can go in straight from the Golan. I think there's enough work for all of us in Lebanon, and I don't intend to watch you from the Golan Heights!"

I meant it; everyone understood that I did not mean to back down. The plans had been finalized, but any deviation was enough to trigger modifications. Furthermore, as everyone knew, there were too many forces and headquarters in a narrow field of action.

The division was arrayed as follows: Barak Brigade under Dagan; Golani under Irwin; one line brigade on the Lebanese border under Mofaz; a special task force comprising a Golani battalion, Golani reconnaissance, a Golani engineering company, and a company of tanks, all under Golani Deputy Brigade Commander Gabi A.; the divisional artillery group under Itzik Gazit; the supply group under Sal'i and the engineering battalion under Eitan. Division staff officers were Yossi R., Operations; Jackson, Maintenance; Meir, Intelligence; Shpira, Adjutant; Tzvika, Supply; Ilan, Communications; Rower, Ordinance; Mizrahi, Engineering; Avi Doktor, Air Coordination; Gazit, Artillery Group Commander; and my second-in-command, Yodke.

The 7th Brigade was transferred to the neighboring division under Emmanuel Sekel. The sector intended for me was too small for two tank brigades. I accepted this fact with the anguish of a father forced to part with one of his sons.

The master plan, "Oranim", from which we designed comprehensive operating plans, incorporated several objectives. To create a new situation in the field, Northern Command was to destroy terrorists and infrastructure in Lebanon by zero hour plus 48. To meet this timetable, we would have to plan movement along a large number of routes. Command was also instructed to be ready to respond to Syrian interference in the Beka'a Valley.

On June 6, Command's order was amended as follows:

A. Northern Command will occupy southern Lebanon as far as the Awali-Dalfi-Kafr al-Zeit -Miu'erat line, destroying terrorists and infrastructure and preventing artillery fire on Israeli settlements, by zero hour plus 24.

B. Command will be on alert to complete Operation Oranim in keeping with the accumulation of forces.

During the preparation period, the division's major intended axis crossed the Litani via Khardale Bridge. Only a few days before "Peace for Galilee", we obtained permission to use Akiyya Bridge, disregarding, of course, the French UNIFIL battalion stationed in the area. According to the plan as approved, my division was to enter the territory by two routes: via both Khardale and Akiyya bridges. The division would capture the Nabatiyya highlands and move north, crossing the Zaharani River on several routes, toward Sidon. The division would then be ready either to occupy Sidon or to circumvent it and head up the coast toward Damour. From there it would participate in the occupation of Beirut — if so ordered.

Itzik Mordechai's division would move up the coastal road and meet mine in the vicinity of Sidon. Itzik and I waged a tacit contest: who would be the first to cross the Zaharani on the coastal road? The idea was to bypass Sidon rapidly and head north as fast as possible before political factors brought us to a halt. Admittedly, my division had no role in the Sidon occupation plan, but I knew I had to be ready for it. OC Command preferred to entrust this city to Itzik, thus letting me move north faster to step up the pressure on Beirut. As for taking Beaufort Castle, Command was of two minds.

According to the original plan, Golani Reconnaissance was to take the fortress from the direction of Khardale Bridge. I objected to this consistently and stubbornly. Every time it was discussed, whenever Amir had approved one of its particulars, I engaged

Command operations officer David Agmon in stormy dispute about the meaning and significance of the approval. I saw no need to take the terrorist bastion on foot, advancing from the bottom to the top. Now that we were allowed to enter the area via Akiyya Bridge, Golani and I could reach Beaufort in motor vehicles. I did not, and still do not, understand why Amir insisted on two courses of action, why he did not decide once and for all. Orders being orders, I prepared Golani to approach the area on wheels and to take all the Arnon highlands, including Beaufort, on foot.

On Saturday the 77th Battalion, under Dubik, took up positions near Marj 'Ayoun, a pro-Israeli Christian town just north of the tip of the Galilee Panhandle, and began to shell targets on the ridge where Beaufort stood. By my order — without approval from the chaplaincy, I was warned — the forces trained even on the Sabbath. I visited the area to observe the battalion in its positions, assessing the quality of preparations first-hand and gauging the men's morale. I also made sure everyone knew it was serious this time. In similar situations in the past we had always suspected that the operation would be scrapped at the last moment, sending us back to our bases until the next time around.

I was apprehensive about crossing the Litani, a difficult obstacle. I set up special units including tanks, infantry and engineering, that would cross the river with confidence and without snafus. The key was painstaking preparation. I had pieced together a multi-unit structure of forces, complete with interlocking components that required perfect coordination. Thus, we moved to the headwater of the Jordan and performed a maneuver virtually duplicating the crossing of the Litani. The war machines advanced in just the right order: tank before personnel carrier, personnel carrier before engineering, engineering before bridge tank, bridge tank before the others. Of paramount concern to me was the well-being of my men. I had to let them train until the last moment. The secret of success, I have always believed, is to assemble the forces correctly and train all their components together in an accurate simulation.

On Friday, we summoned even those men who had gone on Sabbath furlough back to their units. As civilian Israelis sat down to their Sabbath feasts, we read and reviewed the orders with all the formation's commanders and staff officers. On Saturday morning Command headquarters ran through the orders again for the division commanders.

The call-up of reserves began on Saturday afternoon. We waited for nightfall, when the Cabinet would meet in the home of Prime Minister Begin. The Cabinet's communiqué appeared in all the media: Begin would meet the U.S. special envoy Philip Habib on Tuesday. More important to us, however, was another secret Cabinet decision handed down at the same time: the operation was still on. Amir and his staff officers contacted my headquarters to reconfirm the plan. For the umpteenth time I repeated the details worked out in innumerable discussions. A few problems remained, but, as was my habit, I did not trouble OC Northern Command with them. After all, he would head out the next morning to command one of Israel's wars!

I had not been home for more than two weeks. I had promised to come for the Sabbath — but Dalia and the kids had to make do with a phone call. Because the IDF uses wireless phones, anything that discloses Army secrets simply cannot be said. Blabbermouths on the verge of spilling classified information are known to receive warnings by field-security people who break into the talk. Sometimes conversations are cut off; a unit may even lose the use of its phone for several days. With all this in mind, Dalia and I devised a code for the many times I had to inform her that an imminent furlough had been canceled. Just before the Yom Kippur War I had stopped laying the shingles on my roof to rush to the north; ever since, "roof" was our codeword.

"There's a problem with the roof, " I told Dalia again.

"OK, but what about tomorrow? We're having family over and promised everyone you'd try to come!"

"I think there'll be problems with the roof tomorrow too."

"Even by tomorrow it won't be OK?" Dalia asked, puzzled.

"Dalia, you've got to understand. The roof just blew off. There's no roof."

Dalia fell silent. I could not know whether she realized that war would break out the next day.

I told the division's training officer, Capt. Yagil, about Oranim and gave him instructions on how to safeguard Division Headquarters. Throughout the night I called all the commanders, verifying that preparations had been completed and the forces' crews assigned. We were to cross the border at 1200 hours the next day. I sat in my office, making sure one more time that I had done everything I needed to do before the war. I transferred command of my sector of the Golan to another force now stationed there. I cleared away some of the gear in my office so my successor would find it hospitable.

Late that evening I got a call from Maj. Goni Harnik. Goni had been commander of Golani reconnaissance until two weeks previously, when he had gone on leave prior to demobilization. Now he wanted to join the war effort. I was amazed. Why had he called me, of all people? After all, he could have gone directly to the Brigade; they would have found him a place. Goni, however, had something else in mind: command of the reconnaissance unit. He knew the ropes, he said, and had participated in all the preparations and drills on a Beaufort model we had contrived.

"That's not how we do things," I answered. "Once you've handed over command, you don't get it back — even if war breaks out before you're out the door!" After a moment's thought, his disappointment noticeable, he requested, "Maybe you could ask the commander of Golani to let me join him?"

That was logical. Golani was not far from the Lebanese border. within a few minutes I forwarded Goni's request to Golani commander Irwin, asking him to let Goni join the Brigade's command group and adding, "But don't set up a special force for him!"

I was stunned by Irwin's furious reply: "So Goni goes over my head? I won't let him in my brigade!"

I acknowledged Irwin's sensitivity but pleaded with him not to offend Goni.

"He wasn't jumping the chain of command," I explained. "He couldn't get you on the phone, so he made use of my 'good offices'. I mean it: let him join the Brigade!"

We finally agreed to assign Goni to the Deputy Brigade Commander's force, whose tasks included the capture of Beaufort, and Goni raced north to join up with Golani at the point of incursion. I knew very well why he had appealed to me. He had been under my direct command in Operation Hotem, when we had handed out ID cards to the Golan Druse; ever since I had a great deal of affection for him. I liked the way he undertook missions and the youthful vigor he displayed in carrying them out. I had witnessed his leadership ability in the recon company, where he had built an inchoate formation into a large family. His soldiers, among the IDF's personal and professional best, would do anything for him.

I tried to sleep and recharge batteries; who knew when I would be able to do that again? I had to be wide awake, able to absorb, think, and take decisions. Only two hours were left for sleep. I crawled into bed, but my thoughts deprived me of rest... Above all I feared that the Litani crossing would fail. Even the slightest foul-up would stall an entire division. There it would sit, nicely lined up, unable to cross that terrible obstacle. The operation was incomparably complex. the possibilities of error were innumerable. Just one snafu — by a tractor or bridge tank driver — would be enough to leave us stuck south of the litani, unable to discharge our duty.

I wished the river were behind me already.

Sunday, June 6, 1982

At 0530 hours all the division's commanders reported for a final briefing in the Northern Command War Room, a last run-through of the orders before heading for war. Alongside OC Command Amir and his staff officers were Defense Minister Ariel Sharon, Chief of General Staff Rafael Eitan ("Raful"), and, of course, in view of the importance of this encounter, historians, members of the IDF spokesman's staff, General Staff Officers and branch commanders, as well as reservists who served as advisers to OC Command.

Amir and his officers handed the final plan to the Minister of Defense and General Staff for approval. First describing the enemy's final deployment in the sector, Command's operations officer presented Command plans down to the division level, and updated those present on matters of artillery, engineering, air, maintenance, communications, etc. Searching the Command staff officers' faces, I could see their excitement at the occasion and their tension about the weighty mission that would be theirs within a few hours. As if to compound the tension, the Operations Officer stressed that the terrorists were on top alert, and the Syrian Army too had been placed on high alert in anticipation of an Israeli attack.

The Minister of Defense, like ourselves, was troubled about crossing the Litani, and the Command's engineering officer, Ishai, could do nothing to encourage us.

Itzik Mordechai, in command of the western sector of the Lebanese front, presented his plan for the occupation of Tyre and the coastal highway up to the Zaharani River.

"I hope it's clear to you," Sharon said, "that you don't stop in Sidon. You keep going as far North as you can!"

It was my turn. Spreading my maps on the map board along with everyone else's, I first described how the division would come down from the Golan Heights and estimated the magnitude of the forces remaining on the Heights for the defense of that area. Then I presented the division plan, the forces, and their tasks. When I reached the part about opening the Khardale Bridge axis, Sharon interrupted me.

"When are they going to cross?"

"When it's ordered," I answered. "I estimate that if we get the OK, it could be 1500 or 1600 hours..."

"Menahem Einan's division," Amir interrupted. "If it goes in, then the plan will be to bring it in over Khardale Bridge..."

"I recommend," I added, "that if we sit on the highlands, that we bring in Mehahem Einan's force and push toward the interior with the rest of the forces."

I went on, describing how we would clean up the Nabatiyya area the next morning. The Defense Minister interrupted me again.

"I think your division's timing is too optimistic," he stressed. "It'll be very hard to get to the Zaharani crossing today... It's very, very hard to move on those narrow, winding roads. Here you've got people who saw them in Operation Litani. Just going anywhere, without doing anything operational, takes a long, long time."

I tried to explain that the forces would bypass the Nabatiyya area, but the Minister insisted.

"I know there's no other way. I'm just saying... I think it's optimistic. I see no other solution here but to start an hour earlier. Where do you run into Syrians for the first time?" the Minister of Defense asked.

"I don't meet them unless I move toward..."

"It would be better not to meet with them," Sharon rules, turning to OC Command. "Shall we move zero hour up from 1200 to 1100?"

We agreed. Telephoning the Prime Minister from the war room, Sharon got Begin's go-ahead. The operation would start at 1100 hours.

The atmosphere in the war room changed: zero hour was one hour closer! Now Emmanuel Sekel presented his plan, followed by Menahem Einan. Menahem would cross amid my forces on the axis I had opened, using either Khardale or Akiyya Bridge. He would advance toward 'Arb Salim and would station himself on the Beirut-Damascus highway in the area of Dahar al-Bidr.

Raful stood up to summarize.

"The goal, as you know, is to push the terrorists' artillery out of range of our northern settlements. Time is a major factor in everything we do from this moment on, because the international political forces — the UN, the Security Council, the whole bunch — are already starting to push for a cease-fire. The terrorists asked them to. So what matters now is not how perfect the frameworks are or how nicely the convoys are lined up. What matters is that we begin to roll at 1100 hours. In the end, success depends on what we leave behind, whether the territory is full of terrorists or not. If they stop us and their artillery is still in firing range of our settlements, it's like we never started out on this operation." Raful warned against engaging UNIFIL forces. "Don't forget that these are European forces — French, Dutch, Norwegian — and they're liable to stop us. If you run into them, settle things with straight talk," he stressed.

Now Raful changed the subject. "We've already talked about civilians and civilian infrastructure. That means not only to avoid injuring civilians. It can also mean public buildings or private homes or facilities on the way. They have got to serve the population... After all, what we do here had got to serve us for a long time."

There was one exception: the Nabatiyya highlands.

We were to clean up that area but good. This seemed of special importance to Raful, and he explained in great detail how to go from village to village, house to house, flushing out the terrorists.

"Now, Syria," he continued. "I emphasized this matter in the previous operation, too. The plan was to draw up so that we don't engage the Syrians, at least not in the first 24 hours, which are the decisive ones... The Syrians will scream to the whole world that the Israelis are assaulting them — and that means political trouble!"

Finally, a few technical details for the reserve division commanders. The depot equipment had to be treated well: "Take care of it, hold it, put it in order," Raful emphasized. Then another matter: " I ask you to let the reservists take care of other reservist's private vehicles themselves, because there's no telling what shape they'll be in when they come back to pick them up... Good luck."

The Defense Minister stood up and moved to the operation map. Gravely he picked up the pointer next to the board and looked down for a moment, weighing his words.

"I know you're all tired, and time is short," Sharon began, vigorous and to the point as usual.

"Men, pay attention to what I say. These guidelines have got to go from you to all the ranks below... We wouldn't go out on an operation like this to set up a Lebanese government that might be able to sign a peace treaty with us... Even though the Syrian presence in Lebanon is very inconvenient, very dangerous for us, I wouldn't set out on this operation just to get them out of there. Absolutely not. If I'm here, with you, that means it's a moment of truth... Nobody is eager for this war... We wanted to avoid it as much as we could. That's got to be stressed. You've got to look people in the eye and explain. The escalation in the area left us no choice but war. It can't be that we're in a state of "peace" and even so Jews are being attacked — in Israel and elsewhere!"

Sharon apologized for not having time to talk with the fighting men. He had to rush back to Jerusalem, where members of the opposition were waiting in the Prime Minister's office for an update. He continued:

"The purpose is to destroy the terrorist infrastructure, at the range at which they're endangering us... I don't believe we'll reach the Sidon line. That's the 40 kilometer line. That's where the guns will stop firing... But everyone's got to be ready to continue... From the political standpoint, the plan speaks about getting the settlements out of artillery range. So they decided to have another Cabinet meeting where we can take further decisions."

The Defense Minister seemed troubled by the possibility that we would not have time to advance far enough to put our settlements out of terrorist artillery range. We were liable to be stopped by foreign political factors, thus frustrating the operation. He also stressed the complexity of what we were about to do, with many sides taking part to one extent or another — the Syrians, UNIFIL, the Americans and the Russians, and the local population, with which we would have to live subsequently.

"I want to mention this matter of the Syrians. If we've got to attack the Syrians head-on in the Beka'a, we'll do it as late as we can! I know they'll say — perhaps they'll even blame us afterwards — that the Galilee panhandle was being shelled 24 hours a day. Maybe it will be. But our intention is to wait as long as humanly possible before engaging the Syrians. In general, we have no intention of getting into a full-fledged war with the Syrians, but that might not be up to us..."

"What I mean is this: in Lebanon, in my opinion, there will be no choice but to do it. They won't retreat from there in any case, so we'll have to take a different, an additional Government resolution. After all, we won't leave them, the terrorists, there under any circumstances!"

I had expected Sharon to say this. Thus far I had not fully understood how we could carry out the plan without engaging the Syrians. The multi-colored arrows on all our operation maps ran through Syrian forces stationed in Lebanon.

Now Sharon, speaking quickly, began to brief the formation commanders, as if he, personally, were about to command us.

"I want you to know that any step like this has political decisions behind it. I'm ready to point here at every military action we took in the last 30 years. After each of them we were weakened, because right after it Jews began to scream and press and apply sanctions."

We grinned. Arik Sharon replied with a grin of his own, then quickly returned to the briefing to emphasize several further points.

"When you're in UNIFIL territory, you've got to be real careful that the terrorists don't find shelter there... It's important to advance quickly... to make every effort to avoid casualties... not to let Major Haddad's people* commit massacres after we move on. To enlarge Haddad's strip... Don't fire too much

* Major Sa'id Haddad commanded Arab forces in South Lebanon in cooperation with the IDF.

artillery, because there's hardly anyone to fire at, and you'd have to organize ammunition convoys."

Finally: "Men, use your heads... It's up to you to untangle this thicket. We're going to be here with you, and we'll coordinate everything with the Government! We have to get ourselves a long period of quiet... The terror that's emanating from Lebanon to the whole world has killed a thousand people and wounded 4,500," the Minister summed up, turning to Amir, OC Command. "If you want, I'll give you the exact numbers!"

With that, Sharon stepped out of the war room.

I parted from my fellow division commanders with a handshake and best wishes. On the way back to my headquarters I stopped at the Golani encampment, observing the men as they prepared to move and wishing them well. Soldiers were strapping equipment to the vehicles; platoon and company commanders were delivering final briefings. I was proud of them. I congratulated the brigade commander and battalion commanders. One of the men I found there was Goni; he was tying his gear to the personnel carrier of Deputy brigade Commander Gabi A. So he had found his place after all.

"Don't forget to take the Golani banner!" I grinned at Gabi, and he answered with a knowing smile, remembering the half-serious warning I had given the brigade's men: "I'm sure the Golani flag will fly over Beaufort Castle. But don't get so excited that you forget to put up Israel's flag too..."

During the trip, next to my driver Gabi, I had several moments for random thoughts. In another few minutes, by my order, this tremendous force would burst into action. What a heavy responsibility the commanders had to bear, one that would become many times heavier if they failed. The thousands of soldiers alongside their war machines at the side of the road believed in their commanders and would do as they were told.

I studies their faces. Most of them seemed a little nonchalant as zero hour approached. Behind that facade were fears and questions: who would have the privilege of coming home from this war, and who would not? Who would come back in one piece... and who would bear physical or psychic scars all his life?

The sight of the young fighting men made me aware of my maturity and experience. Still, how could I really know the thoughts that were flashing through their minds at that moment? Could they tell my feverish thoughts as I surveyed them, waving them farewell?

I felt almost as though this were a war movie: the General reviewing the long columns of armor awaiting his order, at which they would spring into motion. It was the false calm before a tremendous storm that would erupt in another few minutes. Israeli aircraft would split the skies. Artillery would issue its thunder far beyond earshot. The columns of tanks and personnel carriers would send clouds of dust skyward. At that moment, however, everything was silent. I derived my strength from my fighting men. I looked them straight in the eye and believed in them. I had done everything I could to prepare them for this moment.

In Division Headquarters, spread out in the field, everything was ready. Ilan, the division communications officer, greeted me with a confident smile as I entered.

"Ilan, can we hear everyone, and can everyone hear us?" I had to make sure the basis for all control of forces — communications — was solid.

Ilan spread his arms wide. "Sir, have you got any doubts about the Communications Corps?"

"Ilan, my friend, I believe in the Communications Corps only when all the forces answer me on the radio. Are they answering?!"

"Right now there's radio silence, but there's no reason anyone wouldn't answer. We checked all the sets, and I gave every commander a spare radio."

"So what's left is to pray... Ilan, I want your technical man to make sure that my own personnel carrier is functioning. I don't plan to stay with you too long in these big tents," I smiled, looking around for my armored vehicle.

Yossi, the Operations Branch officer, was sitting in the war room tent, sandwiched between two APCs, satisfied with what he saw. Maps embellished with multi-colored war arrows were spread over large boards. Microphones and loudspeakers were mounted on the APCs' flanks, permitting two-way communication with each of the division's formations. The table, stationed in the middle of the tent and surrounded with general-issue folding chairs, creaked under enough phones and mikes to permit us to talk with anyone we wished. A map of Southern Lebanon was spread out on the table, without its clear plastic cover. It was for my personal use. With it I could talk to the forces and monitor their locations at all times.

Yossi, like a proud housekeeper, gave me guided tour of the war room. He introduced me to the men — I knew most of them — and showed me all the accessories, from the detailed maps to the last of the radio networks that he intended to monitor.

The war room was a comfortable place in which to work. It was clear to me, however, that within a few hours I would take my APC, gather a few staff officers in additional APCs, and head north to join the forces. I had worked with the APC crew in the past: the driver, Ohayon; the operations sergeant, Kobi; the radiomen, Rafi and Amiram; the communications officer, Ilan, and the operations officer, Tzvika.

At 1100 hours, I gave the order: Cross the frontier!

Several thousand soldiers and 300 armored vehicles went into action. Any loose ends that remained would have to be dealt with *en route*. The Air Force was indeed thundering overhead, bomb bays ready to let loose. Artillery shells emitted a powerful rumble as they struck distant targets. Suddenly, I felt an urgent need to contact the battalion commanders and wish them well personally. I broke into the battalion radio networks, identifying myself as "Kodkod Dror" as in times past. The network was now called Anefa, but I considered Dror, the name I had acquired years ago as commander of the 7th Brigade on the Golan Heights, a matter of personal significance, profound and special, so I kept it.

One after another the farewells reverberated on the air. Spiegel, battalion commander in Golani, promised not to let me down; his formation would take any mission to its end. Amiram, Commander of Barak, which had been transferred to Golani Command, quipped, "Sir, did they allocate motor hours for this operation?" A few days ago I had to cancel some of Amiram's maneuvers because his battalion had overshot its quota.

Hastily looking around the War Room, I made sure every order had been recorded and updated, and that all the soldiers, listening in on the radio,

were following the formation's movements and recording their situation and location on the map. In
reply to my inquisitive gaze, the Command representative in the War Room confirmed that he was updating headquarters regularly and was in constant touch
with his War Room. "*Dir balak*," (Arabic for "Watch
yourself"), I called to him with a smile, "Update who
you want, but don't tattle on us!"

I stepped out of the giant tent and observed the
forces moving west and north. Clouds of black smoke
billowed on the other side of the Litani. I hoped the
shells had indeed hit their targets. I could also see
some of the armored columns advancing. It was a hot
summer day, the air clear and visibility good. I beheld an impressive, powerful sight. No enemy would
stand up to them.

Returning to the tent, I found myself swamped
with the hubbub of multiple communications networks — rasping commanders' voices and the racket
of telephones ringing one after another.

The first formation to reach the Litani belonged to
Golani; the next was a Barak spearhead. Both were
slightly behind schedule. According to the plan, these
two major forces were to reach the river at roughly
the same time, along separate routes, and cross it at
different places. Although the water was shallow
enough to permit crossing without the help of tractors — these had nevertheless gone ahead — we found
Akiyya Bridge intact and guarded by a French contingent of UNIFIL. The UN people cleared out of the
way, presenting no particular resistance. That was
totally unexpected.

Once the vanguard forces had crossed the river, I
assembled my Advance Command Group and headed

for the crossing point. An ACG is headed by a division commander and includes intelligence, air coordination officer, and artillery coordination officer. It moves about in approximately five personnel carriers. An ACG is a highly mobile unit that can reach any point on the battlefield at a moment's notice. With its communications equipment it controls all forces in the field and can converse with both its own subordinate commanders and those in the rear.

I passed a large force inching along the axis. With a siren I could have ordered them off the road, but I did not have one. Tailgating me was Z., an aide to the Intelligence Officer. With him was Brig. Gen. Matan Vilana'i, who had returned from study leave and was slated to replace me as Division Commander. In a third personnel carrier rode Niutek, a reserve Air Force colonel, a devoted and professional officer whose girth was a matter of renown. Behind Niutek was a radio personnel carrier. Bringing up the rear was Col. Itzik Gazit, commander of the artillery group. It was a platoon of sorts, capable of defending itself and generating fire in any direction. Before the war I had insisted on integrating the ACG into maneuvers just like any other formation. Several times we had gone out together, mounting mock assault and ordering fire in all directions. Now I informed Itzik and Niutek that I was heading for the battlefield; they could join me or not, as they wished. I knew they would be more effective in the War Room, but they refused to pass up the opportunity and rushed to join my personnel carrier.

Having reconnoitered the area at the end of Operation Litani, and having studied maps and photos intensively, I knew my way around. Again I looked in the direction of the Litani and beheld the impressive scene of armed forces, bristling with might, fording the surging river. We could see exactly who had already mounted the opposite bank and who was still crossing. Traffic jams had developed at the crossing points. I radioed the brigade commanders and alerted them to this problem; they would have to spread out the forces so as not to provide enemy forces or Syrian aircraft with easy targets. At about the same time, even a little earlier, we had sent Mofaz's force into action in the Khardale Bridge sector and the Arnon highlands, where Beaufort Castle was located. From a hill overlooking Marj 'Ayoun, our tanks and artillery fired at and around the castle. This was a feint, meant to pin down enemy forces in the Nabatiyya and Arnon highlands That way they would not move toward Akiyya Bridge and interfere with our progress there. The ruse worked beautifully. The terrorists stayed put, readying themselves to engage our forces crossing the river right there. Mofaz himself was supposed to ford the Litani to the right of the bridge. Later, however, he found the bridge intact and captured it.

Late that afternoon, I realized that the forces crossing the Litani at Akiyya Bridge area were taking longer than expected. Gabi, deputy commander of Golani, began to pressure me; he wanted to head for the field before the tail end of Barak Brigade had crossed the river. Otherwise he would fall behind schedule with his own objective, capturing the Arnon highlands and Beaufort Castle. As I overlooked the crossing area, tensely observing the dangerously slow and heavy traffic, I considered the possibilities. I thought about inserting Gabi into the Barak column, but things were in such a tangle that if I allowed the formations to intermingle, they might mix up their objectives.

After lengthy consideration, I decided to stick to the original plan. Gabi sat down in his place on the axis, crossing the river only after Dagan, Barak Brigade's commander, had done so.

At 1500 hours OC Northern Command Amir radioed me:

"Hi, Dror. We're going to visit you in a little while."

That was unexpected. "My operations officer is at the border point," I answered, adding, "I'm moving in. Over."

"Roger. See you. Over and out." Who was "we," and where did Amir intend to land?

A few minutes later I was summoned to the radio again. This time the voice was garbled.

"Identify yourself," I requested.

"Repeat. I didn't get you," the anonymous speaker replied. Then I identified the voice, which I had known from the Yom Kippur War, when it had forwarded orders to my brigade commander over the brigade airwaves. It was Raful, Chief of General Staff.

I briefed Raful on our location and situation.

"That's real good," the Chief of General Staff answered. "We're here with you, and we're seeing it. You'll have to be ready to turn northwest, when you get the order." The intention, of course, was to move up the coastal road toward the mouth of the Zaharani.

"Roger. All right. I'm moving north toward the mouth of the Zaharani. Over."

"That's OK. What concerns me are those people who write all kinds of things, and they're already here with you, inside."

Those "people", I understood at once, were from the IDF Spokesman's office. They had been sent to follow events in headquarters on the front. I knew Raful hated it, but I had been given orders in these matters and believed I had carried them out properly.

"Roger. Those people who were here set it up in advance. For the moment they're not leaking anything," I argued. "But when I showed up," Raful asserted, "they were thrown out." He hinted that he had already ordered them to leave.

"Roger. I don't know. But in any case — 'the ones who were here' coordinated it with your man in advance. Right now they're not leaking anything."

"I said they're *with you*. Right there in your tent!" Raful raged. "They didn't coordinate it. They are infiltrators, and they know where to infiltrate!"

Now I too began to lose my patience. Evidently Raful had set his helicopter down in my headquarters, attracting journalists who were interested in his company at just that moment. Headquarters was just off the road and easily accessible.

Amir grabbed the radio handset and asked when I could begin moving north toward Khardale Bridge. Checking briefly, I made sure that Mofaz controlled the river crossings and had begun to open the axis to the north.

"Roger, let him keep on going," Amir said, satisfied. "Let him use artillery. That way you can follow him, and if he can cross the Litani, that's OK too."

"Dror here. Roger. There's a problem with Gabi (deputy commander of Golani). He's still moving toward his target."

"Make them all move faster. Over and out." Amir signed off. It was 1530 hours.

I ordered the Operations Branch officer, Yossi R., to translate the guidelines into action. "Check with Gabi of Golani. Find out where he is," I added. "But I want to see the schedule right here — what it says about when he's supposed to turn toward Beaufort. Have him report to me. Over and out."

In the background I heard Yossi ordering Gabi to make better time toward the Arnon highlands and Beaufort. Then came Gabi's reply:

"I figure that'll take me lots more time."

The forces continued to inch along the mountainous twisting roads. The enemy personnel with rocket-propelled grenades delayed our tanks now and then, but not for very long. The hardest part was to move through the villages. Most were crossed by one main street, sometimes narrower than a tank.

Movement took place along four major spearheads. Mofaz advanced in the area of Khardale Bridge, starting from the slopes around Marj 'Ayun and heading northward. Golani Brigade crossed the Litani and continued northwest toward a-Dawir. Barak Brigade headed north on a route parallel to Golani's, with the intention of circumventing the Nabatiyya area and capturing the Zaharani River crossing near the village of Habush. The fourth spearhead, under Golani's deputy commander, crossed with some delay but advanced toward the Arnon highlands and Beaufort Castle according to plan. I personally supervised the area of the Litani crossing around Akiyya Bridge. I considered Akiyya Bridge the most important position of all; from it one could direct each of the forces on its axis and also spot "traffic jams", clearing obstacles and prodding stragglers. I felt bad about Gabi but could do little to save him. I was at peace with my decision not to insert him into the Barak Brigade forces. All I wanted at that time was to see the whole division on the other side of the river.

Rocket-propelled grenades struck one of the Barak

326 • AVIGDOR KAHALANI

tanks, wounding two crewmen. There commenced a
lengthy, exhausting procedure over the radio to obtain a helicopter to evacuate them, since the traffic
was too heavy to permit any possibility of overland
evacuation. My operations officer, Yossi, talked again
and again with officers in Command headquarters
until we finally got word that the chopper was on its
way to the stricken tank.

Then, although the Barak force's commander had
specified the casualties' exact location on the map,
the helicopter headed for another destination represented by the identical code. I cannot remember another instance of two points marked with identical
codes on one map! Thus the chopper landed in en-
emy-held territory, northeast of our forces, just outside Nabatiyya. It was attacked, all seven crewman
and medical personnel aboard were killed, and the
helicopter was destroyed. All of us — Command,
division, and brigade headquarters — came under
heavy pressure to act, because of the chopper acci-
dent, but we could only wait until we had wrested
the area from the terrorists. Interminable hours later,
the remains of the chopper and the bodies were recovered. Only then did we report to Northern Command.

At 1700 hours Gabi asked me for permission to begin
advancing toward Beaufort Castle and the positions
around it. Instead of waiting for stragglers on the
road heading upland from the Litani, his force would
embark on capturing its objective. After making sure
I understood everything, I gave Gabi the go-ahead.
On his way to Beaufort he informed me that he had
encountered an enemy reconnaissance vehicle and
destroyed it with the first round.

"I've got some journalists here in a Peugeot; they're driving me out of my mind," Gabi added.

"You've got to get to Beaufort fast," I reproached him. "As for the journalists, let the air out of their tires!"

Controlling a division from a moving armored personnel carrier in enemy territory is no simple matter. The division commander sits in the rear, his head and trunk outside the vehicle. An officer or some other commander navigates and directs the driver from one point to the next. In front of the commander, on a large plank, is a coded map of the war zone. With a blue marker I marked the forces' locations as reported to me during the fighting.

After I crossed the Litani and advanced several kilometers north, enemy forces reopened fire on my APC. I was moving alone, the command group carriers behind. Thus I had to devote much time to navigating, at the expense of attention to my map and radio. I asked an aide to the division intelligence officer, driving behind me, to pass me and lead us to the next point. I trusted him in any case, but since Matan Vilna'i was with him I had no doubt whatsoever that we would reach our destination.

Yossi, our operations officer, informed me that Mofaz was crossing Khardale Bridge and progressing well. I asked him to contact Command and request that they insert Menahem Einan's division into the column after Mofaz at some later time, to add momentum to the spearhead.

At 1745 hours Gabi reported that he was advancing toward the Arnon highlands with most of his forces. "Will you engage Beaufort soon?" asked Yossi.

"Fifteen-twenty minutes, I think."

That was good news. I understood that the Golani

deputy commander would succeed in eliminating the
delay caused earlier by the traffic jams. However, a
report from Mofaz from Khardale Bridge at approximately 1800 hours was not encouraging. Heading
north, he had come across dozens of mines along the
road, slowing him down. Progress was almost impossible. Since Mofaz' axis was supposed to serve
Command, I instructed Yoss to update Command
and explain the ramifications of these difficulties for
Menahem Einan's division.

"Ask for extra Engineering to help Mofaz, and
check the physical location of Menahem's division,
which is following us. That could be part of the considerations for continuing," I told Yossi.

My concern was for the force that was to pass
through ours. Troubled by the possibility that Northern Command would not be informed in time, I decided to report to OC Command personally.

"Akiyya Bridge is clear, if you want to use it for
Menahem Einan," I informed him.

"Can he cross in that area?" Amir asked.

"Affirmative. But not before dawn; there's lots of
traffic backed up," I answered.

"That's a pity. Can he pass you around Nabatiyya
tomorrow morning?" Amir pressed.

"OK. We'll coordinate it that way. Is he already
behind me? Over." I asked.

"He was instructed to move, but it's dark now and
it takes time..."

"All right," I answered. After a quick thought I
added, "OK, because I said there's a possibility of
inserting him around Khardale Bridge, too... I think
the bridge could be open within an hour or so." I
continued to stick to the original plan, keeping in
mind the route that I believed to be faster.

"All right. Open up the Khardale axis, and after that extend it toward the Nabatiyya axis and the mouth of the Zaharani. That's going to take time, too, so move it. Maybe you'll be able to get him across in the morning via Arnon highlands and Beaufort. Over," answered Amir. So it was indeed possible that Menahem would cross at dawn via Khardale Bridge, as stated in the original plan.

"OK. I'm going to take care of my tanks."

"All right. Go on. Make 'em all run. Real good. Over and out."

All the talks were recorded. Anyone who listens to the recordings must conclude that Yossi, the operations officer, and I knew nothing about the final order given to Menahem Einan's division to advance via Akiyya Bridge only. Yossi, situated next to the phone in the War Room all the time, in direct contact with Northern Command, received no such instruction. Other officers were present too and had heard the Command War Room speaking with us about one sector of the front only. They too overheard no instructions in this matter.

At 1822 hours I contacted Gabi for an update.

"Gabi here," the deputy commander of Golani answered.

"I've got all my forces with me. I went down into all the positions. The only problem is light. It's night, like you said! In terms of location, I'm not far from the objective right now. One unit is already engaging Kaf Arnon..."

"Where's your spearhead that's going to Beaufort?" I interrogated him.

"It's already crossing the road from Beaufort to Nabatiyya. In a little while I'll begin working on Beaufort and the antenna position south of it."

I could tell from the tone of Gabi's voice that he was in the midst of a battle. I knew I should not pressure him too much just then. I too never liked the idea of my commanders bugging me in the middle of an engagement with the enemy. Gabi's task included the capture of four objectives. The southernmost was the antenna, a few dozen meters south of the fortress. The second was the castle itself, and the other two positions that dominated the Beaufort zone and the area to its east, Khardale Bridge, and the "oil route" leading to the mouth of the Zaharani, where a major oil depot was situated.

"OK. Real good, real good," I answered. I was excited: so often had Golani reconnaissance practiced taking Beaufort on models, and here it was on the verge of the real thing!

"Are you putting up the flag today?" I asked Gabi.

"Affirmative. We'll do it. It'll be dark by then, so maybe you won't be able to make it out. We'll take a bunch of pictures. I'd like you to approve additional artillery ammo, because for some reason they've used it all up."

Gabi's report about an ammunition shortage surprised me. Now of all times, as he was about to storm Beaufort Castle! I ordered supplementary ordinance for artillery and issued instructions to see if the air force could bomb the fortress and the whole area again. Itzik and Niutek, the officers in charge of these matters, reported that Gabi was getting everything he wanted.

I contacted Command and clarified to the Command communications officer, who had answered in place of OC Command, the meaning of the large number of mines that were holding Mofaz back. The communications officer promised to pass this information on to Amir. I wanted to have the plan amended so that Einan would prepare an additional option for crossing the Litani.

The Arnon Highlands and Beaufort Castle Fall

The Arnon highlands loom over Khardale Bridge and overlook the Litani on its western bank. Beaufort Castle sits on the crest of the plateau, 700 meters above sea level. Beaufort, built in the early 12th century by the Muslims, is known in Arabic as Kala'at al-Shakif — "Observation Redoubt." The Crusaders made use of it during their stay in the area, and a Druse emir, Faher a-Din, used it to control the area in the 17th century. Until it was damaged in recent years, the castle was 120 meters long and 60 meters wide. Its strategic importance is tremendous; it overlooks and controls all routes leading to Sidon and the coastal plain.

Ever since the terrorists had taken over the place, Beaufort was emblematic of the terrorist threat against Israel's northern settlements. Over the years the IDF knew that terrorists and advance observation officers were digging in there and directing their fire from Beaufort at Israel's northern Galilee "panhandle," especially our border village of Metulla. Our air force and artillery often hit at the castle, but we never succeeded in finding out whether those inside it were injured, had fled, or had stayed where they were, continuing to scheme against us.

Gabi's Golani force had been ordered to take the entire Arnon plateau, including the castle. The force

divided into two formations. One, of battalion
strength and commanded by Maj. Amar, was to take
the ridge north of the Castle, where fortified positions controlled Khardale Bridge, the "oil route," and
the Litani River from the east. The second formation
was to take the fortress and the area south of it. This
force, composed of the brigade's reconnaissance company and the rest from the brigade engineering company, was commanded by Maj. Koplinsky of the recon company and his second-in-command, Tzvika,
commander of the engineering company. This force
itself was split in half. Engineering would take the
antenna position slightly south of the castle, and the
recon unit would take the castle and the fortified
combat trench along its southern flank.

In last-minute planning it was agreed that Beaufort would be taken by daylight, assuming that we
would enter Lebanon at dawn. However, the forces
trained on their Beaufort model by both day and
night; I attended some of those drills. They also practiced crossing the Litani on foot and climbing to the
objective from the east. I opposed this method once
we had received permission to use Akiyya Bridge. I
preferred an armored offensive from the west to the
very threshold of the objective because of the small
difference in elevation.

The first Golani breakthrough force under Maj.
Amar advanced in the dark toward the areas north of
Beaufort Castle, coordinates 548 and 571 on the map.
The men stormed these area, entered the trenches,
and began to clean them out. In hand-to-hand combat the battalion commander was seriously wounded
in the face, his personal radioman killed, and another
four soldiers (including the commander of the leading company) wounded. Despite his grievous inju-

ries, the battalion commander heroically continued to lead his men by radio for some time. Despite the artillery barrage that preceded the onslaught, the terrorists put up stubborn resistance throughout.

The deputy battalion commander, Shuki, took over for his disabled superior. One of the forces stumbled into a minefield; many of its men were injured. Some of those who went in to extricate them were wounded themselves, remaining prostrate in the field. A medic attending to the casualties was killed in action. For more than three hours the wounded men lay in the minefield until their comrades drove a tank into the minefield to evacuate them. The Golani men laid their injured comrades on its deck and took them to waiting helicopters that brought them to the rear. Koplinsky's force then regrouped to capture the castle and the antenna position.

Then Koplinsky, immobile in his personnel carrier, took a bullet in the chest. Making a quick decision, Gabi sent Goni Harnik to take charge of the battle. Goni, who knew every detail of the mission, set out for the area at once. His personnel carrier flipped over twice *en route*. Goni proceeded the rest of the way on foot, in agonizing pain from a back injury. When he finally met up with Tzvika, commander of the engineering company, they decided to change the plan: Tzvika's force would lead; Goni's would follow.

Ready to fire, Tzvika headed for the objective on foot. It was a clear night with a full moon; one could make out silhouettes and shapes at some distance. Crossing a minefield, Tzvika led his men to the antenna position. Within its trenches his men, with himself at their lead, fought with the terrorists hand-to-hand. The company doctor was wounded, as was

Erez, commander of the reconnaissance team. Nevertheless, with help from several recon soldiers, the antenna position fell.

Goni's forces followed the engineering company toward the menacing redoubt. His presence among the fighting men improved morale. Over the radio Goni identified himself by his previous, familiar code name, "Nokem" — the Avenger. Every fighting man knew that Goni was in charge from that moment on. When it came time to begin the ascent, the force crossed a white dirt path near the road leading to the castle. Exposed, the force came under heavy fire. Three recon men — Yaron Zamir, Yossi Oliel and Gil Ben-Akiva — were killed. The next objective was the southern edge of the combat trench leading to the fortress. The force continued under relentless machine-gun fire. Fortunately, the gunners could no longer see them and they could move freely.

The first two men who entered the first trench were Razi Kuterman and the squad commander, Avikam Scharf. They found, to their surprise, that the trenches were very narrow; the men, encumbered with equipment belts and weapons, found movement extremely difficult. Avi and Razi began to eliminate enemy personnel in the trenches until two bursts of enemy gunfire killed both of them. Motti, a recon officer following them, assumed command as the mopping up operation continued.

Accompanied by Goni, Motti headed for the castle entrance. The men fired in all directions and tossed grenades into the trenches. Many terrorists were killed; others could be seen fleeing the area. Then one stubborn foe, concealing himself on Goni's path, opened fire on Goni, killing him instantly.

The rest of the fighting men demonstrated impressive perseverance, cleaning out the trench to its very end.

The recon group took Beaufort Castle. One of its men, Roni, took the blue and white Israeli flag from one of the personnel carriers, climbed up the antenna, and affixed it to the top. I was pleased that it was Gabi of all men who had commanded this battle. I found him to be a superb, valorous officer and an outstanding leader.

At roughly 2200 hours the battle was over. Some time later I was informed that Goni had been killed. I couldn't accept it. Surely it was a mistake; surely another message would come, canceling the first one. It never came.

The day after Beaufort fell, after the dead and wounded were evacuated, the Prime Minister's helicopter landed in the field. Menahem Begin was accompanied by Defense Minister Ariel Sharon and Maj. Sa'id Haddad, commander of the Lebanese forces in southern Lebanon. Although I was responsible for the territory, no one had coordinated the visit with me. I knew nothing about the landing and learned the facts behind it only after the war. Interviewed about Beaufort on Israeli TV, the Prime Minister proclaimed that we had taken the fortress without suffering casualties — no men killed, none wounded. What was the origin of this tendentious assertion by the Prime Minister? The responses were embarrassing and harsh. The bereaved parents correctly considered his statement an insult to themselves and their sons. Military circles who knew the facts expressed astonishment at the fact that Mr. Begin had not been kept up to date. Later, discussing the affair with OC Command, I was told by Amir that he had been informed neither of the Prime Minister's landing nor of why Mr. Begin had not been updated. Making some casual inquiries after the fact, I found that while aloft, Begin had been in contact with General Staff Operations Headquarters, where the officers did not have the latest information. This, perhaps, was the source of the miserable error.

After the war it was my turn for criticism. Why had I ordered the capture of the Arnon highlands and Beaufort Castle the night of the first day's fighting, instead of waiting until the next morning?!

Everyone knows that a formation is assigned its duties by the headquarters in charge of it. Thus only headquarters can modify those duties. While the field commander is given some leeway to modify plans and change the directions of advance, he had no right to alter the mission in its general sense. Neither can he even change the schedule as dictated by headquarters.

My division had been ordered to take the entire Arnon highlands and the plateau near Nabatiyya. Furthermore — and this is important — the division had been ordered to cross the highway at the base of Beaufort via Khardale Bridge and advance along the "oil route," the path Menahem Einan's division would subsequently take. The understanding that Einan would use these axes was clear in all the orders. On the morning of the first day of the war I presented my plan to the Minister of Defense, the chief of General Staff, OC Northern Command, and General Staff officers, emphasizing that I was opening this axis for Menahem Einan and that taking Beaufort Castle was part of the plan. My plan attracted no adverse comments that morning. On the contrary: even Menahem, presenting his own plan, noted that he would cross the Litani at Khardale Bridge.

After the war, I asked David Agmon, Northern Command Operations officer (G-3), "Who in fact instructed me *not* to take Beaufort?"

"OC Northern Command Drori visited your headquarters by helicopter," Agmon replied. "He told you personally." Yes, Amir had landed at my headquarters, but no, we had not met.

When Amir arrived, I was with the advance command group. I had spoken with Amir only on the radio, and these talks, reported here word for word, attest that I knew nothing about a change in route of movement of Einan's division' moreover, I was never informed that my mission had been altered in any way. Had I known before Gabi had engaged the enemy at Beaufort that Menahem would move in the Akiyya Bridge area, I might well have changed my plan because the castle would not have threatened his advance. I would not have made any changes, however, without express permission from Northern Command.

In one of my radio talks with OC Command, I had pressed Amir Drori to encourage Menahem Einan to follow Mofaz. I believed Menahem would reinvigorate Mofaz's force at Khardale Bridge and thus help him open up the axis. Beaufort Castle and the objectives surrounding it dominated the Khardale Bridge crossing; were this not so, it would be reasonable to assume that the basic plan for the capture of the Nabatiyya and Arnon highlands would have required the surrounding of Beaufort, not its capture. Just by surrounding Beaufort we would have been able to pin down the enemy forces on the highland. That, everyone agreed, was essential: the highlands had to be under our control by the Time Khardale Bridge was opened. Listening to the radio talk, one finds that Command's operations officer asked us not to take Beaufort before getting the go-ahead from Command. The talk took place at 2104 hours, by which time the Golani fighters were already in the castle trenches, on the verge of winding up their task. When I received this information from the division operations officer, I sized up the facts in the field and ordered the forces to keep going according to plan. I even alerted Command that this was my decision.

After working together for many years, Amir Drori and I knew each other well. As his long-time subordinate, I had come to know his weaknesses and strengths. I cannot imagine that Amir had not intended to communicate to me the order not to capture the Arnon highlands. Contrary to Agmon's assertion, and as stated, Amir and I never met at that time. Moreover, personal encounters are no substitute for orderly staff work.

The IDF has plenty of communication and documentation systems. Almost every order is backed with telegrams, written communiques, etc. The men in the Command war room, which is equipped with facsimile, teleprinters, two-way radio, telephone, and other devices, are responsible for converting plans and commanders' guidelines into orders for the field formations. In the divisonal war room, in direct contact with Command at that time, were officers who were told nothing about any change in plans. Therefore I can only conclude that the snafu originated in the Command War Room. Command's war room also knew about the casualties we had suffered in the battle for Beaufort, and even gave the division everything it needed for their evacuation.

After the war I came under a cloud of accusations. To my disadvantage, no one set up a commission of inquiry or even appointed an examining officer. All around me there were whispers, but no one would look me in the eye and say what he thought. I knew how to reply to my army colleagues in their own language. With the bereaved families I treated the issue sensitively. I shared their pain — and still do.

In late 1988 I asked the Chief of General Staff, the head of General Staff Instruction Department, and the head of the History Department to verify whether the Basalt Division had been ordered not to take the Beaufort Castle on June 6. After painstaking inquiry, the head of the History Department sent me the following letter.

> History Department
> Office of the Department Head
> April 18, 1989
>
> To: Brig. Gen. Avigdor Kahalani
> Re: The Battle for Beaufort Castle (pursuant to your letter 595, December 1988)
>
> Pursuant to your question and according to the authorized material kept with the History Department, it would seem that the division commander (you) knew only in the middle of the offensive against Beaufort Castle that Command had asked you to wait for permission before taking the castle. Therefore this instruction was given too late (at 062115), whereas the battle itself had begun at 1900 hours.
> Sincerely yours,
> Lt.-Col. Benny Michaelson
> Head of History Department

Perseverance

The Hebrew expression for perseverance is "sticking to the target." It's a phrase we in the IDF use constantly. In the battle field it is the bridge that spans the abyss between the giving of orders and the difficulty of implementing them.

On the battlefield we frequently find that orders to rush an objective, capture it, or cleanse it of enemy forces are not carried out for lack of perseverance.

Perseverance is more than a cliche rasping over the radio waves. It demands sacrifice, sublime courage, and abundant use of judgment. In defensive battle, everyone knows, the soldier goes out to protect his own little acre at any price, knowing that his country and his own home are at stake. In the course of an offensive, things are different. Under life-threatening fire you are ordered to attain certain objectives whose nature and importance you may not understand. Often you ask yourself whether it's really necessary. That's a legitimate question. Then, however, comes an additional question, an inevitable one, the most important of all: do you do it at any price? Is it within the prerogatives and the ability of the man in charge of execution to estimate the number of casualties his action will entail, and according to this criterion, reconsider whether to obey the order?

Having accepted a mission, commanders must not decide whether to carry it out on a basis of the price they're willing to pay. When you go on the offensive, you aim to cause injury and you'd better be willing to suffer it too. The decision to call off an entire mission or parts of it belongs only to the party who decided on it. Only he has the right to modify its schedule, route of advance, and objectives. I prefer it that way, rather than to set up a framework depriving commanders of the right to think for themselves.

I once thought it best to let the persons in charge of execution sit with their commanders in the planning group to help formulate the plans. Experience, however, has shown me that such cooperation is usually undesireable. In the Yom Kippur War, for example, the ordr to enter Syria and close in on Damascus was given once the enemy had been stopped. No one consulted me about the timing or the need to make this move. Had I been asked, I would surely have been a thorn in the brigade commander's side. As a battalion commander ordered to occupy territory under difficult conditions — one swarming with enemy forces — I would have found it hard to swallow an incusrison into Syria. My concern at that moment was the state of my battalion. The men were exhausted, we were not sure who was alive and who was dead, and the tanks were in pitiful condition and few in number. Had I been consulted, I probably would have recommended postponing the action for a few hours or a few days. After the fact, however, I am convinced that the order and its timing were correct.

There is no doubt that decisions on missions such as this should be made by people with vast experience, who have the ability to think profoundly, clearly and analytically, and who possess large personal libraries of dog-eared history books. Such decisions require a long-range view, unaffected by fear of the mission and independent of the structure, size and organization of the force. Only thus can objectives and schedules be determined. The plan should be drawn so that the war ends with the fighting men standing at the best possible point for the beginning of political negotiations. Even the most valorous and daring of commanders cannot insulate himself from the impact of his immediate environment; thus his point of departure is the local problem — not the national need.

Israel's fate depends on fighting men who persevere — who "stick to their targets." The course of Jewish history is paved with the exploits of those who believed in what they were doing and persevered to the extent of the ultimate sacrifice.

Golani Brigade continued to advance into Lebanon through the night. I ordered it to stop for regrouping only when it reached the road heading west, downhill, toward the mouth of the Zaharani River and south of it. We were about ten kilometers from the water's edge, which was approached by two main roads. I and my advance command group positioned ourselves within the leading force, Amiram's tank battalion. Without warning, as I prodded my driver to advance with greater speed, we found ourselves on the front line of an engagement with the enemy. Spattered with heavy machine gun fire, we were forced to withdraw.

I was gripped with a sense of impotence. When I had come under fire in the past, I knew I could swivel my cannon, take aim, and blast the menace away. Here, in a personnel carrier, everything was different. Studying the maps in the back of the vehicle, as a division commander I was not supposed to instruct the driver. My sole means of defense was my phalanx of radios and their thicket of antennas.

Some time later we reached the junction of the

road heading for the mouth of the Litani. A warning reverberated over the airwaves: the junction was about to come under enemy artillery fire. We usually treat warnings of this kind casually. We wait and see where the shells will fall; then we hop into open territory. That way we avoid overcrowding. Accordingly, I ordered our unit to put distance between itself and the junction. Hardly had we advanced five meters, however, when an artillery shell fell on our position. My personnel carrier was hit from the rear, and that of Itzik, the artillery group commander, was hit on its side. Again we were lucky. No one was wounded.

Barak Brigade also continued to move through the night. I insisted as vehemently as I could that Barak reach the vicinity of Habush, a village south of the Zaharani. I was concerned that the terrorists might seize the only crossing in the area, enabling them to hold our forces back or pin them down. Nor did I disregard the possibility that the entire area had been mined. If it had, the enemy could seize the areas overlooking the road and prevent our spearhead forces from passing through freely and without casualties. Our men were tired; I had to prod Dagan, Barak Brigade's commanding officer, and did not relent until I'd made sure that his first battalion had occupied and taken control of the crossing.

Mofaz used the night to regroup, ordering his lead units to continue clearing mines from the "oil route" and to ready it for movement by our forces.

Sometime after midnight, Yossi, the division's operations officer, asked me for permission to insert supply convoys (fuel, ammo, food, water, and other needs) into the column. I gave my consent, adding a warning:

"I'm indeed concerned about running out of fuel," I told him. "It seems to me that this can't be done in an amateurish way. The operation's too involved, too complex. If it's not handled carefully, we're going to get stuck here, out of gas."

Yossi, who knew me well and understood what I meant, summoned all the supply officers and began to coordinate the matter with them.

Transporting supplies in the wake of combat forces is an incomparably complicated and difficult operation, involving long truck convoys laden with sensitive, vital equipment. They have to be protected by combat troops, and need navigation personnel to steer them to the meeting points with the field units. They have to be given the latest communications protocols, coordinated with the field formations. The convoys have to be divided proportionately among the forces, with each convoy carrying the right quantities of the right equipment to the right formation. The convoy has to be led by a force or a liaison officer familiar with the course of the fighting otherwise the convoy might deliver its wares to the enemy.

I have always feared the possibility that field troops might run out of fuel or ammo on the firing line, in the course of battle. Supply forces must be trained to reach every point on the battlefield, in full coordination with field forces, and should be instilled with a sense of responsibility and concern for the fighting man's every need.

The convoys did indeed set out. Quickly checking the next morning, however, I found that they had not joined up with the forces. I was worried.

I spent the night in the field with the command group. We had chosen a place at some distance from the main highway, so we could deploy the personnel carriers in a manner that permitted easy peripheral defense and nevertheless keep the vehicles close enough to maintain telephone contact among them. I turned the radio dial to the brigades' frequencies and used the hours off to ask Northern Command for an update on its plans and the next day's tasks. OC Deputy Command, Maj. Gen. Uri Simhoni, asked me to describe the location of my forces in detail. Between the lines I understood that Menahem Einan was indeed moving north toward the Beirut-Damascus highway and that I would be ordered to head for Sidon.

Shortly before 2300 hours I conversed with OC Command Amir Drori. Thus far I was not sure about my final destination. I knew I might be told to go north toward the Beirut-Damascus highway, using the Basri Crossing to reach Dir al-Kamar and continuing north from there to Dahar al-Bidr. Now Amir clarified that I was to move toward Sidon. We had not yet decided to occupy the city. Rather we would surround it from the south and east; the other two directions fronted on the Mediterranean Sea. In the morning I would acquire another tank brigade, one belonging to Itzik Mordechai's division, operating on the western sector along the coastal road. The reduced-strength brigade, commanded by Col. Eli Geva, was composed of Merkava and Patton tanks. They would add some variety to the tanks presently under my command, all of which were British Centurions that the IDF had modified in many ways.

Throughout the night Command radio emitted an unending stream of instructions, orders, and coordination guidelines. Yossi, the operations officer, pressured Command time and again to send us helicopters for evacuating the wounded from the Beaufort area. As of 2300 hours the wounded were still lying in the field.

"You sure Beaufort is ours?" Uri Simhoni asked Yossi, repeating the question as if in doubt whether to believe what he had heard.

Yossi's reply was unequivocal. He added, "We've also been waiting a long time for helicopters to get the wounded out!"

About ninety minutes later I broke onto the Command airwaves. It took some time to get a hold of the Command Communications Officer, Shalom A. Shalom, who had been the 7th Brigade's communications officer in the Yom Kippur War. He tried to placate me. Time and again Command radiomen answered my signal, called out "Wait!" and abruptly signed off. That aroused my anger. For some time it was my impression that our counterparts in the Command War Room were not functioning properly. Many of my queries were left unanswered; others never even reached their destination. After it had occurred several times, I deduced that the Command officers' liaisons with my division were being replaced too often to coordinate their succession, meaning that each new liaison had to be presented with the same queries again. OC Command and his operations officer, I assumed, were preoccupied with planning the war and coordinating with the General Staff or the Minister of Defense, and all I could do was to continue puzzling about the questions that troubled me. First, how urgent was it to move toward Sidon? After all, I had to know how to plan the soldiers' rest time and the pace of the advance. And when would Gabi's casualties be evacuated from the Arnon highlands?!

Only at 0200 hours, after another talk with Amir, were priorities brought into line and the timetable finalized. Northern Command headquarters was obviously unable to issue clear orders covering the next few days or even the next 24 hours. Because of political constraints and the involvement of the Defense Minister and Chief of General Staff in every step, we could move and operate only up to certain lines, after which we needed further approval to proceed.

At 0300 hours Yossi was still negotiating with the Command War Room. Rasping — he'd shouted himself hoarse — he complained that one of the two helicopters he'd been promised had not yet arrived. That reassured me. At least one helicopter was about to land at Beaufort Castle at long last. I climbed into my personnel carrier, unrolled my sleeping bag between the benches, and closed my eyes.

Monday, June 7, 1982

At the break of dawn I could make out details of the landscape. The houses of Lebanese villages seemed to be close by, and cultivated fields stood out against the otherwise stony terrain. The air was crisp and clean. Silence prevailed — a silence whose significance I understood well. It meant that we had regrouped for another day's fighting and were ready to move. After a quick cup of coffee, served by a member of my personnel carrier crew, I was ready to get back to the microphone.

In one of my first communications I greeted Eli Geva, whose brigade was moving northward along the coastal highway. Once it met up with my division, it would operate under my command. Eli and I had worked together in Battalion Oz 77 before the Yom Kippur War and had defended the Golan Heights together during that war. Later Eli had commanded a brigade in my reserve division. Now he was a few kilometers north of the Litani River on the coastal road. I instructed him to head for a *rendezvous* with Golani Brigade, which was heading west, downhill toward the coastal plain.

According to the plan for the second day of fighting, the advance into Lebanon was to continue as far as the city of Sidon. I was to join up with Amos Yaron's division at the Avali River. Golani was to come down on two axes — one heading toward Mazra'at al-Aquabiyya and the other along the southern bank of the Zaharani, ending at the oil refinery at the mouth of the river. Golani would subsequently cross the Zaharani, move toward Sidon, and engage the city.

Barak Brigade would cross the Zaharani near the village of Habush and move along two axes toward Sidon — one via Sarba, 'Anqun and Ma'adusha south of the Siniq River, and the other via Jaba and the village of Majdalyun to its north.

The deputy commander of Golani was instructed to secure the Arnon highlands by leaving a force behind, and to capture the Mazra'at-'Ali-Taher ridge overlooking the area east of the town of Nabatiyya. That would facilitate the subsequent capture of Nabatiyya itself.

Mofaz was to overcome the many obstacles in his path and climb the Nabatiyya plateau. There he would take charge of the force left behind by Gabi, deputy commander of Golani, and he and Gabi would occupy Nabatiyya together. Thus the force wielded by Mofaz for the capture of Nabatiyya would include Battalion Oz 77, as well as an infantry formation, half of an engineering battalion, and all the units under Gabi, the deputy commander of Golani.

Thus far I had not selected any defined task for Eli Geva. I instructed him to continue moving north toward the mouth of the Zaharani, from where he would subsequently take part in the campaign for Sidon — if my division was assigned to carry it out.

Division headquarters was still in the rear, as was my operations officer, Yossi. The quiet, convenient location had its advantages. It permitted high-quality communications with Command, both by wireless and by telephone, and excellent contact with Command's operations officer and the forces in the field. My command group could easily size up the situation at any time and drew up a plan for the next 24 hours. We were provided with all intelligence by the divisional intelligence officer, M., and our maps were updated regularly. M's assistant, D., worked at my side and discharged his duties in exemplary fashion.

Once I had finalized the plan, I ordered my operations officer, Tzvika, who was sitting next to me in the personnel carrier, to organize the group for further travel. As for the unit we would travel with, I had to choose between Golani and Barak Brigades and finally decided on Golani. Its southern approach route to Sidon would permit me to rendezvous with most of the forces arriving from the south along the coastal highway.

The division was deployed over a vast area, moving along dozens of routes and crossing a great number of villages. The typical Arab village has one main, bisecting street which is also the main highway. This street is rarely wider than a tank. A disabled tank or personnel carrier on the main street — and its men — would be very hard to extricate and would stop the entire force in its tracks.

Before entering each village, our forces had to ascertain whether it was friendly or hostile. Fortunately, most of the villagers waved white flags from their homes, and our ready-to-fire alert remained merely an alert. In several villages, however, we came under fire from the windows of houses as we passed through the narrow streets.

According to standard battlefield technique, one tests every area suspected of harboring enemy gunners before going in. If it turns out to be an enemy stronghold, it will get a heavy dose of aerial, artillery, and tank fire. In Lebanon this technique was useless, for everything was suspect. At the same time, every place was populated by civilians who might be wounded, and we did everything we could, danger notwithstanding, to avoid injuring innocent civilians. We considered it of utmost importance to maintain fair relations with the local population, so that their impressions of us would include more than devastation. After all, we would want them to cooperate with us later on.

From my position in the personnel carrier I enjoyed the unfamiliar scenery, proud of the tremendous might that was traversing the area precisely as planned. Again I marveled at the capabilities of our state-of-the-art two-way radios, with which the commanders controlled their forces perfectly, changing direction and modifying tasks even at distances of dozens or hundreds of kilometers from the forces doing the work. I was pleased with the sound of conversations between field commanders in my division and my staff officers; this was a well oiled, finely tuned machine. I forced myself not to interfere too much; I had to let my operations officer conduct his share of the campaign. But because Yossi was far away and did not always know the considerations behind the decisions, I was often the man behind the mike. At times I felt that I could not take the earphones off even for a moment; an urgent problem might arise and I would be unable to resolve it. I was always troubled by the possibility that commanders might try to contact me or one of my men and fail to get an immediate response — a too-typical occurrence in most headquarters.

I left it up to the commander of Barak Brigade to coordinate with Einan's division on how to divide the sectors in the area of the village of 'Arb Salim. Gabi of Golani reported that he had taken Mazra'at 'Ali Taher and could see white flags fluttering in the vicinity of Nabatiyya. Mofaz was still encountering delays in his climb to the Nabatiyyan highlands. He said he would need "lots more time," perhaps it would take him until the afternoon to join up with Gabi. His remarks disturbed me: I wanted Nabatiyya to fall that very day. In the meantime, Gabi took Golani Brigade across the mouth of the Zaharani and prepared to continue north toward Sidon. Then, concerned about his supplies, Gabi asked permission to stop and refuel. Once he got the go-ahead, he found a superb solution: a gas station across the Zaharani that supplied the brigade's needs.

Later on, Eli Geva too complained about a serious gas shortage. I asked him what had become of his supply convoys; Geva did not answer. Wishing to prevent any delay by Elik, whose force constituted the division's reinforcements, I decided to give him Golani's fuel tankers. They had been delivered to Golani but were no longer needed urgently, since the brigade had filled up on Lebanese-supplied fuel. By my instructions, and over brigade commander Irwin's vigorous opposition, the fuel went over to Eli.

Thick black smoke billowed over the giant fuel depots at the mouth of the Zaharani, and flames of unknown origin were consuming two of them. The cloud was visible for many kilometers. I was worried that the burning fuel gushing from shattered depots would reach the river crossings and obstruct them. Fortunately, that did not happen; the forces advanced unimpeded.

We were approaching Sidon. Irwin, commander of Golani Brigade, ordered his tank battalion to lead the brigade toward the 'Ein Hilweh refugee camp. He requested and received permission to take and hold the areas overlooking the region, with the intention of opening up alternate routes into the center of town.

At approximately 2300 hours, Brig. Gen. Amos Yaron contacted me. Yaron's forces had arrived by sea and had captured the northern outskirts of Sidon in the area of the Awali River crossings. Yaron himself was in the vicinity of Damour, several kilometers up the coast, and his forces controlled the axis leading north from there to Beirut. He was alone, and I was concerned that he was under enemy attack or some other pressure. We had always tried to plan so that forces sea-borne into enemy territory, far from the land forces' routes and cut off from assistance and supplies, would have to spend as little time as possible waiting for the other forces to join up.

Amos, however, was calm. He and his forces sat and waited for us — for Eli Geva, to be precise — to join up with him according to plan as soon as possible. The vehicle and personnel carriers designated for the link-up with Amos were *en route* to Sidon, where they were to cross the city once we had occupied it. Amos' deputy, Yitzhak Zamir, commanded a long convoy that carried everything Amos needed. I could not help but notice his impatience when he asked when the axis would be open.

Then Dagan, commander of Barak Brigade, informed me by radio of the death of Uzi Arad, the leading company commander in Ayal's battalion, now advancing toward the village of Jaba. Uzi had been appointed to his position shortly before the war. I had known him personally, but to Danny, my bureau chief, he was like a brother. Danny, orphaned as a boy, had been "adopted" by Ruthie and Arye, Uzi's parents. A little later, Danny himself radioed me and asked for permission to go home. I agreed, of course.

Suddenly Dagan, commander of Barak Brigade, came on the air with a tone of undisguised alarm. Spiegel, commander of the brigade's infantry battalion, had run into Syrians!

Spiegel reported having engaged "men wearing the other kind of uniform" several kilometers north of Jaba. I checked my watch: it was approximately 0100 hours.

"Dror here. Did they open fire?" I asked Dagan. I could almost picture how the incident would end.

From the information available to me I thought it unlikely that the Syrians had reached that point. We hoped they would clear out once they spotted us approaching the area.

Dagan answered at once: "The Syrians opened fire on Spiegel!"

Immediately I tuned into Spiegel's frequency and broke in. The battalion commander, agitated but decisive, had made up his mind to continue advancing. He would attack the Syrians.

"Stay away from them!" I quickly dampened his enthusiasm. "Under no circumstances are you to go down toward them from your firing positions!"

After their engagement with Barak, it seemed as if the Syrians were trying to retreat. I decided to let them pack up and look for new positions; in the meantime I would talk it over with OC Command Amir Drori. Drori responded to the new battlefield developments with several questions.

"What makes you think they're Syrians?" he asked skeptically.

"Baruch took a few PoWs, and there's no doubt about their identity."

That seemed to satisfy Amir, but he continued to interrogate me, anyway. He had not really made up his mind about how to treat the Syrians. We had met them several kilometers further south than we had expected.

After Drori completed his questioning I said: " I understand. For now I'll maintain contact but nothing more."

What I understood was that Amir himself needed his superiors' permission to let me attack the Syrians.

"Is he OK there? Has he got problems?" Amir pressed, concerned about the Golani Battalion and its commander, Spiegel.

"You know the kid. His morale's OK; he's in good shape."

Now we finalized matters: our forces would wait in place and prepare for defense. I was very eager to continue advancing in that sector; I could not let the Syrians deploy on a new line from which they would be hard to dislodge. In a case like this one should continue applying pressure so that the enemy cannot reorganize. Still, the matter was unquestionably sensitive. I contacted Dagan and Spiegel, passing down the order: maintain contact and no more.

I had more urgent problems on my mind just then. The 'Ein Hilwe refugee camp was putting up very stiff resistance to Amiram, commander of the Golani tank battalion. I was also increasingly concerned abut the capture of Nabatiyya and its vicinity. Mofaz was still trying to climb the plateau near Nabatiyya, and it seemed that he would not succeed in fulfilling the objective.

I updated OC Command Amir Drori: "I'm going to have to take the place with just Gabi." Drori talked me out of it. We agreed that I would wait until the last possible moment on the schedule. At the same time I gave Gabi, about 30 kilometers from me, some forewarning. He was to make all preparations and present me with a plan. Only when I approved it would he be allowed to move on to the town.

I ordered my operations officer, Yossi, to head toward me at approximately 1200 hours. The personnel carriers of the advance command group were suitable for a gathering of all headquarters; there we would plan the coming battles. It took Yossi several hours to move toward the mouth of the Zaharani, his large headquarters following him. Throughout that time I had to sit still, serving as one stationary address for all our formations, now in mid-combat across a vast theater of operations.

Then Barak Brigade split in half. One force continued to confront the Syrians and waited for Menahem Einan's division, which had been delayed for unexplained reasons at 'Arab Salim. The other force began to move toward Sidon. I urged Dagan to press ahead at maximum speed. This he did not do. Making inquiries, I found that he was short of fuel. Eli Geva,

listening in on my talk with Dagan, was heartened
and calm after acquiring Golani's fuel. Now he broke
into the conversation. "If he's running out of gas, he
can have a little of mine," he offered, hoping that
Dagan was listening.

The next exchange was a long talk with Gabi,
deputy brigade commander of Golani. Gabi presented
his plan for taking Nabatiyya. I set a number of "red
lines" that he was not to cross without my express
permission. I suspected he might get bogged down in
the Lebanese town, even though he stressed that he
had spotted hundreds of white flags in the windows
of its houses. After verifying his report, I gave him
the green light to occupy the city.

Veritable throngs of visitors had begun dropping in
at my headquarters, disrupting the course of work. I
ordered all of them to content themselves with "observer status" and stay away from maps and other
equipment. Even the field formations had to queue to
speak with me. Each commander referred his specific
problems to me, compounding my burdens and forcing me to answer questions that should perhaps have
been resolved at the brigade level. Most of the visitors were troubled commanders who faced delays in
schedule or had been handed "impossible" missions.
After our talks, each one went away satisfied.

I clutched the microphone all the time, monitoring
the conquest of Nabatiyya and intervening only when
necessary. I listened to developments in the area
where contact had been made with the Syrians, and
coordinated the exchange of duties between Menahem
Einan's division and Baruch's Golani battalion; the
latter had to rush off to Sidon. I had to intervene to
make sure Dagan got his fuel; otherwise he might

have fallen behind schedule. Even so, I did not expect him to reach Sidon before midnight. Eli Geva's force, advancing toward Sidon by an alternate route, suddenly ran into a steep grade of which Geva had not known. He had to take the brigade to the rear in a complex and difficult operation. Golani was pressing for air and artillery support as it moved in on the 'Ein Hilweh camp. My staff officers now worked at my side; no longer did I have to use the two-way radio to refer problems to my staff and tell it how to resolve them.

At dusk, I allowed Golani to ease up on 'Ein Hilweh. Another Golani battalion, under Motti, was on the main road to Sidon; it was also looking for a more convenient place to spend the night. Motti's force had been attacked several times from nearby citrus groves and had suffered several casualties. Gabi called in with more pleasant news: Nabatiyya had fallen with relative ease — and with no casualties at all!

I discussed with my deputy Yodke the problem of how to provide Barak with fuel. His plan was somewhat reassuring. I wanted to reach the point where everyone, but everyone, had full fuel tanks. Fuel shortages, I knew, would keep me from continuing with the next day's missions.

We spent the night planning the occupation of Sidon, sharing our uncertainties with the brigade commanders by radio. Command had still not ordered us explicitly to take the city. Every packet of orders read out before the war had given me the impression that the area toward Damour and Beirut would be my responsibility, while Itzik Mordechai would take Sidon. I had no idea what was happening in Itzik's sector; I didn't even know what Command had in mind for him for the next day. I went to sleep only after I had planned Sidon down to the last detail.

At 0200 hours my operations sergeant woke me up.

"An order has come in from Command: we're going to take Sidon!" he said excitedly.

I took the news calmly. I had received warnings of this the previous night, and I had shown the plan to my brigade commanders. Now all I needed to do was to forward the command verbatim.

The capture of Sidon would begin at dawn. Examining the situation briefly, I found that Dagan was still waiting for fuel and that Baruch's battalion, now freed by Einan's division, had not yet joined up with Dagan.

"You're going to start this battle on the wrong foot," I complained to Jackson, the division supply officer. "I've known you as the man who gets things done, but now it looks to me as if supplies are going to hold back the war!"

That put him under pressure. Now, I was sure, he'd break his back to find solutions.

Working in the illuminated war room along with Yossi were M., my intelligence officer; Itzik, commander of the artillery group; Niutek, the commander of air support; Ilan, the communications officer; Mizrahi, the engineering officer; and their deputies. Each had mastered his role; all would work in coordination.

As for air support, I decided to remove responsibility for its activation from the brigade's hands. I preferred to have the Air Force operate up to a certain line within the city, according to its own timetable. All that mattered was that it attack the targets that I needed it to, upon my request. That was the most convenient way for both sides. Anyone who knows that aerial bombardment is no substitute for artillery advancing with the ground forces, will never restrain the Air Force from carrying out its missions. Communication with the Air Force is no simple matter; it requires special skill. Directing an aircraft to its target by wireless is a complicated, difficult task, sometimes dangerous to both parties. Occasionally the air and ground forces fail to understand each other, leaving the planes to circle around and around until it's their turn to attack.

Niutek, my air support man, informed me frantically that the Air Force lacked aerial photos of Sidon of the kind that we had, with each house given a number. There was no point in calling Air Force headquarters. Niutek made several phone calls from the field and sent a few telegrams. That resolved the matter.

Sidon was full of enemy targets and concentrations. We had to assign each plane a defined target, so each pilot could load up with the right kind of bombs and, before takeoff, become thoroughly familiar with the nature and contours of the target. The Air Force has a major role to play in the capture of any objective, but I had not yet decided to use all the force now available to me.

Under cover of darkness we moved our artillery battalions up to the mouth of the Zaharani River. By dawn, the cannon could cover any range we might need.

The order to capture Sidon included information that a paratroop brigade which had passed through Itzik Mordechai's sector would be transferred to my division the following day. Its commander, Gotzi, a familiar figure among the paratroops, had mastered his duties long before the war. Itzik, who was to engage in taking Sidon, had approved this plan at that time. Such a supplement of manpower and firepower means alot to a commander facing such an engagement in urban territory. I looked forward to receiving it.

Sidon falls: June 8-9, 1982

We divided the Sidon sector into the mountain slopes and the coastal strip. The heights east of town began at 100 meters above sea level and gradually rose as one moved inland from the coast. The city was surrounded with areas of natural vegetation, cultivated fields, and extensive citrus orchards. The terrain east of town was heavily fissured with channels and streams; it could be crossed, and the town entered from that direction, simply by using existing roads and paths. To enter town by either of the two roads from the south, down the coast, we would have to pass through the 'Ein Hilweh refugee camp and the center of Sidon, although we would not need to enter the lower part of the city. The city's important neighborhoods ('Ein Hilweh, al-Halaliyya, al-Kinya, Kiyya, al-Khara, and Meah-Meah) and the villages on its outskirts fortified the city. For planning purposes, we had to deal with a Greater Sidon, population 150,000.

About 1,500 terrorists — most members of Fatah, the major PLO faction — were deployed in the Sidon area. They dominated the thoroughfares and positioned themselves in tent encampments and recently erected, fortified bunkers. Also active in the area was an armored *fujj* (something like a reduced -strength brigade) of the Palestinian Liberation Army, composed of some 40 tanks and several dozen personnel carriers. Several headquarters were sited in the built-up part of town, including that of the Kastel Brigade, which served as headquarters for all the terrorist organizations in the area. The various organizations also had depots of ammunition, fuel and equipment in the city. Lebanese forces were deployed east of town. We did not consider them especially important. However, not knowing how they would react to our operations, we were ready to deal with them too.

Our basic assumption in planning the occupation was that at least 3,000 terrorists were holed up in the city. Furthermore, many terrorists fleeing the IDF from other areas had retreated to Sidon. We knew, also, that the terrorists were inclined to fight it out in town. They were deployed in many positions in the densely populated area, so we would have to treat every street, alley and house as an objective to occupy.

I was surprised by Command's decision to entrust the capture of Sidon to my division. Thus far I had believed that Command would prefer to make use of my regular armored division for rapid advance, either toward Beirut or toward the Beka'a Valley. However, we took this as a compliment; one of the war's major objectives was ours to attain.

According to the conception that took shape in my headquarters, as based on the existing Northern Command plan, we would enter Sidon from two directions: south and east. The Navy could be integrated into the campaign, too, by landing assault forces from the west. We would leave open the roads heading north, allowing the terrorists to flee town. Leaving the terrorists an escape route would reduce their resistance and make the occupation easier. I intended to finish the job as quickly as possible. It was of utmost importance to open the streets crossing Sidon, for without them our forces could not move north, toward Beirut.

Gotzi's paratroop brigade was to open the main highway into the city, permitting our forces to advance northward. Golani, struggling to take the 'Ein Hilweh camp, would open and secure a parallel route for the movement of forces who would flank the center of town on their way north. Barak, descending from the highlands eastward on two major axes, would capture the villages and neighborhoods east of town and the hills overlooking that area. From there Barak would be ready, by my order and with my go-ahead, to "slide" into town. Eli Geva's brigade would cross the Siniq River, climb the plateau, pass through Barak, and advance in the direction of Amos Yaron's division, waiting in Damour. After joining up, Yaron and Geva would head for Beirut together. Yisrael's regular paratroop battalion, which had landed at the Awali crossing with Amos Yaron, would follow the main highway south and block terrorist forces heading north.

Two formations were left out of the plan. One belonged to Gabi, deputy commander of Golani; the other was Mofaz's brigade. They stayed behind in the highlands overlooking Nabatiyya. My division also had a quota of about 120 air sorties for targets in and around Sidon; we could also call on many artillery battalions, which had been brought in from the surrounding areas and amassed here in preparation for the occupation. They included regular battalions under Shmulik, Yoram and Yisrael, and several reserve battalions. In charge of all of them was Moshe Ronen, second-in-command to Gazit.

At daybreak the Air Force began to land effective blows on clearly defined targets in town. The strikes were thorough, displaying pinpoint accuracy. Niutek handled the air coordination with impressive skill. From his personnel carrier, parked next to the war room, we could hear him threatening and roaring at Air Force liaisons at Northern Command. Nerves frazzled, he demanded more aircraft and insisted that the Air Force keep its word about adjusting the types of ammo to the targets. We also heard his exchanges with the pilots who were carrying out these missions. Their very fear of his shouts, it seemed, made them descend toward their objectives with greater velocity.

I placed most of the artillery battalions at the brigade commanders' disposal; they would soften up the enemy before the ground forces moved in. We had ample quantities of artillery pieces and shells. Sidon was engulfed in a powerful, intimidating din.

Gotzi, commander of the paratroop brigade, had reported that he would be at my service early that morning. When the time arrived, his brigade was still many kilometers behind. To my surprise, he reported that his fighting men would not catch up before noon. I urged him to prod them on. They had to reach the southern outskirts of the city at once.

Golani Brigade continued to push for a breakthrough in 'Ein Hilweh. I let the brigade commander operate at his own discretion. Leading the Golani forces was the second battalion of Barak, under Amiram. Amiram, of average height and rugged build, had just made the transition from paratroops to armor. He had been wounded in war, and the scars of his burns were well evident on his hands and face. Amiram and I had attended the American Command

and Staff College together about three years previously, but I did not let our friendship keep me from viewing his actions critically. He had found it hard to adjust to the Armored Corps' way of life, and I had summoned him on several occasions to discipline him. Now, to assess Amiram's conduct of the battle, I tuned to the frequency used by his battalion. What I heard was the voice of a spirited commander, advancing with the vanguard of his men and demonstrating laudable courage and leadership. Amiram was driving the spearhead forward, the commander of Golani prodding him from behind. I was proud of Amiram.

The commander of Barak Brigade radioed me again and again. Barak had run into lengthy convoys of vehicles leaving the city, as well as throngs of civilians clutching white flags. We had to decide at once how to treat them. Then came another problem: it was 0630 hours, and Golani had not yet joined up with Barak. According to Dagan, they would not do so for another two and a half hours. I decided to slow down the brigade's advance. Barak was already in radio contact with the paratroop battalion that had landed at the Awali crossing, and the paratroopers sounded calm and quiet.

Eli Geva's brigade was short one battalion, having left it behind in Itzik Mordechai's sector. Eli asked me to do everything I could to get his battalion back before he tried to circumvent Sidon. I recommended that once he crossed the Siniq River he advance by the only available route: up the mountains east of Sidon. Once Eli's brigade cleared the entire axis, I would gather my advance command group and head for the mountains, from which I would be able to look down on the city.

However, I had to wait longer than expected; on the way Eli ran into many problems that impeded his progress. The most serious was that two tanks overturned on the dirt path up the mountain. The road was blocked for hours, the entire brigade waiting behind the disabled vehicles.

I was in constant contact with Command headquarters. I shared with Amir my feeling that Amos Yaron was under pressure and that I had to open the axes as fast as possible. Amir reassured me:

"It's more important not to get tangled up in that town. You'd have lots of casualties. And don't worry about Amos. He's not under attack; he's just waiting for ammo and fuel. They're bringing it all by sea, even his personnel carriers."

Amir's deputy, Uri Simhoni, further reassured me and added words of encouragement: don't save ammo! All eyes at Command were on my division, and everyone was rooting for us.

Now was the right time, I thought, to brief Amir and Uri on my situation. It was almost 1200 hours and Gotzi's paratroop brigade, assigned to open the central axis, had not yet arrived. I knew that my commanders, like myself, could only goad the brigade to pick up the pace. Still I wanted them to know that I was advancing on all axes except for the main street of Sidon. Planning the occupation of the city, I had first thought to concentrate Gotzi's force in the east and take the city from a direction less expected. But once I understood that the brigade was actually intended to move in from the south, and that approaching the city from the east would waste time in replanning and execution, I decided to let Gotzi come in from the south after all.

At 0800 hours another brigade radioed me. Its

anonymous commander, "Shinhav" ("Ivory"), informed me that he was at my disposal. Whose was that familiar voice, and what new formation was annexed to mine? A few more sentences cleared up the mystery. It was my old friend, Col. Haggai Regev, operations officer of the 7th Brigade in the Yom Kippur War and a former platoon commander, along with me, in the late Shammai Kaplan's company. I assumed Haggai was to join up with Amos Yaron's division following Eli Geva, and I sent Col. Yossi Melamed to him to brief him. Melamed had just completed his term as commander of Barak Brigade and had joined my headquarters as assistant for special missions.

Again I marveled at meeting up with the same people in each war. In the Six-Day War, Haggai had been operations officer of a battalion in the 7th Brigade. Back then, Melamed had commanded an armored infantry company in the same brigade, and we had fought together. In the Yom Kippur War, Haggai had been the brigade's operations officer; Melamed had been first deputy battalion commander and later full battalion commander. Eli Geva had been a commander who had fought several battles under my command. Now it was 1982 and here we were again, all in the same sub-sector, coordinating our tasks in pursuit of the same goal.

The divisional radio network operated without let-up. I marked the forces' progress on the open map on the desk in my tent. Giant aerial photos of the city of Sidon were mounted on the wall facing me, and I scanned them every now and then to track the forces and guide them. I talked with Northern Command using the wireless telephone on my desk and controlled the forces with the microphone next to it. Operations sergeants sat along the flaps of the War Room tent, monitoring the radio networks and tracking the movements of the forces. Most of my staff officers, were also within calling distance, ready to receive and forward information. We also had many visitors throughout the day; they joined us at the command table and listened to the battles unfold.

The most surprising visitor was Maj. Gen. Yekutiel ("Kuti") Adam. I was pleased to see him; I had always found him to be a fair-minded, serious, and talented man, whom I liked. Col. Haim Sela, one of my team instructors at Command and Staff College, had accompanied Kuti, who radiated friendship and warmth.

"I've just come from the Northern Command war room," Kuti announced. "They're following your movements all the time in there. They're really excited!"

"Yeah? Who?!" I was curious.

"The whole gang, from the Chief of Staff down. But the most interesting was Begin. He was so proud of you when he heard you on the radio!" I won't deny it: that WAS exciting.

"You're going to make major-general," Kuti added suddenly, patting me on the shoulder. Why did he choose this of all times, in the middle of a war, to tell me that?

"That's what Begin said. He told everyone there that he'd make you major-general after the war."

I smiled, not sure how to respond to Kuti's festive proclamation. The easiest way out was to say, "Thanks," grab the mike and go back to running the battle.

Dagan and I decided then to hasten the surrender of Sidon by ordering several civilians whom the brigade had taken prisoner to return to the city and call on the enemy forces to give up. Armed with precise instructions, the civilians set out for the terrorists' headquarters. I held them back until our Air Force had run a few more sorties on the city. Then I ordered a cease-fire.

"You got POWs?" I asked Dagan.

"Two, over." "Roger. Don't let another Pinto happen!" I reminded Dagan of the scandal involving POW deaths during Operation Litani in 1978.

Our next task was to enter downtown Sidon. The commander of Barak Brigade was full of initiative; he had captured several Lebanese soldiers and used them to summon several of the town notables. He would coordinate the next stage with them.

Reports coming from all sectors made it clear that the civilians of Sidon were panic-stricken, seeking to flee from the terrorists who had overtaken their city. As we advanced, we moved special squads of Arabic-speaking soldiers — defined by the IDF as "prisoner interrogators" — to the head of our forces, and equipped them with powerful public address systems. They ordered the town's residents who were fleeing to move toward the coast. At the same time, our aircraft dropped leaflets instructing the civilians to refrain from cooperating with the terrorists; if they followed our instructions, no harm would befall them. I sympathized with these confused, terrified Lebanese. We had to make it clear to them how to avoid the consequences of our massive offensive.

After thinking it over, I decided to halt the drive on Sidon for a full hour, from 10:00 to 11:00. Only formation in direct contact with the enemy, which could not conceal their disgruntlement upon hearing this decree, were allowed to continue fighting. The aerial bombardment did indeed stop and the artillery fell silent at 10:03. The prisoner interrogators set out with their loudspeakers, and civilians began to throng toward the coast as instructed. Wherever Israeli tanks and forces were stationed, the civilians came out onto their porches to behold the astonishing sight of the IDF entering Sidon.

With Gotzi's paratroop brigade still on the way, I could not set zero-hour for the capture of the main street. The problem began to trouble me. That was the shortest and fastest way north — and the spearhead was taking its sweet time.

Radio communications with Irwin, commander of Golani Brigade, was poor because of his low elevation. Irwin was trying to explain that he was in the midst of an engagement in 'Ein Hilweh and was not making significant progress. I instructed him to grab a few civilians and send them into the camp, making it clear to the terrorist commanders that we intended to come in with full force. The task was clear, and I preferred not to interfere with the conduct of the battle. I believed Amiram would open a road through the campt in the best way possible. The resistance in the refugee camp took us by surprise; all day long we bombarded the camp from the air and with our artillery. Still, I did not put Golani under too much pressure; several of Amiram's tanks had been damaged in combat, and several fighting men had been killed. Apart from this, I felt we were on the verge of opening up the center of town.

"Dror, this is Laor, over," a voice suddenly crackled over the division radio. I thought my ears were fooling me, and I waited.

"Dror, this is Laor, over," the voice repeated.

"Dror here. Is that Zilia? Over."

"Roger, affirmative. Zilia. Is a vehicle approaching you? I'm not mobile. Over."

Indeed, it was Lt.-Col. Ephraim Laor. He had been a company commander in my battalion, Oz 77, in the Yom Kippur War. Then too he had broken into my radio transmissions without warning. Now Laor was freshly released from prison, whre he had been serving time for driving without a license. Laor, a genuine slob, proved himself in the Yom Kippur War, and I remembered this to his credit. As commander of the 7th Brigade, I had handed the 82nd Battalion to him, the IDF's first tank battalion. Subsequently Laor had joined the division and was assigned to one of the reserve formations on the Golan Heights. The formation's leisurely pace of activity was not to his liking, and, relying on his friendship with me, asked me to give him more interesting duties. Now he reported to me, along with Yigal Ben-Shalom, commander of the 7th Brigade's reserve armored infantry company. I issued the two of them a personnel carrier, and they headed for the Lebanese villages to collect weapons from the locals. By nightfall they returned at the head of a convoy of heavy trucks and pickups sagging with ammo and weapons. It took real guts to carry out such a mission!

Eli Geva called in again; he was not succeeding in climbing the mountain. It was not my day. Gabi, deputy commander of Golani, sounded irate about my having left him behind in Nabatiyya: " I don't think I deserve this punishment," he griped.

"Roger. Thus far you've done real good work," I said, encouragingly. "I'm fighting for you right now.

Command wants to send you to the eastern sector, and I'm trying to talk them out of it."

I sympathized with Gabi, but did not want to set him in motion toward Sidon before getting the OK from Command. I put up a stiff argument with the Command operations officer, trying to persuade him to attach Gabi to me and leave Mofaz alone in the sector, according to the original plan. I did not believe I had sold him on this point, and waited for an answer.

"Maybe," Gabi continued to press, "I'll arrange with Mofaz that I go to you — and then I can join up? What's more, we're right on the road, ready to move now!"

"I understand you, but stay where you are and wait for instructions."

A few minutes later we were ordered to part ways.

"Take care of yourself!" I called to Gabi as he headed north toward Jebel Baruch.

Now we received a warning about an aerial attack on our forces. We could not figure out the origin of such an attack until a Syrian aircraft passed several meters over my headquarters' antennas, its thunder shaking the entire war room tent. We ran for shelter. If only I were in a tank, I said to myself. Nattke Nir, chaiman of the Soldiers' Welfare Committee, who was visiting headquarters, ran alongside me. One of his legs was ramrod stiff, the result of an injury in the Six-Day War. Only with great effort did he stagger out of the war room. I offered to carry him to safe quarters on my back. The enemy aircraft did not return.

In the meantime, our own planes circled overhead, waiting to renew the attack on Sidon. Most of the artillery battalions were stationed not far from my headquarters. When the ceasefire expired, they resumed their bombardment of Sidon with renewed vigor. It was noon, and the paratroop brigade had still not reported. I updated Command: we were so far behind schedule that I could not deal with opening the main street of Sidon. No one in Command could do a thing. I continued to pressure Gotzi, the brigade commander; this too proved of no use. Now I gave Barak Brigade permission to come down from the highlands to the railroad track that bisected the fields at their base. To achieve this, they had to coordinate with Golani so as not to run into each other; I attended to that personally. It occurred to me to hand the job of opening the main street of Sidon to Golani, using Motti's battalion. I was losing precious time and might not wind up my mission by dusk — the deadline I had set myself. I asked Gotzi to report for a briefing, but he asked me to let him return to his brigade and push it forward. I let him have his way, and sent my deputy, Yodke, to brief him for me.

I wanted a break from the war room myself. I wanted to get away, head for the field and smell the gunpowder. Intuition told me this would do the forces more harm than good. Heading for low-elevation territory — the only place I could reasonably go — would cause serious control problems, since radio contact with the forces along the coast were very poor.

Instead I decided to relocate to the mountain area from which Barak had descended as soon as Gotzi started down the main street, and I instructed the advance command group to prepare to move. The only axis permitting movement toward the best position for direct control was that being cleared by Eli

Geva, heading for Meah-Meah. That axis, however, was blocked by overturned tanks, and his entire brigade was waiting in the citrus groves until they were evacuated. I had lined up a helicopter for myself and the formation commanders in case we wanted to go anywhere. I refrained from using it; perhaps this was an error on my part. I should have bypassed the immobilized forces, gathered a reduced-scale staff, and flown to an observation position in Meah-Meah. So firmly did I control each formation from the war room, I felt, that I was missing out on nothing. By going into motion I might lose some of that control.

Then my friend Yossi Melamed suggested that we go down together to the forces waiting at the entrance to Sidon.

"I'm sure it'll be fun," he recommended.

"It'll be fun, but I might lose contact with all the forces! Look, we control every aircraft in the sky, and I've got to take decisions every moment. There's a problem of coordinating our forces in town; imagine that one of them hits another one just because we didn't coordinate between them! All I need is for Israeli troops to get killed by other Israeli troops in the middle of an Arab city!"

"So maybe you'll come just as far as the entrance to the town?" Yossi persisted.

"I'll come down the moment Eli Geva clears the road, and then I'll stay in Meah-Meah. You've got to understand that I'm not a battalion commander anymore. It would be irresponsible of me to get stuck down there in the middle of the forces. All I'd see there is the rear end of the tank or personnel carrier in front of me. The division commander would 'feel' the forces but he'd lose control. You think he ought to do that just to fill his nose with the smell of gunpowder?"

Yossi nodded understandingly. Perhaps he was even convinced. If he weren't a friend of mine, I couldn't have been so candid.

"*Kodkod Dror, kodkod Dror*," Dagan's agitated cry came through on my frequency. "We're being fired on by our own forces, from the direction of Golani. Tell 'em to knock it off!"

Dagan indeed sounded like someone who was under fire. I ordered Golani to stop firing at once and tried to find out who was shooting at them. Between conversations I felt I was getting increasingly entangled in coordinating between Golani and Barak. Finally I ordered the commanders to resume fire only after personally coordinating their actions by radio!

At approximately 1300 hours I was contacted by Paratroop Brigade Headquarters. This was the call I had been waiting for so eagerly. Now they said they could not advance toward Sidon; the way was blocked with forces including tanks and personnel carriers. It didn't take much imagination to picture the highway cluttered with army convoys. That phenomenon had always angered me. The root of the evil, I thought, was education — chiefly that of commanders. What they lacked was something we in the armored corps called "get-off-the-road-discipline." One of the first rules I had learned when I began my career in armor was: never, never stop on the road!

I sent my deputy to knock some order into the many straggling forces. Gotzi's brigade, part of Eli Geva's brigade, many units accompanying the artillery battalions, and above all, Amos Yaron's forces, were trying to cross town and move north. There seemed to be no way of imposing control on the bulky, heavily-laden convoys. Just the same, I ordered Yodke to join Yossi Melamed and head for the stalled forces in a personnel carrier. There he would push the forces ahead, guide them, reshuffle them, navigate for them — and get the paratroopers through.

Only at 1500 hours did the paratroop brigade finally begin to enter Sidon, after the various headquarters managed to coordinate their movements. I was apprehensive; there seemed no assurance at all that the road would really be opened. I applied maximum pressure on the brigade commander not to let anything delay him. I explained and reexplained the importance of opening the man street of Sidon. Gotzi was always able to give me an "it'll be all right" feeling — but the clock was running and the mission was not. I did not care why. What mattered was that he open the road before dark.

I contacted the Barak Brigade forces that had come down from the mountains and sealed off the city from the north, ordering them to retreat to the rear so they would not be hit by the forces approaching them from the south. Aware that Dagan's path of advance might take him to the coast, I set a "red line" that he was not to cross under any circumstances. I preferred to let the paratroopers reach the coast from the south.

The commander of Golani Brigade asked my permission to enter 'Ein Hilweh for the purposes of extricating Amiram. Resistance in the refugee camp was fierce and the casualty toll high. Amiram had come under hellish enemy fire from the school in the center of the camp. His lead forces had fallen into an ambush. One tank and two personnel carriers were seriously damaged, the tank's loader-radioman had been killed and fourteen crewmen were wounded. With great difficulty Amiram succeeded in rounding up the other vehicles and sought shelter in the camp alleys after the engagement. The previous day's toll had been two crewmen dead and three wounded.

Extricating Amiram's forces from 'Ein Hilweh took a great deal of effort, and it was done under incomparable pressure. Biber, deputy commander of Barak Brigade who was stationed in the middle of a tank battalion overlooking the camp, helped move the men out and covered them as they retreated. At long last the force worked itself free and moved south, stopping only when it reached the highlands south of the Siniq River.

After the fact, we found out just what had happened: 'Ein Hilweh was filled to overflowing with terrorists, who had holed up among its houses. They had ammunition of all kinds, and enough food and equipment to withstand a lengthy siege.

They had secured themselves in underground bunkers, some of which were equipped with ammunition caches. Amiram's tank shells, fired at the houses overhead, detonated the ammo with a tremendous racket. The battalion absorbed deadly fire: machine guns, sniper rifles, rocket-propelled grenades, anti-tank missiles. A missile hit the front end of Amiram's own tank.

I gave permission to extricate the force from the camp, after the commander of Golani had insisted on it. It has always been my custom to heed my subordinates and meet their demands, as long as they acted in the spirit of my instructions and in accordance with orders. When a division commander decides to intervene in his subordinate brigade commanders' operations, he had to know how detailed his intervention needs to be. A brigade commander with a mission should be told which way to head, what to aim for, and when to get there. The brigade commander's orders to a battalion should be more detailed, including routes, defined objectives, and the force's structure in motion and in combat.

After the dust settled over 'Ein Hilweh, I drew the inescapable conclusion that the camp, after being softened up by aerial and artillery bombardment, should have been entered by infantry. Infantrymen are ideally suited to missions in heavily populated territory; they can advance from house to house skillfuly, protecting themselves in the process. By contrast, tanks moving along narrow streets are vulnerable and defenseless.

Amiram spent the night regrouping far from 'Ein Hilweh. I now handed the commander of Golani all the aircraft I had, and threw in some artillery battalions as well. This was meant to encourage him and stiffen his backbone. "We've got all the ammo you need. Use it!"

Among the visitors who continued to stream into my headquarters was Maj. Gen. Dan Shomron, who had completed a term as OC Southern Command and had gone on study leave while being considered for the post of Chief of General Staff. He sat down next to me in the war room and followed events as they unfolded.

"I envy you, Kahalani. I'd be ready to take over for you right now," he said. I nodded in sympathy.

Combat commanders are always afraid that war will break out only to find them without a formation to command, forcing them to settle for an advisory function to some other commander. Combat experience is the fuel that propels field commanders up the career ladder. Others, never given the opportunity to prove their ability under fire, have to find other ways

to get their superiors' attention. A commander's greatest privilege is to lead fighting men on the battlefield.

The paratroop brigade began to fight on the main
street of Sidon after 1503 hours. It was clear from
the first that the daylight hours might not suffice to
wind up the mission and open the axis. That put me
in a rotten mood that I could share with no one. No
matter how crucial my presence in the war room
might be, this was the time to go out and command
the city from one of the points overlooking it. I
checked with Eli Geva again: the road up the mountains was still blocked. To gather the advance command group, hop into a personnel carrier, and join
the forces *en route* to Sidon on the coastal highway
would be patently irresponsible. So I stayed in the
war room.

The paratroopers were advancing on foot and had
begun to occupy the first houses on the main street.
The tanks I had placed at their disposal progressed
with them in the middle of the street, in step with
them, providing close cover. As the forces moved
northward, the artillery units and the air squadron
were ordered to keep away.

I contacted OC Command Amir Drori, describing
the situation as it stood and the expected schedule for
opening the axis. Somewhat apologetically I reported
that Eli Geva was still having problems climbing the
upland bypass route, and that the hookup with Amos
had not yet taken place and would still take some
time.

"Make every effort to push Eli forward," Amir
demanded, "because tomorrow I want to move Amos
from Damour toward Beirut, and I need Eli to open
up the main road as far as the airport south of there!"

This was the first time Amir had gone into such detail with me. He was undoubtedly under heavy pressure.

"Dagan, commander of Barak, had one tank battalion and a reduced battalion of infantry from Golani. Should I send him toward Amos?" I suggested.

"Where will you get the forces from, and what task are you going to give up?" Drori replied in amazement.

"Dagan has almost finished his mission," I answered, happy to have found a solution. "And I'll deploy the rest of the forces over the territory taken by Dagan, under Dagan's deputy."

Drori left it up to me.

"The first forces will reach Amos before the night's over," I promised. By 1700 hours I had already given Dagan his new orders.

"*Kodkod Dror,* 'Boss' here, over." Suddenly the Chief of Staff, Rafael Eitan, broke into the divisional radio network.

"Roger, Dror here, over."

"Shalom. I'm sending you a bottle of whiskey."

"Roger. I'll keep it for after hours; otherwise I'll be soused."

"OK. See you."

What was going on? Raful always loved to pull a good surprise. He seemed to have complimented me in some way, but it was a puzzling compliment for all that. A few minutes later his helicopter landed at my headquarters, and then I understood.

After a brief review we took off together in Raful's helicopter for Meah-Meah. Waiting for us were Barak Brigade forces. The exhausted fighting men greeted Raful with a salute. I could see the glint in their eyes when they were asked to escort us to an observation point overlooking Sidon.

There we watched the terrorists scampering in the streets, trying to flee for their lives. At Raful's request, I instructed the commander at the site to fire at them with the tanks parked in the hills, notwithstanding the long range.

"Give it everything you have," Raful ordered me, referring to the larger operation. "I'm putting no limit on your aircraft and artillery," he continued, binoculars still pressed to his eyes.

"I have unlimited ammo," I answered. "My big problem is the delay of the paratroop brigade in beginning to fight in town."

"Pressure them to get moving," Raful ruled.

"Today is a lost cause, I'm sorry to say. But I believe most of the city will be ours by noon tomorrow." Thus I committed myself cautiously. I observed the city, picturing myself leading the paratroops down the main street of Sidon.

The moment I came back to headquarters I received an excited announcement from Eli Geva: he had succeeded in climbing the mountain! That was a relief. Dagan too had been preparing to move toward Amos Yaron in Damour, north of Sidon. I rejected Dagan's original plan for this operation, since it would have entailed leaving the territory without forces remaining. Only when he reformulated the plan did I allow him to move toward Amos. Perhaps things were beginning to fall into place.

Eli Geva's forces, moving toward Damour during the night, collided with Barak Brigade and opened fire on the brigade's engineering platoon. The reunion had become an engagement. I had to intervene by radio, and only after I defused the tension did Eli continue to advance. At 2130 hours I realized that Barak had not budged. I reprimanded Dagan for wasting precious time. He had gone to take a look at a mobile anti-aircraft missile launcher, fully armed, that had been captured near Meah-Meah. It was an SA9 launcher, the likes of which the IDF still did not have. The information was forwarded quickly to the Air Force, which, I presume, brought the vehicle back to Israel some time later.

The progress of our forces toward Damour by night was complicated. Navigation was hard: the roads were unfamiliar and the mountain grades dangerous. Geva begged me to wait for morning, but I insisted:

"I think you can turn your lights on," I ruled. "You're in charge, you've got the brains. Do whatever you have to do to get there. I gave you lots of codes with lots of marks in 24 hours. Besides, lots of people apart from me are expecting you to get past Sidon. So move, even if it takes you all night. History won't forgive you if you're not on the other side. Over and out."

Geva did not argue. Instead, he reported to Amos Yaron by dawn. A few hours later he was already moving toward Beirut under Yaron's command.

We spent the evening and night preparing for the next day. Tomorrow I would open the central axis at any price, even if I had to man the machine guns in my personnel carrier!

"Tomorrow we're putting the carrier through a test of fire," I informed Tzvika, Division Operations officer and my partner in the carrier. He answered with a knowing smile.

The key to Sidon, I knew, was the paratroop brigade's success on the main street. Most of the city was already ours; all we had left to do was to overrun 'Ein Hilweh and the area from the main street west to the coast. I ordered the commander of Golani to draw up a plan to subdue the camp, and promise to treat his recommendation favorably. Then I instructed my deputy, Yodke, to fly to Meah-Meah by helicopter at dawn; from there he was to control and coordinate all forces operating in that area. I myself would come down to the critical juncture and help the paratroop brigade open the central axis. I handed command of the war room to Uzi, Assistant Operations Officer. He would conduct the battles at night. I gathered the staff officers and went out to recharge the batteries.

Wednesday, June 9

Our aircraft pounced at dawn, and the artillery, which had rained on Sidon all that night, continued to thunder. The paratrooper brigade that had cleared the Sidon area the previous night began to move into the city. Two paratroopers were killed yesterday; now the men advanced with utmost caution. The brigade commander stationed himself on the main road and orchestrated the force, which included tanks that advanced down the road and foot soldiers who progressed from house to house on either side; each covered the other.

I entered Sidon with the command group, parking my personnel carrier about 200 meters behind the first tank of the incursion force. The rattle of gunfire reverberating between the houses heightened the tension. Damage to the city was less severe than I had expected after our aerial bombardments. Our first tank was hit by an RPG. Its driver was dead; its commander, the company commander, had been evacuated to the rear with serious burns. I found to my surprise that he had been a company commander of mine in the 7th Brigade.

When we called a halt to the aerial and artillery bombardment, hundreds of hysterical civilians began running about in the streets. The prisoner interrogators ordered them to move to the coast and wait there. The advancing forces could not open fire for fear of wounding civilians; their routes of advance, too, were blocked by fallen electricity pylons.

I had been told that the town commander had issued a pullback order before dawn. I canceled the artillery barrage that was to land in front of the forces. Observing the civilians as they scampered freely in the city streets, I understood that they knew the terrorists had fled. Only this would explain their confidence. I was surprised to see them evacuating casualties, proferring assistance to their fellows, and clearing the streets to let ambulances through, as if they had coordinated these actions with our forces. I instructed our Arabic speakers to reassure the civilians, to ease the tension further.

I wanted to bring this city under my control at almost any price, and was about to pledge all the firepower I had to the cause. Then I stopped myself. I ordered Itzik, commander of the artillery group, to silence the cannons, and Niutek, air support commander, to stop the bombardment and send the planes home.

Niutek protested. "I've got planes with bombs in the air, and they'll be ready within minutes." He continued to direct the craft to their targets.

"Send them back; it's too dangerous," I answered.

"You know they can't land with the bombs," Niutek tried his luck again.

"Tell them to drop them into the sea. They did that in the Yom Kippur War too." Niutek, who stood next to me, nodded disappointedly. I would not slaughter innocent civilians. It was not their fault that terrorists had settled in the middle of their city.

On the main street, Gotzi was waging the war too slowly for my taste. When he failed to answer my call over "Dror" frequency, I broke into his brigade network to prod him — to his displeasure, I'm sure. Behind his spearhead force a long "tail" trailed, waiting, twiddling its thumbs, its tremendous fighting power wasted.

Work in division headquarters proceeded by the book. The Division Operations Officer, Yossi R., ran the war room with the rest of the staff officers. He was in continuous radio contact with Command, and stayed in his position without moving. My deputy, Yodke, had stationed himself on the mountaintop, coordinating between Golani and what remained of Barak Brigade under the latter's deputy commander, Doron Biber. Col. Yossi Melamed served as a sort of second deputy. I entrusted him with responsibility for the route into Sidon; he would coordinate the forces abut to enter the city, meet with the formations' commanders, brief them on the situation, and schedule the forces' incursion. On the main street, as I have mentioned, was the advance command group with myself in it. Its five personnel carriers followed the brigade commander's advance command group at the most critical point of the campaign.

Throughout the fighting Yodke and I had been in close contact. Long convoys of civilians — men, women and children — pressed toward him, trying to flee the center of town. We agreed that Yodke would let them through, but only after checking each of them, making sure that none was a terrorist who had changed clothes and tried to escape disguised as a civilian. Yodke did, in fact, come across many terrorists in this manner and arrested them all. From his position overlooking Camp 'Ein Hilweh, Yodke devised a plan to attack the camp from the east. It looked good to me. I authorized him to carry it out.

At this juncture Lt. Col. Ephraim Laor visited me on the roof of my personnel carrier. After a warm handshake, he asked me for an assignment. I radioed Amiram, commander of the tank battalion fighting in 'Ein Hilweh.

"Dror here. I've got a problem with a "kod-kod" (Hebrew slang for "commander") who wants to fight. His names' Laor. Can you give him a vehicle or a subformation? Over."

"Amiram here. Negative, I think. I've got spare "kod-kods" and I'd rather not have more. But if it's got to be, anything's possible. Over."

"Roger. He's your buddy. You've got to help him. Give him one vehicle, one tank to command," I suggested.

"Roger. OK. Over and out," and Laor was on his way. What other army in the world has such fighters? — I asked myself. But Amiram had not signed off. He took advantage of this direct contact with me to report his exploits in 'Ein Hilweh, describing in detail the metal shacks that had been damaged and the number of terrorist cells he'd succeeded in wiping out since morning.

Doron Biber, deputy commander of Barak, broke into my network. Excitedly he reported that thousands of civilians were advancing toward him from

downtown Sidon. I knew what this meant: the city
was falling into our hands. I instructed Biber to interrogate a few of the civilians abut what was happening downtown; in response he asked me to send him
a squad of prisoner interrogators. I realized then that
I would not get any quick intelligence from him.
How long would we have to depend on interpreters?
Imagine an Israel Defense Forces officer corps that
could not speak Arabic!

The residents of Sidon were busy with their own
affairs and seemed to accustom themselves quickly
to our presence. I believed we had to exploit the
disarray. The civilians, clogging the streets, were en-
cumbering us as we took aim at dangerous, suspect
targets, but they presumably also made things just as
hard on the terrorists. In any event, the locals no
longer feared for their lives, aware that any terrorists
who had not been found had fled town.

Again Gotzi failed to answer my call on "Dror", and
again I broke into his network. "Keep moving," I said.

"The whole force lined up behind you is going to
waste!" I emphasized.

"I'm preparing missions for them farther on," Gotzi
apologized. I would not settle for that.

Glancing to the right I discovered a broad avenue
which, if opened by our forces, would give us two
simultaneous routes of advance. Gotzi's paratroops
looked like pros. They progressed in groups, covering one another, advancing along building walls and
exercising caution at every door and window that
represented potential danger. A tank advancing between their two columns fired as it rumbled forward,
reminding me of my experience in Khan Yunis in the
Six-Day War, 15 years before.

I ordered Gotzi to form an additional force that would open up another street about 100 meters east of the main road. Gotzi forwarded the order, and I summoned the deputy brigade commander and the commander of the force-to-be for a briefing. I pointed at the street, making sure they knew their job. Before giving the go-ahead, I listened to a brief explanation about the breakthrough force's structure, composition and operational methods. My concern was that the new formation would collide with the brigade commander's force, advancing on a street that converged with the new axis near the end of the densely populated part of Sidon. I was not at ease until I had made Gotzi and the deputy brigade commanders swear they would coordinate their actions, and until I knew that they had in fact done so. A wonderful feeling overcame me at the sight of the paratroopers marching alongside the houses, escorted by tanks in the middle of the street, the latter firing occasionally for the benefit of the former as if the two were appendages of a single body. Sidon would soon be ours; our grip on the downtown area was tightening with each passing moment. True, a pocket of resistance remained in 'Ein Hilweh, but I gave it no thought at that time.

At 1200 hours Gotzi reported that he had occupied the downtown and that the streets were clear of enemy forces. Elated, I instructed my deputy, Yodke, to conduct our forces through the town northward, up the coast toward Damour, with all possible speed.

Our movement through the city was like water pouring through a crack in a massive dam. With deep satisfaction I observed the lengthy convoys that had waited so many hours and were now crossing the city on their way north. Fighters waved as they passed me. But it was not yet time to relax. Everyone clutched his weapon, eyes searching for the enemy.

The streets were still obstructed here and there with electricity pylons and damaged cars, but our drivers circumvented them easily and kept the tanks, personnel carriers and trucks moving. The town had taken a beating. Windows were shattered and the upper stories of some buildings had collapsed under aerial bombardment. The artillery barrages preceding the breakthrough had made their most evident impact on the town's vegetation and cars.

The paratroops maintained their deployment in the city streets. We controlled the intersections, and the brigade dispersed in the streets of the lower city. Thus far the IDF had not really damaged Sidon, but it would take the city many days to recover and put the ordeal of war behind it. The city's high-rise buildings gave Sidon a modern facade. Its shop-lined streets reminded me of south Tel Aviv, a commercial center with a few high-rises. Most of the shops were closed. The residents evidently preferred to slam shut the shutters and stay home.

Itzik Mordechai reached Sidon in the middle of the fighting and was waiting for us to finish. Then, he could take command of Sidon, as stated in the plan finalized the previous day. Yanush, still waiting in the Beka'a Valley with his forces for approval to advance, paid me a brief visit in the center of Sidon. I radioed Command to update Amir Drori. Drori seemed to be in a good mood this time. Crisply, he instructed me to hand command over to Itzik Mordechai and move north in one of two possible directions. One would take me up the coastal highway as far as Damour, from which I would head eastward toward Jebel Baruch and down into the Karoun Valley, where I would help Yanush fight the Syrians. The other would have me follow Amos Yaron toward Beirut. Amir's underlying assumption was that Amos, assisted by Eli Geva's brigade, would reach the airport area by evening.

Although I did not know what duties Amos Yaron had assigned Dagan, I handed the orders down. By instruction of Amir Drori, I would take all the forces with me: Golani, Barak, and Haggai's brigade. To secure Sidon, I would have to leave Gotzi's brigade with Itzik Mordechai.

I instructed Gotzi on how to secure the lower city so the forces could continue passing through on their way north. Then I invited Itzik Mordechai to join me on the terrace of one of the houses, from which I showed him how the forces were deployed in town. Itzik asked me to leave behind some of my forces. Too many, I thought, to secure the city until the last of his units reached him. I agreed to hold back enough forces to meet the need for that day. Than I briefed Mordechai on the difficulties in 'Ein Hilweh. The camp would not fall easily, I said; he would pit an especially massive force against it, one that would go about its work in an orderly way. Thus Mordechai intercepted several additional infantry units that reached Sidon and pointed them in the direction of 'Ein Hilweh. Wishing Itzik good luck, I handed him the keys to the city.

It takes many days to restore normal functioning in an occupied city. First you take the main intersections and key areas. Then you occupy public institutions such as city hall, schools and banks. Finally you control the supplies of water, electricity and food. All this had to be done to attain the residents' cooperation and bring the city back to its routine. To this end the IDF establishes a special administration that runs the city as soon as it is occupied. We set up such a body in Sidon too, as soon as Itzik's forces rid the town of the last enemy personnel. Our forces knew how to foster constructive cooperation with the locals, and so Sidon reverted to its role as the capital of all of southern Lebanon.

Our forces spent another five days or so in 'Ein Hilweh. In theory it was possible to go from house to house, making absolutely sure no enemy was hiding there. In fact, I knew, it was altogether unrealistic. I was glad to get out of town and head north.

My personnel carrier progressed slowly. So far I had known Sidon from maps and photos, and now I sought to learn it by sight. Again I pictured scenes from my favorite war movies: Allied forces thrusting into Europe along burning streets. My regular paratroop brigade, which had moved into Sidon from the north, passed me by. Yisrael's battalion had landed at the Awali River with Amos Yaron and it too became part of the division for the purpose of taking the city. I studied the faces of the soldiers I met, and found no little sadness there. Two of their comrades had been killed as they fought their way through profuse vegetation into Sidon.

Amir Drori came for a visit late that afternoon, landing his helicopter next to the division's advance command group several kilometers south of Damour. Ordinarily introverted and taciturn, Amir was relaxed, at ease, and overtly excited this time as he greeted me with a broad smile. It was our first meeting since the war began. With great circumspection he disclosed that our Air Force would set out within a

few minutes to destroy some batteries of Syrian surface-to-air missiles stationed in the Beka'a Valley.
Then he provided further details: "Yanush is moving
north with Emmanuel and Giora, and they're going
to attack the Syrians on the ground." I was surprised
that they were going to attack Syrians, although the
action was certainly warranted. Then, even though
Command had not yet formulated any plan for the
war's subsequent stages, Amir tried to describe the
assignments that might become mine.

"I think Amos Yaron will stop in South Beirut,"
Amir explained, drawing imaginary lines on my map.
"If he does all right with Jaja (commander of the
regular paratroop brigade) and Eli Geva, they'll stop
just around the airport line, and I think Jaja will keep
on going and join up with the Christians. I don't
know how Yanush will do in the Beka'a. You have to
be ready to move east from Damour toward Jebel
Baruch and from there down into the valley. You're
going to blindside the Syrians from the west."

Amir drew arrows with his finger. Then, studying
the map again, he continued:

"A second possibility that you have to master is
for you and your division to stay in the area from the
coast eastward, just after we've taken Kafr Sil. That
could be tomorrow at daybreak. For all planning purposes, your force is Golani and Barak, and you'll also
get Haggai with his brigade."

The directions and goals were clear. Although I
preferred more specific duties, I understood that the
situation in the field was still vague. Not until that
evening would Amir join the Chief of Staff's planning group and get the go-ahead for his plan for the
next stage. After spending a few more minutes describing the events behind the big arrows, Amir re-

turned to Command. No sooner had he taken off
than some accurate mortar rounds landed no the advance command group. Unhurt, we leaped into our
personnel carriers and roared away. The shelling reminded us that the war wasn't over yet.

On Wednesday, June 9, our aircraft attacked a phalanx of nineteen Syrian land-to-air missile batteries,
destroying seventeen of the batteries and damaging
the other two. In a dogfight that developed during
the sortie, twenty enemy aircraft were downed.
Yanush's force began to move north toward Lake
Karoun at 1300 hours. Amos Yaron's division progressed in the western sector, and Jaja made his way
along the mountainous axis via Kafr Matta toward
Beirut. Eli Geva headed for the Beirut airport along
the Damour-Beirut highway, while my force waited
south of Damour until ordered to continue north.
    Then, south of Kafr Šil, Eli Geva's force ran into an
ambush, suffering heavy losses in equipment and
men. His request to retreat was approved. Amos
sounded upset on the radio. "I'm afraid the terrorists
or the Syrians will get their hands on some tanks of
ours that were left behind," he confided. The
headquarters in our sector radioed each other back
and forth. Rumor had it that a battle-worthy Merkava
tank had been taken into Beirut after Eli Geva's retreat. This made our skin crawl; the all-Israeli tank, in
its first war, had fallen to the enemy! Morale aside,
the Merkava contained original Israeli inventions and
unique attributes, information of which had to be
kept out of enemy hands. I entered Eli Geva's radio
network, listening well into the night as his retreat
proceeded.
    Early in the morning of Thursday, June 10, I re-

ceived a communique that shortly turned into an order: I was to send Barak Brigade ahead to complete Eli Geva's mission. Asking Command for verification, I was told that I was to prod Dagan, who would join up with Geva and continue up the highway to the airport, about three kilometers away. For lack of choice I forwarded this instruction to Dagan, who went over to Amos' command. That reminded me of orders in the Yom Kippur War that were disobeyed, of commanders who had failed to transfer forces to other formations as instructed. At that moment I wondered whether they had not done the right thing after all. I felt as though part of my body had been torn away.

So Dagan, leading two reduced-strength tank battalions and one Golani battalion, went out that morning to open the road to Beirut. After a few hours on the move, Moreno's tank company leading the force, along with an engineering company from the division, ran into a Syrian ambush that devastated the spearhead. Scores of crewmen in Alon Company under Effie — seminarians in the IDF's combined religious study and active duty program — were wounded and killed. Engineering men from Eitan's battalion who had come to help them were mauled as well.

Moreno's tank battalion had been the spearhead of Barak. I was sure it might have been handled differently. I felt like a father who had sent his children to help their friends and discovered that they had been injured — and that he could do nothing to help, not even offer advice. Because of my many talks with the forces before the war, I had known most of the commanders and some of the soldiers personally. I had trained them, assigned them targets and missions, and above all, gave them something of my essence and psyche, to prepare them in the best possible way for the worst possible war.

There I was, on the sidelines, observing Barak Brigade, engulfed in the middle of the campaign. then an additional order came in from Command: I was to transfer Golani Brigade to Amos Yaron. Golani would open an axis parallel to and east of the coastal road, in the highlands. I almost refused, but held myself back. First, I would talk with OC Command Amir Drori, and only then would I transfer the force.

"Amir, I don't understand the order," I complained over the phone.

"No choice," Drori answered. "You know our forces are in a sticky situation, and Amos has lots of casualties. We have to reach the airport. They're talking about a cease-fire, and we have to surround Beirut." Amir sounded tolerant and sympathetic, but firm and resolute.

"So let me do it. I'll command the battle. I promise you I'll open the road!' I pressed. "Those are my forces and I should command them."

"I understand you, It makes sense, but I can't switch command between two division commanders on one axis."

"So let Amos go ahead and join up with the Christians. That's a tough mission in itself, and I'll open the axis," I gave it my last try.

"Avigdor, send them for now, and we'll see what happens," Amir ruled. Then he added, "I'll see you today in the field. By the way, get in touch with Eli Geva; he's going to be under your command again."

I parted with Golani and set up my advance command group on a towering hill overlooking the battles on the Damour-Beirut road. Then Eli Geva, in his tank, reached the command group for update and orders.

"What are you doing in a tank?" I asked, puzzled. "Isn't a personnel carrier or a jeep more comfortable?"

Eli answered without hesitation: "Don't you remember Kahalani? In the Yom Kippur War you wouldn't step out of your tank even for a moment . As you see, I had a model to emulate..."

That Thursday above Damour, I had so little to do that I visited Amos Yaron and his advance command group on the coastal plain. It was an amicable reunion. Amos, surrounded by staff officers, was preoccupied with running the battle. He had set up shop in a house under construction, several kilometers south of Kafr Sil, offering an excellent view of the road. Seated next to Yaron was the Chief of Staff, Raful. Sighting me he stood up to shake my hand. "Your people are fighting real good," he asserted, complimenting Barak and pouring salt on my wounds.

I parted with Raful and Amos and went to the neighboring house, where Maj. Gen. Yekutiel Adam and Col. Haim Sela had been shot to death the previous day by terrorists who had holed up inside. I stayed there a few minutes, upset, communing with their memories.

The cease-fire went into effect on the afternoon of Friday, June 11. By that time, Golani and Barak Brigades were operating under Amos Yaron. In our sector the cease-fire lasted more than 24 hours. Amos' forces stopped in their tracks; only the next day, Saturday, did they continue toward Kafr Sil and the position we called "Radar Hill". Golani, spearheaded by Amiram's battalion, took Kafr Sil. Once again Amiram proved his leadership ability and courage,

wiping out Syrian tanks and other enemy vehicles at
ranges of several hundred meters or even less. They
fought in the village streets and in between the houses.
Barak Brigade opened up the main road to Beirut,
wiping out enemy along the highway. As Amiram
was taking Kafr Sil, a paratroop battalion took Radar
Hill, next to the village. On Sunday, immediately
after completing their missions, the two brigades returned to my division. To give the wayward sons a
proper homecoming, I ordered my staff officers and
the supply group under Sal'i to pamper the brigades
in every way possible. They deserved it.

The battles over, my attention turned to several
soldiers who had suffered shell shock. I approached
this task with supreme caution.

Combat reaction syndrome

The fighting man on the battlefield is in a state of
perpetual internal conflict between the need to do his
duty and his instinct to survive. A fighter who lacks
the psychological strength to resolve the conflict displays limited, faulty performance. It is under these
circumstances that combat reaction ("shell-shock")
manifests itself.

The syndrome surfaces in various ways — among
them violence, amnesia, indifference, inability to
speak, and physical disturbances. It is induced by
various kinds of pressure. Major among them is the
fear of death. A soldier can become so anxious that
he loses his self-control and ability to function. He
may deny himself food, drink, and sleep, causing
physical distress that further reduces his ability to
cope.

At times the soldier reports for duty with unresolved problems from home or work in his kitbag. These gain intensity at times of danger and compound the battlefield pressure. Past traumas repressed thus far are liable to resurface under fire.

Trust in commanders and comrades has much to do with one's ability to cope with the pressure of combat; a soldier whose trust is undermined will be less able to confront danger. The death of close friends also reminds one of his own vulnerability, magnifying his own lack of confidence and adding to the pressure.

A different kind of pressure arises when the fighting man questions the professionalism of those around him, the quality of the weapons being issued to him, and the correctness of the actions taken in battle. Fear is further amplified if one feels he does not belong to the formation. This kind of fear besets soldiers whose role in the course of the fighting is passive.

Psychologists and mental health officers are assigned to every brigade and unit in the Israel Defense Forces. Their duties are twofold: to enhance the fighting man's ability to cope with his internal conflict on the battlefield, and to get those affected back to their units. These specialists also advise the commander, who attempts to treat victims of the syndrome or take preventive action.

It was my division's mental health officer, Maj. Rothenberg, who taught me the three cardinal rules for the treatment of combat syndrome victims: treat them near the zone of combat; treat them as soon as possible after the symptoms first appear; and make them expect to return quickly to full performance in their units.

Commanders ought to know the factors that cause combat reaction syndrome. Reliable and correct leadership, personal attention, and actions meant to reassure the victims will give them relief and increase the prospect of their resuming their duties.

The war winds down

The division regrouped in the South Beirut sector near the airport, and I divided the area between Barak and Golani. Both brigades kept a force on the front line as formations of considerable size reorganized in the rear. With so much of the situation unresolved, we faced day after day of sublime tension in anticipation of further fighting. The major question was: would we enter the heart of the Lebanese capital?

My division and that of Amos Yaron relied on my division's supply group, which was to meet all the fighters' many needs. The tremendous quantities of food hauled into our zone vanished as if they had never arrived. the soldiers opened battle rations, selected the items they liked, pushed the rest aside, and complained that they were still hungry. This was especially prevalent among Jaja's paratroopers. The supply lines were long and twisting. Lengthy convoys of food, fuel and ammo made their way from Israel into the heart of Lebanon. The quantities of ammunition required — chiefly artillery — were particularly massive. We were under constant terrorist fire from Beirut, but our artillery never failed to return fire. A special problem was the shortage of drinking water. Mammoth tankers were sent to Beirut from the Nahariya area in northern Israel, but they were quickly emptied. In the meantime, regulations prohibited the use of any other source for drinking until it had been checked by a competent medical authority; thus we could not use Lebanese water freely. As the oppressive heart of June, July and August took its toll, however, some of our men began to improvise.

One of those who took the initiative was my friend Motti Friedman, who let the cries for water reach a certain crescendo and then set out to find his own sources for the division. Motti, a private detective by profession, spotted and began to follow a pickup truck loaded with jerricans, making its way from the fuel depot at the mouth of the Zaharani to a water source. He found it: a well that delivered an unlimited bounty. A little later, some ordinance people reached the area to administer the "waterworks", and medical corps personnel came by to check the water. The division's tanks quickly filled.

The supply group was commanded by Col. Sal'i, a division stalwart who had hand-picked a unique team of officers. I summoned the group, intending to put our heads together and figure out how to meet the many demands coming in from the field. The commanders of the medical, ordinance and supply battalions (Romam, Issi, and Talmor, respectively), reported to the meeting looking just like enlisted men with maps in hand, fire-resistant tank suits protecting their bodies, and binoculars around their necks. Sal'i started with a general review. His deputy, Galili, went into greater detail, and others presented and analyzed every detail of concern to me. All of this was done skillfully, carefully, and very thoughtfully. At the end of the meeting I could banish all concern: the division would not go hungry.

Symptoms of "post-war" behavior began to surface quickly. We hardly regrouped when the soldiers began appropriating Lebanese houses to sleep in. Headquarters also began setting up shop in "requisitioned" local quarters. I immediately ordered all the formations to set up tent encampments in the field, and ordered headquarters to organize themselves as if in the middle of a dessert. Division and brigade headquarters, in any case, stretched tent flaps between personnel carriers to serve as war rooms.

The Japanese cars used by the Lebanese Army (and unavailable in Israel) became commodities in demand. They were quickly provided to anyone who placed an "order". Again, I spoiled the party, allowing my men to use standard IDF vehicles only. The Military Police helped out by setting up road blocks and confiscating any rolling booty.

A large number of enemy ammunition caches were scattered throughout the populated area and elsewhere. Appropriating this material was perfectly permissible, and the supply group undertook the mission. The supply convoys that reached our forces in Lebanon returned to Israel creaking under the weight of weapons and ammunition — enough to supply a division and more — that had been salted away by the terror organizations. The quantities of ordinance they had cached in depots and mountain caves astonished us all. It was a special experience to behold hundreds of IDF trucks, filled to capacity with tools of destruction, making their way back to Israel, straight to the army warehouses.

With no battles being waged, one could travel around Lebanon without fear, even in unescorted vehicles. Very quickly, however, terrorists who had remained in the area realized that this was a way to strike at the IDF — and they went to work. It was at that time that our forces mounted the siege of Beirut, trapping more than 10,000 terrorists in the city. Our goal was twofold: to make them leave town or to wipe them out. We had wounded the body of the snake, as it were, but the reptile's head was intact and confident in the heart of the Lebanese capital. Israel's leadership used the threat of entering Beirut as a weapon in its efforts to drive the terrorists out of Beirut. However, no threat can exist without movement in the field, and we made these movements concurrently. We spent that time inching into Beirut: first to the airport, then to the Hai Salem quarter, and later to other parts of the city.

Bashir Jemayel's Christian forces proved seriously disappointing. We had hoped Jemayel would take the initiative, but when I met the Christian fighters and contemplated their clean, pressed uniforms and their sunglasses, I knew only we would bear the burden. Whatever hopes Israel may still have harbored were shattered for good in early September, when Bashir Jemayel was assassinated. No successor of stature stepped forward to exploit the results of the war and establish a strong government capable of taking the reins of power in Lebanon.

In late June, 1982, the division and brigade commanders were summoned to the command group at Northern Command headquarters, now stationed in Beirut. A large map of the city, spread out in front of us, and aerial photographs next to it were marked with multi-colored arrows presenting us with our next operation: the occupation of Beirut.

I glanced in astonishment at Amir Drori and his staff officers. They spoke in an absolutely normal tone of voice, and read these orders with no perceptible change of manner, as if orders of this kind had been given to us on any number of occasions. I knew how much bloodshed this operation would entail, and the thought agitated me. I listened anyway, asking only for clarifications. Afterwards I approached Amir.

"Is this serious?" I asked bluntly, looking him in the eye.

"There's an instruction to get ready," he answered. "We're the army, and we have to obey all of it."

There was no gainsaying that, but even Amir was not sure whether the government had in fact approved our making all the preparations and whether the IDF had been given the go-ahead for the operation. Nevertheless, on my way back to the division I was already pondering routes and operational moves. My division would start gearing up for the breakthrough at once, and I myself would do everything possible to keep casualties to a minimum.

I presented the fighting men of my division with the plan for occupying Beirut in minute detail. In all my talks with the formations, the men expressed surprise that we really "meant business" about entering the city and lashing at the terrorist forces there. The toughest questions of all were asked by the reserve paratroopers, who were older than the others, more experienced, and supremely self-confident. I was not at peace with the move being planned, but I let no one know of the feelings raging inside me. I insisted vehemently that from the moment we entered the city we concentrate only on discharging our duties. In all briefings I emphasized the importance of teamwork among the forces, by which we might attain our objective with a minimum of casualties. The plans were readied and agreed upon, and the men were prepared to march on Beirut. All that remained was to wait for the Government's go-ahead.

In mid-July my division was transferred from the Beirut area to the east, where it took control of a broad sector of the inland Beka'a Valley. The division acquired an additional brigade: the 7th, commanded then by Eitan Keinan ("Kaouli") and subsequently by Zamir. For this brigade too, reassignment to my division was a "homecoming".

We had embarked on hard times, a period of digging in militarily and getting ready for Lebanon's harsh winter. Terrorist cells infiltrated our area almost every night, attempting to attack our forces. We repelled them with heavy losses to them in all but one case, when they killed four soldiers and the commander of an infantry company in a well-executed operation.

My division and that of Emmanuel Sekel, stationed to the east, operated under Maj. Gen. Moshe Bar-Kochba ("Brill"). Together we planned our major action: a day of battle against Syrian forces that were collaborating with the terrorists. In a withering blitz, our tanks stormed the enemy positions, opened fire and destroyed about 70 Syrian tanks and many other vehicles of different kinds. The Syrians got the message: they dug new trenches, deeper to be sure, but farther from our positions. The terrorists stopped operating from Syrian territory, seeking to penetrate our area from other sectors.

In Beirut, the IDF continued tightening the noose we had slipped over the terrorist's necks. One of the participants in these battles was Amiram's battalion. One day in early August the battalion crossed Beirut Airport and dug in to the north of it. In the course of this move, Amiram's tank took an anti-tank missile, and he was seriously wounded. His men radioed me at my position in Beka'a and I rushed to my helicopter. Amiram was evacuated to Rambam Hospital in Haifa, where the surgeons feared he would lose his sight. To everyone's delight that did not happen;

Amiram returned to duty, again commanding combat formation.

In October, 1982, my division was sent back to its regular sector on the Golan Heights. The local residents gave us a joyous, enthusiastic welcome, as if greeting a long-lost member of the family who would put things back in order. Home again.

Operation Peace for Galilee was a bitter and painful campaign that claimed a heavy price in blood. From the day it began, June 6, 1982, until August 31, when the terrorists left Beirut, the IDF lost 345 of our men, in addition to 2,383 wounded. Between September 1, 1982 and June 3, 1985 — the day the IDF left Lebanon and consolidated itself in a "security zone" just north of Israel's border — another 306 perished and 3,883 were wounded. The war broke the nation's heart and shattered its unity. A harsh and protracted public debate ensued between those who believed the war was essential and those who argued to the contrary. The daily reports and color photographs channeled from the field straight into every home further fueled the confrontation and aggravated the domestic discord.

While preparing for the operation and in the midst of the fighting, I too believed the war was essential and just. Never, on the other hand, had I imagined that we would have to stay in Lebanon so long. As time passed and we sank ever deeper into the Lebanese mire, I became a "man of little faith" with respect to Lebanon's ability to marshal a force that would impose law and order and serve as a partner for dialogue with Israel. Only after three difficult years did our forces come home. I watched the fighting men returning with relief and satisfaction.

The flags were flying high in the parking lot in front of my HQ on the Golan Heights. Officers and career noncoms exchanged their work fatigues for gleaming dress uniforms. An ambience of festivity touched everything. However, the winter that had settled in on the Golan Heights, and the ash gray sky that came with it, matched my feelings well. I had just handed the division to Matan Vilna'i. Matan was exuberant and I too smiled every which way, hiding the sadness in my heart. It hurt to part with the division and its men. This time I knew I was leaving the Golan Heights for good. I had become part of its landscape, and it will forever be a part of mine.

17. FROM THE BASALT
STONES TO THE
IRON TRIANGLE *

In January, 1983, I obtained the consent of Chief of
General Staff Rafael Eitan to take leave for study at
Israel's National Defense College. For several months
I had the privilege of enriching my academic knowledge under Maj. Gen. Yaakov Even, my erstwhile
commander. In April of that year, Raful stepped down
in favor of Moshe Levy, who won the competition
with Yanush and Dan Shomron for the highest position in the Israeli Defense Forces. Yanush left the
service and went into business; Dan Shomron stayed
in uniform, aspiring to attain the Chief of Staff's position in the future, as indeed he did.

I had an ambition of my own. Approaching Moshe
Levy, I expressed the desire to command the Command and Staff College at the end of my studies, or to
take up some other position on the General Staff at
that time. And indeed, within days I was appointed
to replace my friend, Amram Mitzna, as commander
of the College. After a brief overlap, Command and
Staff was all mine.

* "Iron triangle" — a nickname for the IDF compounds and
encampments in the Tel Aviv area

The Inter-Branch Command and Staff College was the kind of place where I could impart something of my experience to the successor generation. It was a crossroads through which captains, majors and lieutenant-colonels passed, and I did everything I could to make a term there compulsory for any aspiring lieutenant-colonel. I battled for this with the General Staff and its generals, and eventually the College doubled its student body and became a junction that could not be bypassed.

The Commander of Command and Staff has much to say about the subject matter and the pace at which it is taught. I tried to generate and foster behavior patterns befitting the quality and rank of the senior officers who were the college's best "pupils". For example, I expelled anyone caught cheating on tests. Every student was given defined tasks and asked to set others for himself; that reduced the quantity of subject matter that could be "bequeathed" from one student to the next, to the displeasure of those interested in evading the labor of study. The exercises were as realistic as I could make them. I sought to train each student in the command of a battalion and a brigade, and to prepare him for duties as a senior staff officer in field formations. I also introduced general studies and various enrichment activities.

The College always faces a challenge in coping with new perceptions and keeping its subject matter up to date. However, I found my job at least twice as hard as that, for it was my aim to apply my authority and leadership to hundreds of officers, including several dozen colonels who served as instructors. The College's "final exam" tests the students' ability to express themselves. We gave them no rest. Like all Israelis, the students at Command and Staff missed no opportunity to "run the country" from every possible angle, constantly challenging their commander and instructors.

The Command and Staff College was a school. It would have been natural if, entering it after years of combat, the students did not take classes seriously. But that was not the case, I could only marvel at the scholastic atmosphere and the stress that gripped the students in their ambition to attain high grades and positive evaluations.

In recent years the IDF has become increasingly aware of the importance of higher education. Academic training has become an inseparable part of the officer's career development. In the past, officers took study leave only if they were to forgo the services of certain individuals for some time. Under this method, combat officers were usually at a disadvantage; they were denied approval for advanced studies because they were constantly needed in their units. The army has since learned that a well-educated officer is a better officer, and that well-educated combat officers lose nothing of their operational skills.

The IDF struggles to keep good officers in the standing army. One factor contributing to the officer's decision to sign for career service is the possibility that a company commander, for example, would have the opportunity to earn a B.A. during his service. The Inter-Branch Command and Staff College allows even officers who failed to pass high school matriculation to earn a B.A. and do advanced military studies. To do so he must earn good grades at both the College and the university in which he takes his civilian courses. This access to higher education makes the College highly attractive and prestigious. This could change, of course. It may eventually become possible to let candidates complete university studies before entering the College. Then the College will have to reorganize commensurately, adjusting its curriculum to the new situation.

My arrival at Command and Staff was my first encounter with formal, official training programs, drawn up in advance, which permitted us to set forth subject matter and schedules and adhere to them. For the first time I could make plans without having to be ready to modify them at a moment's notice. We were inured to outside events, and no IDF alert could scramble the schedule of classes, drawn up by a staff under Chief Instructor Zion Ziv. A scholastic atmosphere permeated everything and produced beautiful results.

Schedules

We've got a slogan in the IDF: "Every plan is a basis for changes." You hear it everywhere. It lets you modify your plans without excessive pangs of conscience. Much time is lost because schedules go awry; senior officers lose precious hours waiting at closed doors for discussions set for certain times and delayed again and again.

The first victims of this constant reshuffling of schedules are the staff officers, the commander's executive arm. These men, ready to leap with every ring of the phone and willing to set out for a meeting at any moment, ultimately find themselves needlessly waiting on the other side of someone's door until the commander inside manages to clear his desk. Staff officers also spend too much time redrawing plans that had already been finalized and passed on.

Another slogan of ours: "The commander isn't late — he's been delayed." Indeed, many commanders are delayed, but not always for good reason. Truth to tell, this author has also been known to perpetrate such injustices. The army's highest echelons, frequently asked to cope with changes in schedule, arrogate to themselves the right to bounce the changes down the ladder, sometimes without thinking twice. Once it had become legitimate at the top, the practice filters down to the lowest-ranking commanders.

The army pays a steep price for these unplanned changes in schedule. Commanders and formations who try to hold to schedule as a way of life eventually stop treating it as a matter of life and death. On constant maximum alert and under subliminal stress, we tend to plan badly or concentrate on the short term only. Commanders and staff officers feel there's no point in drawing up a monthly plan, or, in many cases, even a weekly plan.

The scheduling and timing of most matters is entrusted to staff officers, office chiefs or secretaries. A commander who fails to keep an eye on the plan until it has gone into effect finds himself in a whirlpool. He has to adjust to the situation that has come about, cancel tasks for which there is no time, and settle for putting out fires only. Cancellations and changes in schedules are most prejudicial to the image and reliability of the person who makes the pendulum swing.

Even though everyone knows this is true, most IDF commanders and officers are unable to coordinate matters and meetings for any period of time exceeding one week. Their ability to attend private functions, likewise, is dubious. Home and family always take second place to the head-of-household's recurrent, incontrovertible assertion : "The schedule might change — after all, I'm in the army!"

Admittedly, unplanned changes in schedule are justified in isolated cases, usually involving front-line fighters. They are on the alert, always wound up, ready for any change. However, there are few of that sort in the IDF.

There's a time and a place for everything. In war, as in peacetime, one must determine at every stage where things begin and where they end. Working halfway through the night is such a norm in our field formations that it has become a philosophy. These units treat night time as "spare time", in which one completes whatever he failed to accomplish during the day. Soldiers are entitled by standing order to six hours of sleep each night. Our combat units honor that privilege in the breach, arguing that "The missions are not accomplished; they've got to be done tonight!" At times,we also confront our soldiers with what we call a "white night," i.e., a sleepless night.

You cannot train a soldier to function without sleep. We can only teach him to work through the suffering that comes with sleeplessness. Lack of sleep impairs a soldier's ability to absorb messages. Our practices in this regard are such that much of the material presented in the IDF training courses fails to reach its objective.

"Time is money." That key sentence, the public sector's first commandment, gives business its sense of order and efficiency. Public services, operating without the profit motive and unconcerned about maximizing the use of manpower and time, are always less efficient.

Unlike the public services, however, the Israel Defense Forces periodically stop and compare the number of people with the tasks to be done. Nevertheless I believe that any attempt at giving everyone a job definition must result in under-employment. We can and should economize on manpower by giving one person several duties. I have often seen large numbers of soldiers twiddling their thumbs while their units' staff officers and commander stay up half the night. Streamlining means reducing the number of positions. However, commanders are loath to do this, for when they do so there is no reward.

The only way we can discharge the duties thrust upon us is to cultivate and maintain a high work ethic and make full use of every working hour we've got. Six-day Israel gives us plenty of hours — from Sunday morning through Friday afternoon.

During my tenure as commander of Command and Staff, my first born son, Dror, reached the age of 18 and was drafted. When I saw him in uniform for the first time, I knew a generation had gone by. From then on, I felt like a father when I faced my own soldiers. No longer was I a big brother, an experienced colleague accompanying them in their army careers.

When Dror told me of the regular doses of injustice and petty harassment dished out to him and his comrades, I refrained from interfering. I was well aware of the kinds of mischief a junior commander could wreak upon his subordinates, but I kept my thoughts to myself. Perhaps it was better to be just a soldier's father rather than someone who knew exactly what went on in each and every unit in the middle of the night.

When he went out to operational activity or was

placed in a dangerous situation, I sensed his ordeal and was discomfited: Dror out there and I at home?! Now I understood my parents' concern throughout my army service. Now I knew the dread of a father who sends his son to war.

At this time I was given a second assignment: command of a division in time of emergency. I had vehemently insisted on this appointment, an exceptional move in the IDF, so I would not have to "look for work" or become someone else's advisor if war broke out. Divisional command is a full-time job, so my emergency appointment made my tenure at Command and Staff a tough, highly pressured period of time. Col. Tzuk Bustan, serving as my deputy and commanding the division under non-emergency conditions, made it possible.

In the meantime, as I was about to complete my duties as commander of Command and Staff, Chief of General Staff Moshe Levy was promoting other officers with my rank and giving them senior assignments. Since it was standard practice to give priority to field commanders, I was at a disadvantage, which I could overcome only by lobbying more vigorously with the decision-makers. This manner of activity was never to my liking.

What were the COGS's considerations? Cognoscenti hinted that I was not one of "his men" and that I therefore had little chance of being promoted by him. I decided to wait and see.

Itzik Mordechai succeeded Yossi Peled as chief of the General Staff Instruction Division. For the first time, my commander was a man of my own age. Moreover, I found myself under the command of one who had once been my subordinate. That was a first too. I had often been on the other side of that arrangement, commanding close friends or former commanders.

The position I requested at the end of my tenure at Command and Staff was deputy commander of the newly-formed Ground Forces Command (GFC). The commander of GFC, Amir Drori, acceded to my request, thus refuting all rumors about lack of cooperation between us. The Chief of General Staff also approved the appointment. So, after more than three years at Command and Staff, I passed the baton to Yodke, my deputy in the "Basalt Division", and went home. Nobody gave that a moment's thought.

A few weeks later, the Chief of General Staff called me from home. Moshe Levy complimented me for having revolutionized the Command and General Staff College, and requested my recommendations on how to improve the school in the future. The College had become a sought-after destination, the COGS said, emphasizing my personal influence on the students. As we continued to converse, the atmosphere relaxed and comradely, I expressed my wish to serve as head of the General Staff Instruction Division, a position that had recently become vacant.

Levy agreed. "You're a good candidate for that. You're also the longest-standing brigadier general in the army and you deserve a good promotion." Finally he ruled, "We'll talk about it some more."

Several months later I got a phone call from the COGS' Bureau Chief: I was to report to GFC as deputy to Uri Saguy. Uri had informed me a few weeks earlier that he would be pleased to work with me. Less than 24 hours after that long-awaited phone call, I had already pinned the GFC emblem to my sleeve.

I integrated into GFC very quickly. I knew almost all the commanders and formations, and was quite at home among them.

18. EPILOGUE

Like every senior officer, I had reached a crossroads. It was 1987 and I was 43. I loved my work. I set out every morning with the joy of creation. The uniform I wore had become my calling card, an inseparable part of my personality. My language, like that of my comrades, exuded army jargon, turning any simple outing into "movement of forces in the field." As I considered all of this, I was curious about my own future. However, even the possibility offered me of serving as a military attache overseas did not tempt me. I made up my mind to accept no position I was offered, no matter how alluring, unless it had the authority of Major-General rank.

Officers at the crossroads

In the Israel Defense Forces, unlike other armies, officers reach key positions while relatively young. After every war, a large group of officers is promoted in rank and duties — officers who before the war had held lower ranks than those considered standard for their positions. since there is a chronic shortage of officers, an ever-increasing number of young officers are appointed to positions meant for people of higher rank. Thus the minimum time lapse between promotions, among the world's lowest to begin with, decreases. This phenomenon is most conspicuous in the combat units. Battalion commanders are about 27 years of age, brigade commanders 32-35, and division commanders are still on the youthful side of 40.

As in any hierarchical society, the top of the IDF ladder is densely populated. Many officers compete for a small number of senior positions, and those who make the choices have their work cut out for them. Many stay in limbo, waiting for vacancies on higher levels that may earn them a promotion as well.

Every officer believes he can continue contributing to the IDF, that he is able to handle more responsible duties. Inevitably he compares himself with those promoted before him, and reaches one conclusion: he is as good as they are, if not better, and his right to promotion is absolute.

At some stage every officer feels he has to toot his own horn. Striving to blaze a trail to the top, he starts to lobby among those who might be able to promote him, sparing no effort until he has met with anyone who might have some influence. Because there are no clear-cut criteria by which officers' abilities get measured, many believe that the secret is popularity: "Get on the right terms with the right person, and you'll be set for life."

Officers who pass the age of forty without attaining the position they desire inevitably consider retirement. However, like any inert body that tends to stay in its present state, most such officers prefer to remain in uniform. The IDF is a "home" for those who serve it. It sees to their every need and, by paying fair wages, also tends to their economic security.

The prospect of stepping into civilian life evokes all kinds of apprehensions, of which the fear of the unknown is the most basic. Israeli society values the skills and reputations of high-ranking officers. There is no doubt that these men can find their places in the civilian economy. However, the very need to look for a job at the age of 40 or 50 tends to give one a sense of hopelessness. Officers accustomed to senior responsibilities face one inescapable fact: after their kind of army service, there is no promotion. Only a very few exceptional individuals attain a status equal to that which they held in the army. The others have to strike out on a new path, often starting from the very beginning. Since none of us is eager to begin rebuilding his or her life in middle age, we should not wonder that many IDF officers postpone their retirement again and again. Furthermore, having decided to stay in uniform, these officers do everything they can to continue climbing the ladder. The problem is that those whose chances of promotion are slight usually are not explicitly informed of this. It is hard to approach an officer with a glorious past, look him in the eye, and tell him he's reached the end of the line. Many therefore hang on, waiting for a promotion that will never come. Others finally step down with the feeling of being victims of ingratitude.

The IDF does nothing to prepare its fighting personnel for retirement while they are still in uniform. Upon retirement the officer does, however, have recourse to a well-organized retirement department that eases the transition to civilian life. It is noteworthy that former staff or "professional" officers (medical, legal, etc.) quickly find civilian situations. For their comrades in combat units, by contrast, suitable civilian positions are hard to come by. Precisely those men who spent up to a quarter of a century assaulting the training hills, safeguarding the country's borders, or engaging the enemy, find demobilization an especially painful experience.

The civilian market has changed radically over the years. It is not the intimate old boys' club it once was, and IDF officers are finding it harder than before to integrate. A young officer at the outset of his career doesn't need to look for long to understand that he should choose a job in the army that assures him a secure, orderly life after he retires. Priorities change and the shortage of combat officers progressively worsens. The Army is trying to reverse the tide in its informational activities; it even offers officers benefits and grants to those willing to opt for combat careers. The results are not yet evident.

Dan Shomron had hardly had time to warm the Chief of General Staff's chair; he was stationed in a special bureau in the General Staff compound, preparing for his new duties. Even at that early stage, however, I asked to set up a meeting with him. Dan, who had overcome the opposition of the incumbent COGS, Moshe Levy, to become Levy's successor, was up-beat, congenial and hearty. He gave our talk a com-radely, unofficial ambience, and when I stood up to leave I saw light at the end of the tunnel.

In May, 1987, Shomron, newly installed as COGS, summoned me for an official interview. I had no doubt that this *tête-a-tête* would decide the fate of my military career. I had resolved to accept no answer that failed to posit an unequivocal objective. If there was no place for me among Shomron's generals, I would leave at once. Within days. Dan greeted me heartily.

"I've spent the past few days making some deci-sions on the IDF's major functions and how we'll discharge them." Then he got to the point: "You're going to be a senior field commander!"

"When?" I wanted to know.

"Within a month, six weeks at the most, you'll be able to consider the matter sewn up."

Then I expressed my desire to serve as head of the General Staff Manpower Branch. It was in that capacity, I believed, that I could best influence the quality and image of the IDF's major weapon, the human being.

Several weeks later the media reported that my promotion was just around the corner. All my efforts to stem the publicity were in vain. Hundreds of excited well-wishers called me at home the following Saturday. Casual friends expressed congratulations, and close friends griped about my keeping secrets from them. I was embarrassed. To this day I do not know the origin of the report.

After waiting for eight months in ground forces' command HQ, I met with the Chief of General Staff again, at my request. This time Dan Shomron did not look me in the eye; he pretended to search his desk for a document he needed to study. He knew very well why I had asked for this meeting.

"Kahalani, your promotion isn't going to work out for me in the near future," he said, clearly discomfited.

I prodded him to be more specific, to tell me in so many words what had changed his mind and revoked our agreement. Dan groped for words.

"A different order of priorities has come up for me," he said.

I looked away.

I quit, I said to myself. Still , I had the right to

present my case to Defense Minister Yitzhak Rabin, and I stood on my right. Rabin thought I was "out of line" and did not regard my agreement with the Chief of Staff binding. He tried at length to reach me through my emotions. "You've got to be patient!" he thundered, attempting to prove the point by telling his own personal story. Before stepping down as Chief of General Staff, Moshe Dayan had preferred to be succeeded by some officer other than Rabin and tried to send Rabin away for studies. Rabin stayed put.

"And look where I am today — right here," the Defense Minister smiled. Then he stated, "No officer is being promoted until after the elections!"

I did not give up. Would he at least tell me if I was one of those being considered for promotion? It was not fair to depict my retirement — if I followed through with it — as an act of impatience. Nor was it fair to link my promotion to the elections scheduled for the coming November.

The Defense Minister surrendered to my pressure.

"You'll get a clear answer by summer," he promised.

Stepping out of his office, I was of two minds. I had come in having resolved to quit, and I had gone out confused. I decided to wait until the summer, count to ten, and make my move.

In the summer of 1988, Dan Shomron offered me the position of Chief Education Officer of the IDF.

"With your personality you'll be an emblem and a model for youth, and you can contribute a lot — to the IDF and to Israel!" the COGS stressed.

I answered on the spot: No.

"I won't fill another position at the rank of brigadier-general. But I'd be happy to accept the field forces position you agreed to give me more than a year ago, alongside the appointment as Chief Education Officer. In other words, a promotion in duties with the field forces, and I'll handle both jobs at once."

"Not a bad idea," Dan agreed. "I'll let you know."

In late July, 1988, several members of the General Staff alerted me to some inside information: within a week, another officer would be appointed to the field forces position I had been promised. That's it, I decided. I quit. I informed Uri Saguy, commander of ground forces command, that I would be leaving my position within two weeks. I confided my schedule to the staff officers too, wanting to have time to tie up a few loose ends. After having spent years waiting for change, this *dénouement* gave me a sense of relief. The decision to retire was mine alone. I listened only to my conscience, intuition and sense of dignity.

I reported my decision to the COGS' Bureau Chief. "I've got no grudge against anyone," I told the officer who had just assumed the promised position. "Tell the Chief of Staff that I'm leaving. I'll be a good boy about it, I promise."

Shomron reacted through the media, insisting that he had promised me nothing. That was an insult. Yes, he had the right to change his mind, but there are surely better ways to go about such things.

I went to the 7th Brigade, stationed on the Golan Heights. I wanted to depart from the Israel Defense Forces in the place where I had grown as an enlisted man, platoon commander, company commander, battalion commander — and brigade commander. It was an exciting day, and the incumbent brigade commander did everything he could to make it a pleasant one. After visiting my son Dror, who was serving with the brigade on the Golan Heights, I said my farewells and headed home, for Nes Ziona.

One look in the mirror told me that some things had changed after all. By the time I parted with the IDF I had lost much of my hair, and quite a bit of what remained had gone white. The major piece of baggage I took home was a feeling of satisfaction originating from my life's performance. Never have I felt that my efforts were in vain. If I had it to do over again, I would do just that: do it all over.

As much as I gave of myself, the Army gave me more. I left a home, a family in uniform. I stepped away with a wealth of knowledge, experience, and scars.

As a boy, I had heard much about Zionism, about building my country, and about defending it. Today, I feel I am part of all these things — as every scar on my body will attest.